INDUSTRY

The smoking factory chimneys of Halifax, a West Riding woollen town in the Calder Valley. (*Yorkshire Post.*)

MODERN GEOGRAPHY SERIES

BOOK II

THE BRITISH ISLES

D. M. PREECE
LATE SENIOR GEOGRAPHY MISTRESS, CREWE COUNTY GRAMMAR SCHOOL

AND

H. R. B. WOOD, M.A.
FORMERLY DIRECTOR OF EDUCATION FOR WALLASEY, SOMETIME LECTURER
IN GEOGRAPHY, ST MARY'S TRAINING COLLEGE, STRAWBERRY HILL

UNIVERSITY TUTORIAL PRESS LTD
9-10 GREAT SUTTON STREET, LONDON, E.C. 1

MODERN GEOGRAPHY SERIES

A well-illustrated series of eight volumes in general and regional geography for use by pupils in Secondary Schools.

BOOK   I.   FOUNDATIONS OF GEOGRAPHY.

BOOK   II.   THE BRITISH ISLES.

BOOK   III.   EUROPE.
By D. M. PREECE and H. R. B. WOOD, M.A.

BOOK   IV.   NORTH AMERICA.
By A. W. COYSH, M.Sc., and M. E. TOMLINSON, D.Sc., Ph.D.

BOOK   V.   ASIA.
By W. B. CORNISH, B.A.

BOOK   VI.   THE SOUTHERN CONTINENTS.
By A. W. COYSH and M. E. TOMLINSON.

BOOK VII.   AUSTRALIA AND NEW ZEALAND.
By D. C. MONEY, M.A., F.R.G.S.

BOOK VIII.   AFRICA.
By A. W. COYSH AND M. E. TOMLINSON.

Published 1938.   *Reprinted* 1943
Second Edition 1944
Third Edition 1946
Fourth Edition 1948
Fifth Edition 1949
Sixth Edition 1951
Seventh Edition 1954
Eighth Edition 1955
Ninth Edition 1957
Tenth Edition 1959
Eleventh Edition 1960
Twelfth Edition 1961.   *Reprinted* 1962
Thirteenth Edition 1962
Fourteenth Edition 1964
Fifteenth Edition 1967.   *Reprinted* 1968
Sixteenth Edition 1970
Seventeenth Edition (*Revised and Reset*) 1971

ISBN: 0 7231 0557 X

PRINTED IN GREAT BRITAIN BY UNIVERSITY TUTORIAL PRESS LTD
FOXTON, NEAR CAMBRIDGE

PREFACE TO THE SEVENTEENTH EDITION

The British Isles was originally written by the late Miss D. M. Preece, one of the most outstanding teachers of geography in schools, in collaboration with Mr H. R. B. Wood. In subsequent editions, revision has been carried out, amongst others, by Mr W. Hannah, of Crewe County Grammar School, to whom the authors were particularly indebted for help given at all stages in the preparation of the book. The Fourth and subsequent editions have been prepared by Dr L. J. M. Coleby.

The British Isles is the second of a series of eight volumes issued under the general title "Modern Geography" and meets the needs of pupils preparing for the General Certificate of Education at the Ordinary Level, and other examinations of similar standard. The subject is treated in its regional aspects, and an attempt has been made to preserve a balance in the consideration of the physical, human, and economic aspects of each region. In a book dealing with a country such as Britain, where industrialism is of paramount importance, it is natural that much space should be devoted to the manufacturing areas, and to overseas trade.

As in the case of the preceding volume, *Foundations of Geography*, the numerous illustrations and diagrams are a valuable and attractive feature of the book. The half-tone illustrations are in plate form and adequate cross-references have been provided. Many of the illustrations provide suitable subjects for discussion and can be used as the basis for other appropriate exercises.

In the present edition, a new Chapter has been included on Industry and Services, and numerous alterations have been made throughout the text with the object of keeping the book as up to date as possible, and of ensuring that the authors' aim of dealing with current problems against their geographical background is constantly brought before the pupil.

Following Meteorological Office procedure, Centigrade has been adopted as the definitive scale of temperature but Fahrenheit equivalents have also been included in both text and diagrams. These Fahrenheit equivalents have been given in italics. The notation "30 C.°", etc., has been used when referring to a *range* of temperature, to distinguish it from an actual temperature of 30° C. A number of weather and climatological maps are based on information, supplied by the Meteorological Office, which is Crown copyright and is used with permission of the Controller of H.M. Stationery Office.

Thanks are due to the Geological Survey, British Railways, the National Coal Board, Imperial Chemical Industries Ltd, the Nuffield Organisation, the Steel Corporation of Wales, the ESSO Petroleum Company, the Manchester Ship Canal Company, the British Aluminium Company, Messrs Unilever Ltd, Messrs John Brown and Co. Ltd, Messrs Stewarts and Lloyds Ltd, the North of Scotland Hydro-electric Board, and the City of Wakefield Corporation for kindly lending photographs from which some of the illustrations were prepared. The reviser is indebted to Mr E. H. Cooper, M.A., for the use of Fig. 25 (*a*). Examination questions set at the Ordinary Level of the General Certificate of Education have been included by kind permission of the various Examining Bodies concerned.

CONTENTS

ILLUSTRATIONS

THE BRITISH ISLES

CHAPTER 1

INTRODUCTORY

The Position of the British Isles

The British Isles are situated between latitudes 50° N. and 60° N. off the north-west coast of Europe. This position has had a number of direct results on the development and progress of these islands.

Firstly, a study of the globe will reveal the fact that Britain is situated in the centre of the "land hemisphere", so that she has easy contact for commercial and other purposes with the leading industrial and most densely-peopled countries of the world. Whereas Britain, during the Middle Ages, was on the edge of the known world far from the principal trade-routes, to-day she stands on the seaward margin of the densely-peopled industrial region of Western Europe whence radiate the principal maritime trade-routes to all parts of the world, notably to the eastern United States and the Far East.

The climate is neither so hot nor so cold as to prevent people from working either in field or factory throughout the year, and the proverbial variableness of the weather from day to day helps to provide that incentive to work without which progress is impossible. It has been suggested that the British capacity for regular routine work, so necessary in the manufacturing industries, is partly the result of climatic conditions.

Another important feature of the position of the British Isles is that they stand on the Continental Shelf (Fig. 2). The floor of the shallow seas around Britain was once an extension of the great plains of Northern Europe. These plains were submerged at the end of the last glacial period, when the level of the ocean rose because of the melting of ice. The British Isles became separated from the continent perhaps 8,000 years ago and the line which now marks the depth of 100 fathoms was formerly the edge of the continent. One result of the submergence was to produce an indented coastline with deep inlets, thus providing good natural harbours. The continental shelf has also served to increase the tidal range and to produce strong tidal currents which have kept the estuaries free from silt and prevented the formation of deltas. The

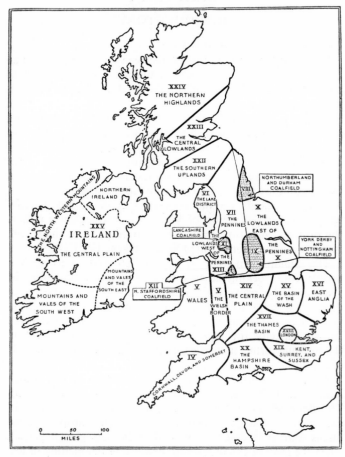

Fig. 1. THE DIVISIONS OF GREAT BRITAIN AND IRELAND.—The numbers correspond to the chapters dealing with each section.

shallow waters of the continental shelf are the feeding grounds of a great variety of fishes, so that the fishing industry has prospered.

The island environment, the good harbours, and the familiarity with the sea fostered by the fishing industry, have resulted in the growth of a seafaring nation, whose peoples have spread to the ends of the earth. Nor must it be forgotten that the sea frontiers of Britain have allowed her to develop her industries and resources, undisturbed by invasions for many centuries. On the other hand, the early invasions of Romans, Jutes, Angles, Saxons, and Danes during the period before the Norman Conquest, served to introduce a variety of racial elements which have been an important factor in the development of the modern British "type".

The Build of the British Isles

Since the British Isles were once joined to the European mainland, it will be expected that there should be some similarity between the rocks and structure of Britain and that of the Continent (Fig. 3).

Fig. 2. THE CONTINENTAL SHELF.
Horizontal shading = More than 100 fathoms.
Inclined shading = Less than 100 fathoms.

(1) The old hard rocks, *e.g.* the granites, schists, and gneisses of the Scottish Highlands, are repeated in the Scandinavian Highlands.

(2) The lowlying plains of Eastern England have their counterpart in the plains of the Netherlands and North Germany.

(3) Chalk and limestone escarpments with the intervening clay vales similar to those of South-East England are to be seen in Northern France. Both the south coast of England and the north coast of France have bold headlands of chalk.

(4) The structure and scenery of Cornwall is very similar to that of Brittany.

Not only are there striking similarities between the rocks of the British Isles and those of the European mainland, but there is also strong evidence of the former connection of Great Britain and Ireland (see pages 234-6).

A study of the physical map of Britain shows that all the

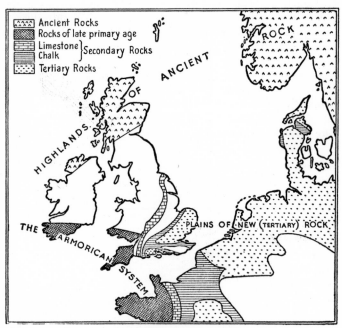

Fig. 3. To Show the similarity of structure between the British Isles and the Neighbouring Coastal Area of Europe.

mountainous areas lie in the north and west, and that in the south-east there is a plain crossed by low ridges of hills. The reason for this is apparent if the physical and geological maps are compared. Such a comparison shows that the mountainous areas correspond to regions of rock geologically old, which have resisted the various forces of denudation and remain as high mountainous or plateau regions. The south-east of England in contrast is composed of newer and less

resistant rocks of the Secondary and Tertiary geological ages.
The mountains of the north and west, too, are the old denuded
remnants of ancient mountain systems; but the rocks of the
south-east have only been subjected to very slight "folding"
during more recent geological times.

The contrasts between the north-west and south-east of the
British Isles are best understood if a line is drawn from the
mouth of the River Tees to the mouth of the River Exe.
Such a line divides the British Isles into two sharply contrasted
regions.   To the north-west of this line lie most of the British
coalfields, and also the highest and most extensive areas
of highland.   In the north-western area the geographical
development depends mainly on the rocks.   Where the rocks
are old and hard there are extensive plateau areas, unproductive because of their thin, infertile soil, their damp chilly
climate, their difficult communications, and their lack of
valuable minerals.   Such areas are the Highlands of Scotland,
the Southern Uplands of Scotland, the Lake District, the
Pennine Chain, the Welsh mountains, the moorlands of
Cornwall and Devon, and the Irish mountains (see plates
facing pages 16, 80, and 81).

Where, however, the rocks, while still old, are somewhat
newer than those referred to above, minerals, particularly
coal and iron, are found.   This has led to the growth of
densely-populated manufacturing regions.   Such areas are:—

(A) On the flanks of the Pennine Chain.

(B) On the flanks of the Welsh mountains.

(C) In the Midland Plain of England.

(D) In the Midland Valley of Scotland.

The chief coalfields of the British Isles are (Fig. 4):—

On the flanks of the Pennines or of the Lake District:

1. Northumberland and Durham.   3. Cumberland.

2. York, Derby, and Nottingham.   4. South Lancashire.

5. North Staffordshire.

On the flanks of the Welsh mountains:

6. North Wales (Flint and Denbigh).

7. South Wales (Glamorgan).   8. Forest of Dean.

In the Midland Plain:

9. East Shropshire.	11. Warwickshire.
10. South Staffordshire.	12. Leicestershire.

In addition to the English coalfields mentioned above, there are two small ones south-east of the Tees-Exe line:

13. Bristol.   14. Dover.

In the Midland Valley of Scotland:

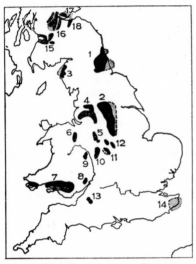

15. Ayrshire.

16. Lanarkshire.

17. Fifeshire.

18. Midlothian.

Ireland:

In Ireland there are small and relatively unimportant coal deposits in Kilkenny and at Dungannon.

Fig. 4. THE COALFIELDS OF BRITAIN.—Coalfields marked in black. The dotted areas show concealed fields. The numbers correspond to the list in the text.

In addition to coal there are also deposits of *iron ore*, such as those of Furness in North Lancashire. Many of the coalfields such as the Lanarkshire, North Staffordshire, and South Wales, also have deposits of iron ore, but these are much less important than they were formerly, and they now provide only a very small proportion of the British supplies. The iron ore deposits of northern Britain have played a great part in the industrial development. The mountainous areas of the north-west also yield small amounts of lead, zinc, and copper ores. The chief districts are the Pennines, North Wales, and the Lake District. There was a slight revival of tin mining in Cornwall when the tin mines of Malaya were in Japanese hands.

In addition to the mining of coal and metal ores, quarrying is also important in the north-west. There are the building granites of Aberdeen and Cornwall, and road metal granites of North Wales (Penmaenmawr) and Leicestershire, the slates of North Wales (Festiniog and Penrhyn), Westmorland, and Cornwall, and the china clay and china stone of Cornwall and Devon. Salt, important in the chemical industries, is found mainly in the New Red Sandstones as in Cheshire. There are also deposits of salt near Droitwich (Worcestershire) and near Greatham at the mouth of the River Tees. Potassium salts (for fertilisers) have recently been found near Whitby.

The portion of Britain which lies to the south-east of the Tees-Exe line is very different from the north-western area which has just been described.

A physical map shows that the south-east is mainly a plain, and that relatively

Fig. 5. LIMESTONE.—1. Cotswold Hills. 2. Edge Hill. 3. Northampton Uplands. 4. Lincoln Edge. 5. North York Moors.

CHALK.—A. Salisbury Plain. B. White Horse Hills. C. Chiltern Hills. D. East Anglian Ridge. E. Norfolk Edge. F. Lincoln Wolds. G. Yorkshire Wolds. H. North Downs. J. South Downs. K. Western Downs. L. Purbeck Downs.

little of the land rises above 600 ft, whereas the highlands of the north-west average 2,000 ft, and rise to 4,000 ft in Scotland (Ben Nevis). In the south-east only in two places do the Cotswolds rise to 1,000 ft. In spite of its general low level this area has a clear arrangement of hills and plains (see plate facing page 32). The hills are arranged in lines which run approximately, from north-east to south-west. A comparison of the relief map with a simple geological map will show that the ridges of hills correspond to belts of limestone and chalk, and that the valleys are composed mainly of clay (Fig. 5). The clay round London is known as the London clay, and is quite different from the Oxford clay in the Cherwell Valley.

The ridges of chalk and limestone are steeper on one side than the other, and the steep side is (with the exception of the

North Downs) always on the northern or western side. Such ridges of hills are called *escarpments*, the steep slope being known as the *scarp slope*, and the gentle slope as the *dip slope* or counter scarp. The limestone escarpment begins at St Alban's Head and runs westwards to Lyme Regis, thence northwards, keeping to the east of the Mendip Hills and through the Cotswolds, Edge Hill, the Northampton Heights, Lincoln Edge, to the North

Fig. 6.   SOURCES OF IRON ORE IN
GREAT BRITAIN.

York Moors which terminate seawards in a rugged coast with limestone cliffs such as can be seen at Whitby.

The system of chalk escarpments is not quite so simple. It consists of four branches, all radiating from Salisbury Plain (really a chalk plateau). These branches run—

(1) Through the Marlborough Downs, Chiltern Hills, East Anglian Heights, Norfolk Edge, Lincoln Wolds, to the Yorkshire Wolds, where the chalk ends in a bold headland, Flamborough Head.

(2) From Salisbury Plain through the North Hampshire Downs, and the North Downs to the chalk cliffs of Dover.

(3) From Salisbury Plain south-eastward through the South Hampshire Downs and the South Downs to Beachy Head.

(4) From Salisbury Plain south-westward through the Dorset Heights and then turning abruptly eastward through the Purbeck Downs and the central ridge of the Isle of Wight.

The rocks of the south-eastern area yield neither the variety nor the quantity of valuable minerals as are found to the north-west of the Tees-Exe line. There are two small coalfields, viz. the Bristol coalfield and the Dover coalfield in Kent. The latter is of recent development and has not yet given rise to any important industry.

By far the most important mineral of South-East England is iron ore. Jurassic iron ores are found along the north-western edge of the limestone escarp-

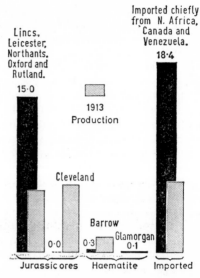

Fig. 7. SOURCES OF IRON ORE USED IN THE UNITED KINGDOM IN MILLIONS OF TONS, 1965. Although Britain provides nearly half of the iron ore she uses, imported iron ore has a much greater iron content.

ment from the Cleveland Hills of north Yorkshire to Oxfordshire (Fig. 6). They are quarried in a number of places, viz. (1) at Scunthorpe and Frodingham in Lincolnshire; (2) at Corby and Kettering in Northamptonshire; and (3) near Banbury in north Oxfordshire. All these are acid ores, and they could not be used until the discovery of the Thomas-Gilchrist process eighty years ago. These workings supply 98 per cent. of the iron ore of Great Britain (Fig. 7).

But minerals do not determine the development of this portion of England. Before the industrial revolution of the late seventeen hundreds, population density depended mainly on the quality and amount of agricultural land. South-east of the Tees-Exe line the only areas of infertile soil are narrow ridges of porous limestone and chalk and there are no large unproductive areas of scanty population like the Scottish Highlands or the Pennine Plateau. Hence the south-east was the richest, most densely populated and most important part of the United Kingdom. The towns were mainly picturesque old market towns of moderate size, many with beautiful old churches or cathedrals, *e.g.* Salisbury, Norwich, etc.

At the start of the industrial revolution the main source of power was water power, but very soon the water-wheels worked by mountain streams were replaced by steam engines using coal as fuel (see pages 102-4). Coal being cheapest on the coal-fields themselves, it was here that industry developed rapidly. So that the coalfields became densely populated areas with large and important new industrial cities. So that during the nineteenth century the population of the north-west increased much more rapidly than that in the south-east.

In the twentieth century the pattern has changed again. Industrial power can now be brought considerable distances quite cheaply, especially by the national electricity grid. In addition, advances in technology have considerably reduced the amount of fuel required in many processes. Industries are no longer so tied to coalfields. New industries have been set up in the south-east, attracted by the vast market available to them in the London region (page 170). Raw materials can readily be imported via London and other ports.

These new industries, *e.g.* road vehicles and aircraft, plastics and chemicals, radio-communication and electronics, are still-growing industries producing commodities that we can readily export. On the other hand some of the industries of the north-west, *e.g.* coal-mining, ship-building, and cotton, are declining in importance in the face of foreign competition. Efforts are being made to establish new industries in the north-west also but there has been for many years a drift of population to the south-east (page 265), a drift that is still taking place and will probably continue.

CHAPTER 2

CLIMATE

Winds, Depressions, and Anticyclones

The climate of the British Isles is determined by their position on the western margin of a land mass in the cool temperate zone. The islands therefore lie in the track of the westerly winds from the Atlantic throughout the year. Records show that, on an average, the wind blows from a westerly quarter (*i.e.* N.N.W. to S.S.W.) on two days out of every three. These

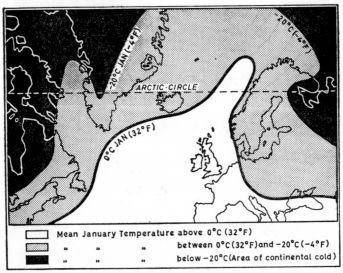

Fig. 8. To Show the Position of the British Isles within the "Gulf of Winter Warmth".

winds not only modify the temperature and cause rainfall, but bring in their track those depressions and anticyclones which account for the variability of British weather from day to day.

The characteristic features of the British climate are its warm winters [more than 20 Centigrade degrees or 36 Fahrenheit degrees higher than the average for the latitude (Fig. 8)], its dampness, and its variability.

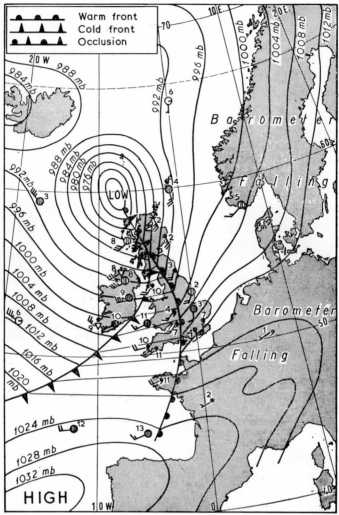

Fig. 9. CYCLONIC CONDITIONS.—30th Dec., 6 h. A deep depression, centred off N.W. Scotland is moving north-east, and the associated warm sector is moving across England and Wales. Note the wind veers at the fronts, the rain in advance of the warm front, the drizzle in the warm sector, and the showers and broken cloud behind the cold front. Temperatures in the warm sector are much higher than those in advance of it. The air behind the warm sector is not as cold as that in front of it owing to its passage over the relatively warm ocean.

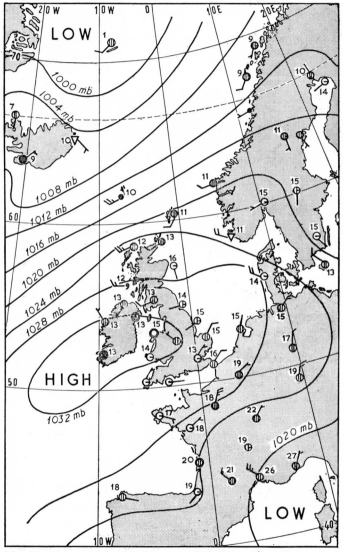

Fig. 10. ANTICYCLONIC CONDITIONS.—17th July, 7h. Forecast of several days' fine weather.

13

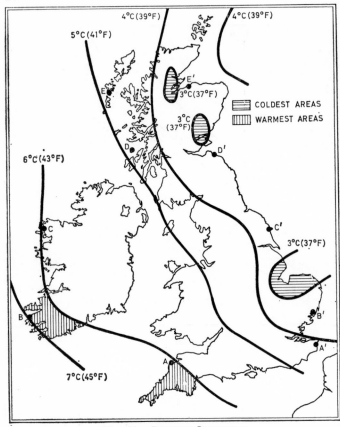

Fig. 11. JANUARY ISOTHERMS.

Depressions, or regions of low pressure (Fig. 9), occur when a stream of warm air from the south or south-west meets a stream of cold polar air from the north or north-east. The lighter warm air rises over the heavier cold air, and, as a result, condensation takes place and rain falls. Depressions are therefore associated with rainy weather. It is estimated that, on an average, about forty depressions pass over these islands each year, but their frequency varies from month to month, being greatest from November to January and least from May to July.

Anticyclones, or regions of high pressure (Fig. 10), are associated with periods of bright sunny weather in summer and in winter with rainless weather (sometimes cloudy), and with fogs and frosts. Anticyclones are of less frequent occurrence than depressions, about twelve passing over the British Isles each year. Nor do they travel so quickly as depressions, but sometimes remain stationary for days and even weeks, giving long periods of dry weather. In summer, anticyclones often give rise to "heat waves" and in winter to spells of very cold weather.

Temperature

Figs. 11 and 12 show the isotherms of the British Isles for January and July.

If, in January, two places are taken in the same latitude, one on the west coast and one on the east coast, *e.g.* A and A′ (Fig. 11), and their temperatures estimated it will be found that the western place is always warmer than the eastern one.

For example, five pairs of stations are marked on Fig. 11. A comparison of their temperatures is shown below:—

WEST COAST	EAST COAST	WEST IS WARMER THAN THE EAST BY
A 6·4° C. (43·5° F.)	A′ 4·6° C. (40·3° F.)	1·8 C.° (3·2 F.°)
B 7·2° C. (45·0° F.)	B′ 3·7° C. (38·7° F.)	3·5 C.° (6·3 F.°)
C 6·1° C. (43·0° F.)	C′ 4·1° C. (39·4° F.)	2·0 C.° (3·6 F.°)
D 4·6° C. (40·3° F.)	D′ 3·3° C. (37·9° F.)	1·3 C.° (2·4 F.°)
E 4·5° C. (40·1° F.)	E′ 3·1° C. (37·6° F.)	1·4 C.° (2·5 F.°)

The average of the last column is about 2·0 C.° (*3·6 F.°*), so that, from the figures it would appear that the west coast is, on an average, 2 C.° (*3·6 F.°*) warmer than the east coast in January. Any number of pairs of stations may be taken and in each case similar results will be obtained, *i.e.* the station on the west coast will be warmer than the corresponding station on the east coast and in the same latitude. In the above table the greatest difference is between B and B′. This is because B is open to maximum sea influence and B′ is very near to the influence of the continental cold.

If the same stations are taken for July (Fig. 12) and their temperatures estimated, the following results are obtained.

West Coast	East Coast	East is Warmer than the West by
A 16·3° C. (61·3° F.)	A′ 17·4° C. (63·3° F.)	1·1 C.° (2·0 F.°)
B 15·0° C. (59·0° F.)	B′ 17·1° C. (62·8° F.)	2·1 C.° (3·8 F.°)
C 14·4° C. (57·9° F.)	C′ 16·0° C. (60·8° F.)	1·6 C.° (2·9 F.°)
D 13·8° C. (56·8° F.)	D′ 14·8° C. (58·6° F.)	1·0 C.° (1·8 F.°)
E 13·6° C. (56·5° F.)	E′ 14·2° C. (57·6° F.)	0·6 C.° (1·1 F.°)

The average of the last column is less than 1·3 C.° (2·3 F.°), so that the east coast appears to be about 1·3 C.° (2·3 F.°) warmer than the west coast in July.

The foregoing examples show that the warming influence of the sea in winter is greater than the cooling influence of the sea in summer. In *winter* the source of warmth is the *sea*, so that temperatures decrease from west to east and the isotherms run roughly north to south (N.N.W. to S.S.E.). For instance, the 5° C. (41° F.) isotherm passes through the western islands of Scotland and Dungeness (*i.e.* the north-west of Scotland is as warm as Sussex in winter). In *summer* the influence of *latitude* is stronger than that of the sea. While the latter does have a cooling effect on the west, the temperatures, generally, decrease northwards and the isotherms run from west to east (S.S.W. to N.N.E.).

Because the sea is warmer than the land in winter, isotherms trend northward where they cross the sea, *e.g.* 6° C. (43° F.) south of Ireland. In summer the land is warmer than the sea, and isotherms trend southward over the sea, *e.g.* 15° C. (59° F.) over the southern Irish Sea.

The January 5° C. (41° F.) and the July 15° C. (59° F.) isotherms divide the British Isles into four quadrants (Fig. 13), of which the N.W. quadrant is the most equable (*i.e.* has the smallest ranges of temperature), and the S.E. quadrant is the most extreme (*i.e.* has the largest ranges of temperature). It must be remembered that temperature decreases with elevation at an average rate of 1 C.°, for 500 ft (1 F.° for 300 ft), so that the actual temperatures experienced in the highlands of

Above: Dartmoor is a granite moorland. Note the rounded outlines, the exposures of barren rock; the "tor"; the absence of trees, fences, and cultivation. (*Valentine and Sons, Ltd.*)

Below: Mamore Forest in the Scottish Highlands, looking E.S.E. from Ben Nevis, a heavily glaciated and deeply dissected plateau. Notice the bareness of the scene; the absence of vegetation; the exposed rock; and the even level of the mountain tops. (*Geological Survey.*)

Above: Part of the plain of Essex, a view typical of the agricultural plain of England. (*Aerofilms Ltd.*)

Below: West Dean, near Seaford, a view typical of the chalk country. The village is situated in a sheltered valley, where ground water is nearer the surface, ensuring a water supply, and making possible the growth of trees. Note the smooth contours of the hills; the absence of trees at higher levels; the unfenced roads; the corn stacks, indicating cereal cultivation on the lower ground; the shortness of the grass and the resultant occupation of sheep rearing. (*F. Frith and Co. Ltd.*)

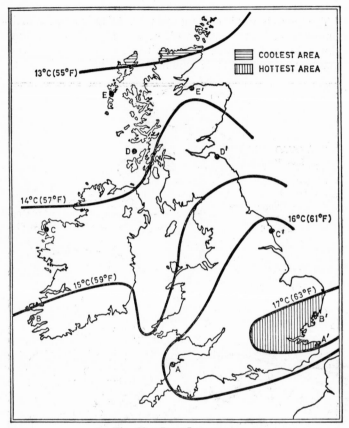

Fig. 12. July Isotherms.

Scotland or Wales are lower than those shown on isotherm maps, where the isotherms have been calculated for sea-level.

Rainfall

The rainfall of the British Isles is due, in part, to the effect of relief on the prevailing winds, and in part to the passage of depressions.

There are marked differences in the rainfall of the western and eastern sides of the islands, both in (*a*) the amount received, and (*b*) in its distribution throughout the year.

The westerly winds coming from the Atlantic are, for their temperature, heavily laden with water vapour. The highest mountains and plateaux of the British Isles lie near the west coast. On reaching these mountains the winds are forced to

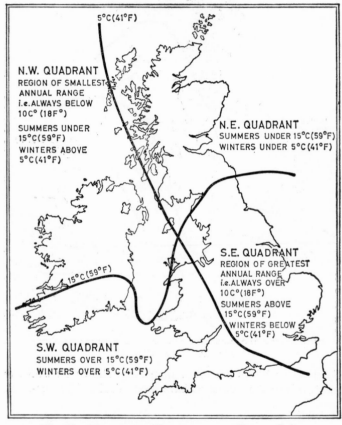

5°C(41°F)

N.W. QUADRANT
REGION OF SMALLEST
ANNUAL RANGE
i.e. ALWAYS BELOW
10C° (18F°)

SUMMERS UNDER
15°C(59°F)

WINTERS ABOVE
5°C(41°F)

N.E. QUADRANT
SUMMERS UNDER 15°C(59°F)
WINTERS UNDER 5°C(41°F)

S.E. QUADRANT
REGION OF GREATEST
ANNUAL RANGE
i.e. ALWAYS OVER
10C° (18F°)

SUMMERS ABOVE
15°C(59°F)

WINTERS BELOW
5°C(41°F)

15°C(59°F)

S.W. QUADRANT
SUMMERS OVER 15°C(59°F)
WINTERS OVER 5°C(41°F)

Fig. 13. Temperature Regions of the British Isles.

rise, and the resultant cooling by expansion produces heavy rain. The winds pass on, but as they have already lost much of their moisture and also because they are descending to the plains and becoming warmer, less rain falls. (Such areas on the leeside of mountains are known as "*rain shadow*" areas.)

However, if the winds should be forced to rise again over hills, however low (*e.g.* Cotswolds, N. Downs, Yorkshire Wolds, etc.), the rainfall again increases.

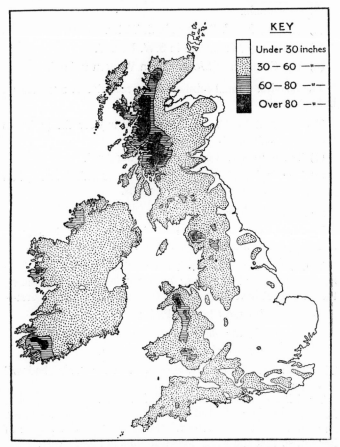

KEY

Under 30 inches
30 — 60 —"—
60 — 80 —"—
Over 80 —"—

Fig. 14. RAINFALL OF THE BRITISH ISLES.—Note carefully the distribution in relation to the highland areas. Locate the six areas of heavy rainfall enumerated on page 20.

A rainfall map of the British Isles shows that most rain falls on the western mountains and least on the eastern plains (Fig. 14). The areas of heaviest rainfall (over 80 in.) are—

(1) The Western Highlands of Scotland around Ben Nevis and including the mountains of Skye.

(2) The Lake District.

(3) Snowdonia.

(4) The Brecknock Beacons in S. Wales.

(5) The Kerry Mountains in S.W. Ireland.

(6) The Connemara Mountains in Western Ireland.

The heaviest annual rainfall so far recorded is over 200 in. in Snowdonia.

The areas of least rainfall (under 30 in.) are the plains to the east of the mountains:—

(1) The narrow east coast plain of Scotland.

(2) The English plain to the east of Wales with the exception of most of the chalk and limestone hills.

(3) Mid-Somerset.

The lowest average annual rainfall recorded is 19·3 in. at Shoeburyness, on the north shore of the Thames estuary.

While, broadly speaking, it is true that the west of Britain has heavy rainfall, it should be noted that three regions on the west coast have light rainfall (under 30 in.). These are:—

(*a*) the Cheshire Plain;

(*b*) the plains around the lower Severn;

(*c*) the plain of Mid-Somerset.

They are all lowland areas, and all lie in the "rain shadow" of mountains to the west or south-west.

The Irish plains have heavier rainfall than the English plains, for Ireland receives the full force of the rain-bearing westerlies, and her western mountains are not so continuous as those of Britain, so that the winds penetrate inland more easily.

The lightest rainfall in Ireland occurs over a small portion of the plain around Dublin.

Depressions are largely responsible for the seasonal distribution of rainfall in the British Isles. In *winter* (Fig. 15) depressions cross the Atlantic from the south-west, and, as Europe is covered with a mass of cold dense air (high pressure), they usually pass either to the north or south of it, *i.e.* in the directions indicated by AB, A'B', EF, and CD. As a rule depressions follow the track AB and A'B' more frequently than they follow the tracks CD or EF. As they pass westward of the British Isles on their journey north-eastwards it follows that, *in winter*, the west will receive far more cyclonic rain

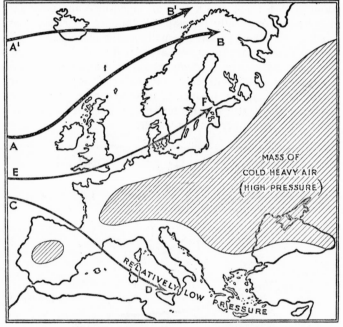

Fig. 15. WINTER CONDITIONS IN EUROPE.

than the east. Thus the western portions of the British Isles have a marked winter maximum of rainfall.

The kind of weather experienced by a place during the passage of a depression depends upon the relation of that place to the path of the depression. A place situated immediately in the track of the depression experiences different weather conditions from one on the northern or southern edge of the depression. Thus when a depression follows a path such as AB, the British Isles experience rainy weather with mild winds veering from south-east to south and south-west. Whereas, when depressions pass along the track EF cold north winds, often accompanied by snow, are experienced.

In *summer* Europe is a region of low pressure to which depressions are attracted (Fig. 16), following such tracks as PQ, RS, TX. As they often pass eastward over England along such a track as TX they are intensified and secondary depressions frequently develop. Secondary depressions are small areas of low pressure, usually on the margin of a main depression, and are frequently associated with thunderstorms accompanied by heavy downpours of rain and possibly hail. Since the secondaries develop as the depressions pass eastward it follows that the frequency of thunderstorms increases eastward also. It is for this reason that Eastern England has more rain in summer than in winter.

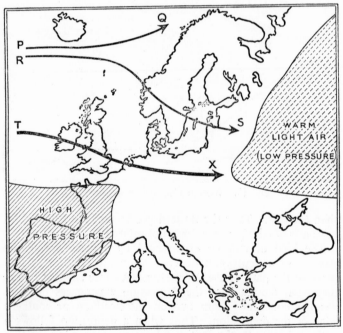

Fig. 16. SUMMER CONDITIONS IN EUROPE.

The amount and seasonal distribution of rainfall in the east and in the west is illustrated by the rainfall diagrams for London and Valentia (Fig. 17).

From these it is clear that:—

(1) Valentia has more rainfall than London.

(2) Valentia has most rain in the winter months, and that London has most rain in the summer months.

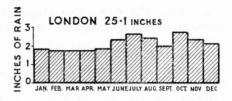

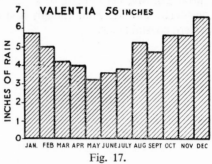

Fig. 17.

RAINFALL FOR LONDON AND VALENTIA.

(3) Although London has a summer maximum of rainfall, the total summer rainfall in London is less than the summer rainfall of Valentia.

Average rainfall figures for the 35 years 1916-1950 show a rainfall 5 to 6 per cent. greater than those for the previous 35 years, 1881-1915, with a rather more uniform spread over the year.

Summary of the Differences between the Climates of the West and East Sides of the British Isles.

(1) The west is warmer than the east in winter.

(2) The west is cooler than the east in summer.

(3) The west has heavier rainfall than the east.

(4) The west has most rain in the winter months.

(5) The east has most rain in the summer months (with a second maximum in October as a rule).

The west with its equable temperatures, heavy rain, and winter maximum of rainfall has a typical *insular or maritime* climate.

The east, with its greater range of temperature, lighter rain, and summer maximum of rainfall has a climate less insular, and approaches nearer to that of continental areas. It must, however, be remembered that, compared with places in central Eurasia, the climate of Eastern England must still be considered insular, even though it differs from that of the western coastal areas.

CHAPTER 3

AGRICULTURE AND FISHERIES

Introductory

About four hundred thousand workers are directly employed on the land, producing goods worth about £2,000 million a year, of which livestock products account for nearly two-thirds. Agricultural workers are just under 2 per cent. of our working population, much the lowest proportion for any country in the world (West Germany 12 per cent., France 20 per cent., world average 55 per cent.). But our agriculture is now the most highly mechanised in the world, so that we are able to produce nearly twice as much as thirty years ago, and with a much smaller labour force.

Only one-fifth of the total area of the United Kingdom is useless for agriculture and this includes towns, factories, and inland water. Over a quarter (mainly in Scotland) is fit only for rough grazing. About one-seventh is under grain crops and one-sixth under other crops, including temporary grass. In terms of cost, we produce about half our food. Nevertheless, more than half of our wheat and cheese, nearly all our butter, and nearly a third of our meat have to be imported, to say nothing of five-sixths of the wool required for our woollen industry, and a good deal of the feeding-stuffs for our livestock.

Throughout the British Isles, the type of farming is of the kind referred to as *mixed farming*, *i.e.* the farmer grows a variety of crops, and rears cows, sheep, pigs, and chickens. In some districts farmers may have more ploughed land than pasture land, while in others farmers may concentrate on the rearing of animals and grow fewer crops.

Because of the dense population, the price of land in Britain is high, and therefore farmers must get as large a return as possible for their land. This is done by "intensive" farming, *i.e.* by the application of up-to-date methods, by scientific manuring, by careful choice of seeds and breeds of animals, and by the rotation of crops, so that the land is not unduly exhausted by bearing the same crop year after year, and so that pests and diseases that attack a particular crop and overwinter in the soil do not find the same crop waiting for them again the next year. It is because of the system of crop rotation that the British farmer has such a variety of crops and animal products. Of recent years there has been some tendency to grow the same crop for several years on suitable land, making good the loss of soil fertility by extensive use of artificial fertilisers. Sooner or later, however, the gradual build up of pests and diseases reduces yields until it becomes no longer profitable to continue with the same crop. Many of the crops grown in rotation, *e.g.* oats, swedes, and turnips, are used for feeding animals, so that farmers with a high percentage of arable land also rear animals, and have some fields of pasture. One of the advantages of mixed farming is that it is comparatively easy to switch the emphasis from arable farming to stock rearing and vice versa as circumstances demand.

Wheat { U.K. Production in 1,000's of Tons
Average 1936-8—1651; 1966-8—3692; 1969—3515

Wheat is grown throughout Britain south of the Scottish Highlands, for in the northern counties of Scotland the summer temperature is not high enough to ripen the grain. The climate of Britain is not ideal for wheat growing, as the summer weather conditions are too uncertain, and we produce somewhat less than half of our needs. Winter wheat, sown in the autumn, gives a much bigger yield than spring wheat, and hence is grown wherever the winters are not too cold, although as a rule it is too "soft" to make good bread. It is used for biscuits or mixed with imported wheat, and about half our production is used as fodder for stock. Extensive wheat growing is therefore confined to that part of England which has the most suitable climate, viz. Eastern England (Fig. 18). Yields are high—over 30 cwt. per acre. Production has almost doubled in the last 25 years.

Wheat requires the following conditions for a satisfactory harvest:—

(*a*) Moisture in the growing season.
(*b*) Warm, sunny weather for ripening and harvesting.
(*c*) Rainfall that is not too heavy, *i.e.* about 20-30 in.

(*d*) Land that is flat enough for the use of large machines.
(*e*) A moderately heavy soil.

Now in Eastern England are found the areas with the hottest summers, and the rainfall is about 25 in. Moreover, although these regions have slightly more rain in summer than in winter,

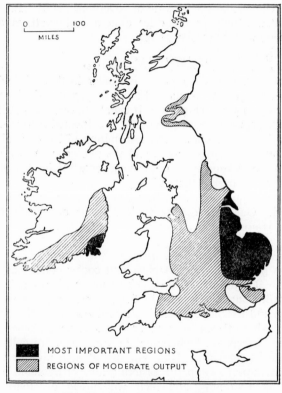

Fig. 18. DISTRIBUTION OF WHEAT

the summer rain is of the thunderstorm type, and is soon over. The area is also a plain, and the soil is mainly a fertile boulder clay deposited during the Ice Age.

The principal wheat-growing districts are Lincolnshire, Norfolk, Suffolk, Essex, Cambridgeshire, Huntingdonshire, and Bedfordshire, the Vale of York, and Holderness. In Scotland the chief wheat region is in the east of the Central Lowlands in the Lothians, Fife, and the east coast plains nearly as far north as Aberdeen. Wheat is also cultivated on the rich sandstone plains round Moray Firth. In Ireland wheat growing has increased in recent years, despite the dampness of the climate, largely because of government subsidies. It is cultivated mainly in the drier eastern and southern areas between Louth and County Cork.

Barley { U.K. Production in 1,000's of Tons
Average 1936-8—765; 1966-8—8642; 1969—8561

Barley grows under conditions similar to those for wheat, so that like wheat its cultivation is largely practised on the drier eastern plains (Fig. 19). It can, however, ripen at lower temperatures than wheat, so that it is cultivated further north and at higher altitudes. The distribution of barley is almost identical with that of wheat, and the two crops play a great part in the rotation system. The east coast plain of Scotland grows more barley than wheat, and barley is one of the principal grain crops of the south-eastern quadrant of Ireland. Our best quality barley, about one-sixth of the whole, is used to make beer, the rest is fed to animals.

Oats { U.K. Production in 1,000's of Tons
Average 1936-8—1940; 1966-8—1212; 1969—1298

Oats grow well under damper and cooler conditions than wheat. Because of this their cultivation is widespread, since they will flourish not only in the damper areas of western Britain and Ireland, but also in the arable lands of the eastern plains, where they enter into crop rotation with wheat and barley. Except on high mountain areas oats are cultivated throughout the British Isles, but special note may be taken of their importance in the eastern plains of Scotland as far north as Caithness, and their widespread distribution in Ireland, particularly in the lowland areas of Northern Ireland and in County Cork (Fig. 20). Production of oats has been tending to fall in recent years.

Sugar-beet { Production in England and Wales in 1,000's of Tons
Average 1936-8 —2763; 1966-8—6759

At one time the root crops grown in rotation with wheat were mainly turnips and mangolds. After 1918, sugar-beet was grown on a considerable scale and many large factories were established.

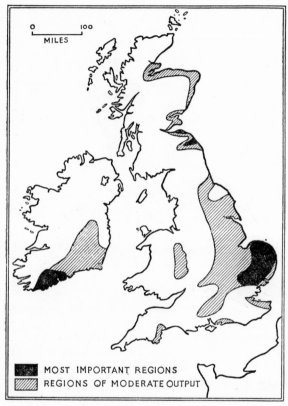

Fig. 19. DISTRIBUTION OF BARLEY.

The sugar-beet needs a good deep soil, with rain from June to August, and a dry harvesting period later in the year. These conditions of soil and climate are satisfied in the plains of Eastern England.

Sugar-beet also has certain advantages from the farmers' point of view. It plays its part in crop rotation, and provides, in its green tops, good animal fodder. The farmer gets an immediate cash return for his beet, and after the sugar has been extracted, the pulp can be used for winter feeding of cattle. One acre of land gives about two tons of sugar-beet.

Fig. 20. DISTRIBUTION OF OATS.

Beet, however, needs very careful cultivation, especially in the thinning, which is done in spring. The yield of crude sugar depends on the thinning being done at the right time, and is usually about 15 per cent., but may be as high as 20 per cent. After refining, about one-eighth of the raw sugar is left as molasses, used to make alcohol.

As shown in Fig. 21, sugar-beet is cultivated in:—

(1) The wheat lands of eastern England from the North Riding to Essex.

(2) North Shropshire and the neighbouring counties.

(3) Fifeshire and along the coast to the Tweed valley.

(4) The Isle of Wight and parts of Hampshire and adjacent counties.

(5) In Co. Cork and other parts of southern Ireland.

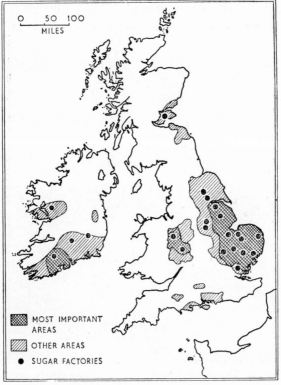

Fig. 21. DISTRIBUTION OF SUGER-BEET.

Sixteen of the eighteen sugar-beet factories of Britain are in the eastern counties, and of these factories, those at Cantley and Ely are the largest. Home-grown sugar-beet now provides over one-quarter of our total consumption of sugar.

Fruit

Another group of agricultural products characteristic of S.E. England is fruit and hops, but it is difficult to draw hard and fast lines, because fruit growing is widely distributed all over Great Britain. For example, there must be very few parishes that do not contain an apple tree, but some areas grow more fruit than others (Fig. 22). Fruit grown in the British Isles is of various types:—

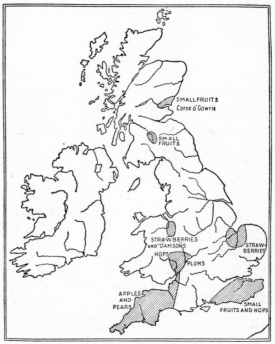

Fig. 22. THE DISTRIBUTION OF FRUIT (CHIEF AREAS ONLY).

(*a*) Small, soft fruits, such as strawberries, cherries, raspberries, gooseberries, currants, etc.

(*b*) Larger fruits, such as apples and pears.

(*c*) Stone fruits, such as plums and damsons.

Above: The Vale of Evesham—a fertile agricultural region with many orchards, especially of plums. (*Aerofilms Ltd.*)

Below: The Fens near Boston. Note the drainage canal and ditches, the straight causeway roads, the absence of hedges and trees. The rich soil is intensively cultivated. Potatoes are much the most important crop. Flower bulbs, sugar-beet, grain, and soft fruits are also grown. (*Aerofilms Ltd.*)

Above: These tree ferns and other semi-tropical plants growing in the gardens of Tresco Abbey, Isles of Scilly, testify to the very mild winters of the extreme south-west of England. (*James Gibson.*)

Below: The valley of the River Lea, a few miles north of London, is a great market gardening area. The photograph shows some of the acres of glass-houses near Cheshunt (*Aerofilms Ltd.*)

(*d*) Uncultivated fruits, *e.g.* bilberries of the moorlands, which have a definite value for dyeing purposes.

Since the small fruits are quickly perishable, it is clear that a dry, sunny period for picking is of more importance than in the case of apples and pears. Hence the most important areas for strawberries, etc., are found in the east of England, where the summer temperature is highest and the rain least.

The principal regions for small fruits are:—

(1) Kent, Surrey, Sussex, and Hampshire.

(2) In the Basin of the Wash near Wisbech.

(3) The Carse o' Gowrie—the fertile, sunny plain between the Firth of Tay and the Sidlaw Hills, with Dundee as a centre.

(4) The Clyde Valley, north of Lanark.

(5) Western Cheshire in the Dee Valley around Farndon. This area is in the rain shadow of the Welsh Hills.

Nearness to markets where the fruit can be sold, and quick transport to those markets, are very necessary when dealing with soft fruits that do not carry well. The nearness of the south-eastern counties to the great population of London is very important. The East Anglian area has quick communication with London and with the Midland coalfield areas; the Carse o' Gowrie and the Clyde Valley with the industrial areas of Central Scotland; and West Cheshire with South Lancashire and North Staffordshire.

The large fruits, such as apples and pears, while having a very wide distribution, are most important in the western counties, particularly in Cornwall, Devon, Somerset, Herefordshire, and Worcestershire. The climate in the west is milder and wetter. Rain is needed to "swell" the fruit, and long dry spells usually result in the apples falling from the trees. Apples are used for the manufacture of cider, both in the south-western counties and in Herefordshire.

Stone fruits are grown to a great extent in the Vale of Evesham (see plate facing page 32). Damsons are the speciality of Shropshire and S.W. Cheshire, where they are rarely found in orchards, but grow in the hedgerows of the cottage gardens.

In recent years there has been a marked change in the activities of the fruit-growing regions, particularly in the centralisation of marketing, in the manufacture of jam, and the bottling, canning, and deep freezing of fruits. Almost every year there are two or three weeks during which there is a great surplus of fruit. Instead of this being sold at very low prices, as formerly, it is now used in the jam and canning factories in the fruit districts. Some of such centres are Histon (Cambridge) Tiptree (Essex), Wye Valley factories (Herefordshire), Dundee, York, and Carluke (Lanarkshire).

Hops

Hops require a rich soil and hot summers. They are grown on poles in fields much after the manner of runner beans. Many hop growers now have permanent wire frameworks to support the hops. Much labour is required during the picking season, and the fact that large numbers of people from the East End of London go to Kent to pick hops during the harvest is one of the factors which has contributed to the importance of hop production in Kent.

Hops are grown in the valleys of the Weald of Kent and Sussex. The only other important district is Herefordshire and the neighbouring areas of Worcestershire. Kentish farms often include the characteristic "oast house"—a round building in which the hops are roasted before being dispatched to the brewing centres (see plate facing page 160).

Flowers

Although flowers are grown in every British garden, there is a great demand for early flowers grown under glass or in specially favourable areas. The trade in flowers is of relatively recent origin. Two districts are of major importance.

(1) The Holland district of Lincolnshire, where not only flowers are grown, but there is also an important bulb-growing industry.

(2) Cornwall and the Scilly Isles, where the extremely mild winters and absence of late spring frosts enable flower growers to send daffodils, narcissi, etc., to the London markets very early in the year.

Market Gardening

Market gardening is the large-scale production of vegetables and salad crops. Such cultivation demands much more labour and care than ordinary farming, and can be carried on profitably on high-priced land near to industrial centres. Moreover, owing to limited garden space in urban areas, it is the large towns that consume the produce. Quick transport, ensuring the freshness of the produce when it reaches the shops, is essential. The distribution of market gardeners is determined mainly by nearness to large industrial areas.

Some of the most important areas are:—

(1) The counties bordering London both on the north and south (*i.e.* the Home Counties), which supply the Metropolis (see plate facing page 33).

(2) The Vale of Evesham, which supplies the Midland industrial areas.

(3) The Vale of York, which supplies the Yorkshire woollen towns, etc.

(4) North Shropshire, Cheshire, and West Lancashire, which supply the industrial areas of Lancashire and North Staffordshire.

(5) Cornwall and Devon.

The last-named region is far removed from the industrial centres, but it has a very special climatic advantage. Its winters are the mildest in the British Isles, and there is little danger of damage being done to the crops by late frosts. Consequently vegetables can be produced much earlier than in other parts of the country.

In recent years there has been an enormous increase in the large-scale production of fresh vegetables, which now amounts to about three million tons a year, worth about £200 million, about one-tenth the value of all our agricultural production. This rapid increase has been associated with the establishment of factories for the canning and deep freezing of such vegetables as peas, beans, carrots, new potatoes, and tomatoes.

Potatoes { Production in England and Wales in 1,000's of Tons
Average 1936-8—5083; 1966-8—6767; 1969—6117

The potato can be used to supplement, or as a substitute for, cereals as human food, as food for animals, and as a starting point for the manufacture of spirits and industrial alcohol. Since potatoes are bulky and do not keep very well, they do not feature in international trade on a large scale but are grown mainly for home consumption. Consumption of potatoes in this country is greater than before the war but is now decreasing. The most important potato-growing area is the Fens (see plate facing page 32).

Potatoes are very liable to certain virus diseases, and hence the best "seed" potatoes are grown in cooler, more northerly, areas (*e.g.* Scotland) which are too cold for the insects which elsewhere carry these infections from plant to plant.

Cattle Rearing

Cattle are reared in every county in the British Isles, but some districts, because of their soil and climate, are much more important than others for cattle rearing. In 1968 our cattle numbered nearly twelve million, more than ever before in our history. Of these, over a quarter were cows in milk.

Cattle are reared for their milk, meat, and hides. Dairy cattle are those reared primarily for their milk, and they require an abundance of rich, juicy grass. For this the following conditions are necessary:—

(*a*) A good average rainfall of 30 in. or over, well distributed throughout the year. Dry periods hinder the growth of grass in the meadows.

(*b*) Cool summers, so that the grass is not parched.

(*c*) Mild winters, delaying the frosts, so that the cattle can be fed out of doors over a longer period, thus reducing the need for feeding stuffs. Grass stops growing when the temperature falls to about 6° C. (*42°* F.), hence the districts with the mildest winters, such as Cornwall and Devon and S.W. Ireland, offer the most favourable conditions for the growth of grass.

(*d*) While not absolutely necessary, a clay soil is an advantage, since clay does not allow the rain to sink quickly into the ground.

The climatic conditions outlined above are clearly those of the west of the British Isles (Fig. 23). The most important dairying regions are—

MOST IMPORTANT REGIONS
OTHER REGIONS

Fig. 23 DISTRIBUTION OF DAIRY CATTLE.

(1) CORNWALL, DEVON, AND SOMERSET. Cornwall and Devon are noted for their cream, and Somerset for Cheddar and St Ivel cheese.

(2) WELSH LOWLANDS. The Plains of Gwent, Pembroke, and Anglesey are the only extensive lowlands in Wales. The Plain of Gwent is noted for Caerphilly cheese, and

supplies milk and dairy produce to the dense population of the South Wales coalfield.

(3) CHESHIRE. This is one of the best-known dairying counties, and has more cattle per 100 acres than any other county. Its sandstones are largely covered with layers of boulder clay, often of a type much too heavy for ploughing. Cheshire is particularly famous for its cheese, but it also produces large quantities of milk for dispatch to large towns and creameries.

(4) SOLWAY FIRTH AREA. The plains around the Solway Firth, both on the Scottish and English sides, form another important dairying region. Carlisle, Dumfries, Wigtown, and Kircudbright are the chief market centres. Much of the dairy produce from this region is sent, via the Tyne Gap, to the north-eastern industrial area.

(5) AYRSHIRE. Milk and dairy produce to the industrial districts of Central Scotland are supplied by Ayrshire.

(6) THE VALES OF OXFORD AND AYLESBURY. In these areas, and in the Lower Thames Basin, the enormous demand of London for milk is one of the chief causes of the great importance of cattle rearing. Some fifty milk trains enter London daily, bringing milk from Oxfordshire, Buckinghamshire, Bedfordshire, Berkshire, etc.

(7) THE IRISH PLAINS. (*a*) In the south-west, in the lowlands of Limerick, Cork, and Tipperary, Kerry, Waterford, and Kilkenny.

(*b*) To the north of the Central Plain, in the counties of Sligo, Leitrim, Cavan, and Monaghan. The great area of lowland which extends between the two regions outlined above is not primarily a dairying region, but engaged in the rearing of cattle for beef (see page 251).

Changes are taking place in the dairying regions similar to those in the fruit and market gardening areas. Whereas in times past farmers' wives used to make most of the butter and cheese in their own dairies, to-day, factories have been established for this purpose in all the principal dairying areas. These factories make butter, cheese, and patent foods. We now produce over 2,600 million gallons of milk a year,

90 per cent. more than in 1939. About one-third of our milk is converted into butter, cheese, cream, etc. This yields less than half of the cheese we eat, and provides about one-eighth of the butter.

The "Little Wilts" dairies of Trowbridge (Wiltshire) are well known. "Ovaltine" is made in Hertfordshire, and "Trufood" in Cheshire. In Cheshire, too, there is a large collecting centre for the United Dairies, and on the Cheshire-Staffordshire border Cadbury's have a large milk collecting centre. Huntingdonshire is noted for its Stilton cheese, and the dales of Yorkshire for Wensleydale cheese.

Very often pig rearing and bacon-curing are associated with dairying, much of the skimmed milk being used to feed the pigs. The pig population of England and Wales in 1968 was over seven million. Bacon production is particularly important in Wiltshire, Berkshire, the Irish Plains, and the Vale of York. About one-third of our bacon and ham is home produced.

Cattle reared as beef or store cattle are found more especially on the Midland Plains (Fig. 24). The climate here is slightly more extreme than in the west. The New Red Sandstones of Warwickshire and the middle Trent Basin produce good pastures, and so these areas supply meat to the Midlands. The Vale of York is also important for cattle rearing. In Scotland three regions are of prime importance, and all are plains of Old Red Sandstone. The first is the triangular lowland of north-east Aberdeenshire; the second the plains around Moray Firth; and the third is the Vale of Strathmore, the long, narrow plain lying between the Highlands on the north, and the Ochils and Sidlaws on the south. This latter district is near to the industrial areas of Central Scotland.

The Central Plain of Ireland is an outstanding area for the rearing of beef cattle, particularly in the region immediately to the north-west of Dublin (Baileatha Cliath). Live cattle are exported to England. The greatest difficulty of Central Ireland is that of communication, which makes the regular collection of milk a difficult problem, hence the excellent damp pastures are used for beef production rather than dairy cattle.

In olden days, cattle rearing gave rise to leather industries in the market towns. Many of the old tanyards have now disappeared, but some still exist, as at Shrewsbury and Nantwich. In the Midlands, particularly at Northampton, Leicester, and Kettering, there are important manufactures of boots and shoes, but little of the leather is actually tanned in these towns. Stafford also makes footwear.

Fig. 24. DISTRIBUTION OF BEEF CATTLE.

Glove-making is another branch of the leather industry. Worcester, Yeovil (Somerset), and Woodstock (Oxfordshire) are among the chief centres. At Hyde and neighbouring towns in North Cheshire, hat and upholstery leathers are manufactured. Thus the chief leather manufacturing towns are never very far removed from the cattle-rearing areas.

This is because the original industries used local supplies of hides. Since the bulk of hides and skins used to-day are imported, tanning centres tend to develop in or near the great ports, *e.g.* around the Mersey estuary, and in London and Bristol.

Sheep

In the Middle Ages, England was a very important wool producer, and exported much wool to Europe. In fact, wool was England's main source of wealth, and sheep were reared on all the fertile plains of the south-east. To-day, however, the population is much greater than formerly, and land has to be used more profitably and cultivated intensively. Sheep are now reared only on areas that are unsuitable for industry, cattle pasture, or agriculture (Fig. 25) and are reared mainly for meat. The highland areas of Great Britain make good sheep pastures. Excessive dampness of the ground is a disadvantage to sheep rearing, because on damp soils sheep develop "foot rot". The western mountains, however, though wet, are well drained. Light sandy soils near the coasts with their rather stiff, dry grass, also provide good sheep pastures, since the sandy nature of the soil allows the water to sink freely into the ground, leaving the surface dry.

The principal sheep-rearing areas of Britain are enumerated as follows. In England, particularly, there is a steady transfer of hill lambs from the North and West via the intermediate heights to the lowlands of the Midlands and South.

(1) THE SCARPLANDS OF SOUTH-EASTERN ENGLAND (particularly the North and South Downs). Chalk and limestone are porous rocks, so that rain quickly sinks below the surface. The result is that the top soil is very dry, and often the only vegetation of these hills is short grass except where layers of glacial clay have given rise to woods, as on some parts of the Chiltern Hills. Kent has more sheep per acre than any other English county, and this is partly because the chalk hills (N. Downs) can be used for sheep rearing, and partly because

of its nearness to London and the consequent great demand for meat. In Kent, sheep are also reared on the salt marshes near Dungeness (Romney Marsh), but these sheep are removed to drier downlands during the winter (see plate facing page 17).

Sheep rearing is also important on the scarplands of Leicestershire and Lincolnshire.

Fig. 25. Distribution of Sheep.

(2) THE PENNINES (and the Cumberland and Westmorland Fells). The limestone districts, being composed of a porous rock, have a dry surface and produce short grass suitable for sheep rearing. Other areas of grassy fells and open moorland are similarly useful.

(3) THE WELSH MOUNTAINS. These mountains are mainly covered with moorland vegetation, and sheep rearing is very important in every county, for Wales contains very little fertile lowland. Radnorshire, with most highland and least lowland, has more sheep per acre than any other county in Wales.

(4) THE SOUTHERN UPLANDS OF SCOTLAND AND THE CHEVIOTS. This is a region very similar to Wales, both in the type of rocks of which it is composed and in the nature of the scenery. There are the same wide, open moorlands separated by fertile valleys. This is quite the most important sheep-rearing area in the British Isles, and Roxburgh has more sheep per acre than any other county in Great Britain.

(5) THE HIGHLANDS OF SCOTLAND. This is the mountainous district lying north of a line from Helensburgh to Stonehaven. This area, useless for cultivation and covered with moorland vegetation, would appear to be ideal for sheep rearing. Such, however, is not the case. In the southern areas, which are drained southwards by the River Tay and its tributaries, there is certainly a great deal of sheep rearing, and Perth has a very important sheep market. North and west of the Tay Basin, however, the area is very bleak and wet, and transport difficult. The northern areas are at a great distance from markets, and so there is less sheep rearing than one would expect, and large areas are preserved as grouse moors and deer forests.

(6) IRELAND. In Ireland there are only about one fifth the number of sheep that there are in England and Wales, and they are reared principally in two areas:—(a) in the Wicklow Mountains, in the south-east, an area with rocks very similar to those of Wales, and (b) in County Galway and parts of Roscommon, where the land surface is composed of limestone, and not covered with glacial soils as in other parts of the Central Plain. Sheep are also reared in smaller numbers on the other highland areas of Ireland, as on the Mountains of Donegal and the Mourne Mountains.

It must not be forgotten that the British Isles rank as one of the most important sheep-rearing countries of the world. We have nearly 30 million sheep, nearly three-quarters as many as there are in New Zealand, but British wool and mutton are used at home and do not enter into world trade as do the New Zealand products. In 1965 the home production of wool was nearly 60,000 tons, about one-seventh of the total quantity used by our factories. Nearly three-quarters of the beef and mutton we eat is home grown. British breeds of sheep are the basis of the great flocks of the sheep-rearing countries in the Southern Hemisphere, and there is a steady export of British pedigree animals to these countries.

Poultry

The most important poultry-rearing districts in order of importance are:—Lancashire, Norfolk, West Riding of Yorkshire, Essex, and Cheshire. The supply of poultry and eggs to large industrial areas is an important factor in determining the distribution of these districts. "Broiler" production is especially important in Norfolk. Nearly all the eggs we eat are now home produced.

Ireland normally produces large quantities of poultry for export, and has a particularly important trade in Christmas turkeys.

Fisheries

The British fishing industry is the eighth largest in the world but has been decreasing in size in recent years. There are some 25,000 fishermen, giving employment in all to perhaps 120,000 persons. The annual catch, over $\frac{3}{4}$ million tons, is worth about £70 million. Until recently almost every coastal village, especially in Devon and Cornwall, had its tiny fishing fleet, but of recent years the industry has become highly concentrated in certain ports with good facilities for rapid transport by rail or road to inland industrial areas.

The chief fish caught are cod, a deep-water fish from cold northern waters as far away even as Iceland and the Grand Bank; haddock, another deep-water fish, caught largely in the more northerly parts of the North Sea; and herrings, a surface-water fish in the North Sea. Of these, cod is much the most important. Of recent years, the North Sea fisheries, especially the herring fisheries, have been over-fished and they are now much less productive than formerly.

The principal fishing ports are Grimsby, Hull, Fleetwood, and Lowestoft; North Shields and Milford Haven are smaller centres. Herring fishing is seasonal in character, and since most of the catch is either cured or exported, good rail facilities are not so important in this case. The chief herring ports are Peterhead and Fraserburgh in Scotland, and Yarmouth and Lowestoft in East Anglia. Herring fishing is also an important occupation of certain small ports in the west of Scotland, *e.g.* Stornoway, Ullapool, Mallaig, and Oban.

Over 200,000 tons of fish are landed annually at British ports from foreign ships, *i.e.* are imported, at a cost of £80 million.

Forestry

Only about 6 per cent. of the area of the British Isles is woodland, and the greatest density of woodland is in the north and east of Scotland and the south-eastern counties of England. Rather more than half this area is Forestry Commission land. Home-grown timber provides only a small proportion of our national requirements and the remainder has to be imported. The Forestry Commission is planning to increase our woodland area by 50 per cent. over the next fifty years, when, it is estimated, it will provide about one-fifth of the timber we need. At present the proportion is less than one-tenth. See also page 228 for forestry in Scotland.

CHAPTER 4

INDUSTRY AND SERVICES

We saw in Chapter 3 that only about two per cent. of people in Britain are employed in agriculture; very much fewer than in any other country. Indeed, taking the world as a whole, nearly three-fifths of the population depend directly on agriculture.

Britain is the most highly industrialised country in the world, and only by selling manufactured articles abroad are we able to pay for the food and raw materials we have to import (see Chapter 28).

Although there are no towns and few villages of any size that do not have some manufacture, manufacturing tends to be concentrated in various "industrial" areas. This localisation is due to a number of factors. Every industry needs—

(1) Power;

(2) Raw materials;

(3) Labour;

(4) Customers.

In addition, certain industries have special needs, *e.g.* shipbuilding demands access to navigable water, aircraft assembly plants must be adjacent to airfields, heavy chemical industries require large quantities of water, and so on.

In Britain, as in nearly all industrial countries, the chief source of power is still coal, although oil is now not far behind. Coal is a heavy and bulky material and is expensive to haul considerable distances except when carried in bulk by water. Hence industries using large amounts of coal are generally located on coalfields. It is true that Greater London, the biggest single industrial area in the world, has developed at a considerable distance from a coalfield, but London has always been able to obtain coal cheaply by sea from, *e.g.*, Northumberland and Durham coalfields.

Industries requiring very large amounts of electric power are sometimes most economically located in areas where hydroelectric power is available. A British example is the extraction of aluminium from bauxite at Lochaber (pp. 241-6).

Electrical power generated from coal or other sources of energy can be sent considerable distances comparatively cheaply by cable, and the development of the National Electricity grid in recent years has assisted industrial growth in the south-eastern half of England.

If an industry uses large amounts of raw materials it is clearly an advantage to save cost of transport by operating as close to the source of the raw materials as possible. Hence, for example, we find iron and steel works on those coalfields where iron ore is also found; a considerable proportion of our bricks are made on the Oxford Clay belt between Bletchley and Peterborough; and cement works are almost invariably very close to their supplies of chalk and clay. When raw materials have to be imported from overseas, the industries using them are often to be found at or near the ports. Thus there is much smelting of imported ores in South Wales and on Merseyside; all our petroleum refineries, with the exception of Llandarcy, are either at ports or on estuaries, and many of our ports have flour mills.

Improved communications—in the nineteenth century the development of railways, and in the twentieth the growth of road transport—are factors reducing the dependence of an industry on nearness to its raw materials, and hence are factors tending to assist the wider spread of industry.

A large new factory built in an agricultural area will have great difficulty in obtaining work people. Hence there is a big tendency for new works to be set up in, or very near, large towns, *i.e.* in existing industrial areas, which therefore tend to grow more and more industrialised, spreading out further and further and engulfing agricultural land in the process. Again, existing towns can offer services not so readily available in the countryside—water, gas, transport services, and facilities for education or entertainment.

An industry, if it is to survive, must be able to sell its goods; *i.e.* it must have customers, or what we call a "market". It will clearly be an advantage if this market is close at hand, although the degree of advantage varies greatly with the commodity and is in general very small for articles of high value for their weight or bulk. It does not usually pay, for example, to cart gravel or sand more than ten miles. It is because of the local market that the manufacture of agricultural implements is often the first type of engineering to develop in a hitherto non-industrial area. It also accounts for the growth of, *e.g.*, textile machinery manufactures in South-East Lancashire (p. 123). Obviously the biggest markets are the existing densely-populated industrial areas, which therefore again attract further industries. It is largely because of this that the huge industrial area of Greater London has grown so rapidly and so large.

It is very difficult to draw a hard and fast line between different industries, especially in the chemical and engineering trades, as in many cases the finished product of one industry is the raw material of another. Thus textiles are the raw materials of the important clothing industry; coal and iron ore those of the steel industry; bricks, cement, etc., those of the building industry. A number of industries, *e.g.* shipbuilding and vehicle manufacturing, are largely concerned with the assembly of components made separately elsewhere.

We shall divide the main industries of Great Britain into—

(1) Mining and Quarrying;

(2) The Smelting of Iron and Other Ores;

(3) Textiles;

(4) Engineering;

(5) Chemicals;

(6) Building and Construction.

There are, in addition, many other smaller industries, some of which make a considerable contribution to our export trade, *e.g.* whisky distilling (£175 million).

Mining and Quarrying

It is obvious that mining and quarrying can only be carried on in places where the requisite ore or material occurs. Nevertheless, other economic factors, such as the richness of the deposit and ease of access from the centres wishing to make use of the raw material, will decide which of the possible sites will be worked, or worked first.

Above: The Helford River, Cornwall, an example of a "ria" or drowned valley. The picture, taken at low tide, shows the stream meandering over the alluvial flats. At high tide the estuary is full of water from bank to bank. (*Judges Ltd.*)

Below: Land's End, a rugged coastline eroded by the Atlantic waves. (*Valentine and Sons, Ltd.*)

Above: Brixham in Devon (*Valentine and Sons, Ltd*), and
Below: Polperro in Cornwall (*B.R.*).

Many coastal villages and towns in Devon and Cornwall formerly had their fishing fleet and occasionally a little smuggling was a profitable sideline.   Now these places are main engaged in catering for holiday makers.

By far the most important mineral mined in Britain is coal. The location of the coalfields is described on pp. 6-7 and 210-222 (for relative outputs see Figs. 36 and 105). The coastal coalfields have obviously an advantage from the point of view of exporting. They are, in order of importance, South Wales, Northumberland and Durham, Fifeshire, and Cumberland. Nowadays, however our export of coal is very small although there are still appreciable coast-wise shipments.

The Lanarkshire, North Staffordshire, and South Wales Coalfields also have iron ore deposits but these are now to all intents and purposes exhausted. Almost the whole of our home supplies of iron ore now come from the oolitic limestone areas of Oxfordshire, Northamptonshire, and Lincolnshire (pp. 151, 117).

Apart from iron ore there is little mining of ore of other metals except small quantities of lead and tin. Salt is produced in Cheshire and Worcestershire (see p. 7) for domestic use and as a raw material for chemical industries. Annual output is about 2 million tons.

Very large quantities of non-metallic minerals are quarried. Production of limestone and chalk, mainly from the escarpments of the south-eastern half of England, is about 40 million tons. Some of this is mixed with clay and converted into cement. About 6 million tons of limestone are used annually in blast furnaces as flux. Large quantities are used as raw materials in the chemical industry and in agriculture as lime, while in some limestone areas the rock is quarried for building stone (*e.g.* Bath and Portland).

Deposits of sand and gravel are widespread and over 40 million tons a year are dug mainly for use in building construction. Slate is obtained from North Wales and Cumberland. Some 12 million tons of igneous rocks are quarried mainly for road metal. Other important minerals are sandstone (2 million tons), fire-clay ($2\frac{1}{2}$ million tons), gypsum ($2\frac{1}{2}$ million tons), and china clay (1 million tons).

The Smelting and Refining of Metallic Ores.

Most metallic ores are converted into the metal by heating in blast furnaces with coke, made from coal in coke-ovens.

The coking of coal also yields valuable coal-tar products, an important raw material for certain chemical industries.

To produce a ton of iron, there is needed on the average about two tons of ore, nearly a ton of coke and about 6 cwt of limestone, which is used as a flux. Larger amounts of ore and coke than this are needed for low-grade English ores, which have a low iron content, smaller amounts for high grade imported ore. It is clearly more economical to bring the coke to the ore, rather than the ore to the coke. In earlier days, however, when owing to less efficient smelting much larger amounts of coke were required, the pull of the coalfields was greater.

British iron-smelting areas can be divided into three classes: (*a*) coastal coalfields using mainly imported ore; (*b*) inland iron-producing areas away from coalfields, and (*c*) inland coalfields without local ore. These last are mainly engaged in remaking scrap iron. Of the three largest iron-smelting areas— South Wales (p. 78), North-East England (p. 96), and Lanark- shire (p. 217), the first two are coastal. Less important centres in this class are on or near the Manchester Ship Canal, the Dee, and in Cumberland and Barrow (p. 87).

The two inland iron-smelting areas away from coalfields are centred on Scunthorpe in Lincolnshire (p. 117) and Corby in Northamptonshire (pp. 151-52). These use the local Jurassic iron ores.

Much of the iron produced in blast furnaces is turned into steel in mills, which for economy of operation are built adjac- ent to the blast furnaces. The remainder is sent to steel works in many centres throughout the country, or is exported. Sheffield is a steel centre which buys iron from Scunthorpe and elsewhere, and now makes nearly ten per cent. of Britain's steel. Birmingham is the centre of another important steel region. Both Sheffield and Birmingham make considerable use of "scrap" which is obtained from dismantled machinery, worn out railway track, old motor vehicles, and so on.

The iron-smelting areas centred on Sheffield and on Birming- ham are in class (*c*), on inland coalfields and with little or no local ore. The Sheffield district is much the more important. It ranks fourth in output for the British Isles and makes nearly all the British output of special steel and steel alloys.

Since our supplies of non-ferrous ores are almost all imported, the principal smelting and refining areas for these are, as we should expect, on or near coastal coalfields. The South Wales coalfield, especially round Swansea and Llanelly (p. 78) is the most important area, particularly for copper and zinc. Other important areas are Merseyside, Clydeside, and the London and Birmingham industrial districts.

Textile Industries

Cotton goods were our principal export some fifty years ago. Owing to foreign competition and the rise of artificial fibres such as rayon and nylon there has been a falling off of production and the amounts exported are only a quarter of those before the War of 1939-45. South-East Lancashire is still the world's most concentrated cotton manufacturing area but cotton goods are now down to twelfth place in our export list (nearly £40 million) and we produce only one-fifth as much as India. Another important cotton manufacturing area is around Glasgow.

The factors affecting the location of the cotton industry and the various processes employed are described on pp. 119-23.

Wool. The location of our woollen industries is described on pp. 101-3. Wool, unlike raw cotton, can be produced at home; but most of our raw wool is imported as home supplies are insufficient. The value of our woollen exports is about twice that of our cotton goods, although the quantity exported is rather less than before the War of 1939-45.

Rayon is a form of cellulose and is made chiefly from the naturally occurring cellulose in wood pulp by a process involving the use of chemicals and very large amounts of water. Britain is the world's third largest producer (after the U.S.A. and Japan) with an output of about half a million tons, and our exports are worth about one quarter those of cotton or woollen goods. The industry is not so localised as those of wool and cotton. The principal areas are south-east Lancashire, the Midlands, especially in Leicester, Flintshire, and at Pontypool. Pontypool also makes nearly all our *nylon*, a purely synthetic fibre.

Linen is made from flax. The linen industry is carried on throughout Northern Ireland, the chief centre being Belfast (see pp. 245-6). Northern Ireland is the most important linen-manufacturing area in the world.

Jute. Sacks, canvas backing for carpets, rope, and other products are made at Dundee from raw jute imported from Pakistan.

Silk. Silk manufacturing is not an important industry in Britain. It is carried on in Flint, in Macclesfield, and the surrounding district, and in London (Spitalfields).

The Clothing Industry. The manufacture of clothing is a very large industry employing over a quarter of a million people. London is the most important centre, followed by Lancashire and the West Riding of Yorkshire (especially Bradford and Leeds).

Engineering

Engineering includes the manufacture and assembly of a great variety of metal goods, such as machinery, engines, boilers, tools, locomotives and rolling stock, ships, vehicles, aircraft, dynamos, motors, etc., and employs over 4 million workers.

Heavy engineering is largely found in the large industrial areas of the north of England and of Central Scotland, light engineering in London and South East England and in the Midlands.

SHIPBUILDING. Britain is the world's fourth largest shipbuilder, constructing about five per cent. of all new ships (largely oil-tankers these days). Our exports of ships in 1969 were worth £67 million.

Three-quarters of our total output is produced in two main areas, Clydeside in Scotland, where ships of all kinds are built, and in North-East England on the estuaries of the Tyne, Tees, and Wear, which tend to specialise in tankers and "tramp" steamers. Of the smaller areas, Belfast specialises in liners and motor ships; Birkenhead and Merseyside to these adds also naval vessels. Naval ships are built also in the various naval dockyards. Most large ports also do a little shipbuilding and all have repair yards.

Large shipbuilding areas are all on estuaries and usually near steel-producing areas, as the heavy plates and girders used in the construction of ships are bulky, heavy and costly to transport, except over short distances. Considerable deep-water frontage is also needed and this is not usually available at coastal ports.

MOTOR VEHICLES. Although far behind the United States in volume of production, Great Britain is among the world's largest exporters of motor vehicles (cars, lorries, and buses). The industry employs about 100,000 people and exports were worth £600 million in 1969. The industry is located mainly in in the Midlands and the South-East, with Coventry, Birmingham, Derby, Luton, London, Oxford, and Bristol as important centres [see Fig. 25 (*a*)]. There is a factory in the Irish Republic at Cork. Much of the work consists of assembling components manufactured in numerous smaller factories. Most of the component firms are found in the Midlands and the London area, and are thus well placed to supply assembly plants. The industry relies on a steady flow of components which cannot readily be stock-piled because of the space required. The industry is therefore very much at the mercy of strikes in component factories.

AIRCRAFT. Aircraft manufacture, the newest of the vehicle industries, has grown very rapidly and employs nearly a quarter of a million people. Assembly plants must be on or close to airfields, the components and engines being made elsewhere. Derby, Bristol, and Crewe are important aero-engine centres. Exports of aircraft in 1969 were valued at £180 million.

RAILWAY VEHICLES. The chief centres for the manufacture and repair of railway locomotives and rolling stock are Swindon, Crewe, Darlington, Doncaster, Derby, and Eastleigh (near Southampton). Exports were worth £12 million in 1968.

ELECTRICAL ENGINEERING is another rapidly growing industry and includes the manufacture of, *e.g.*, dynamos and motors, wires and cables, lamps, telephone and telegraph equipment, radio, radar, and television apparatus, and so on. It employs nearly a million people and exports products to the value of over £400 million. London is much the most important centre, followed by Lancashire and the West Midlands.

MACHINERY MANUFACTURES are a very wide group and include agricultural machinery and tractors, textile machinery

(South-East Lancashire, see page 120), civil engineering plant, office equipment, and machinery for all other industries. Machinery is our second largest export, second only to vehicles.

London is the most important single area, but all industrial areas share in the making of machinery. Agricultural

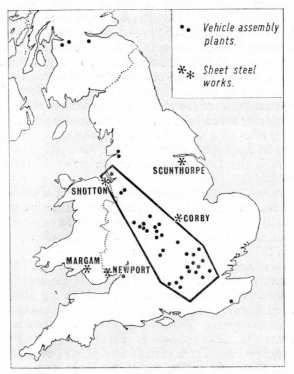

Fig. 25 (*a*). LOCATION OF MOTOR VEHICLE PLANTS IN THE BRITISH ISLES AND THE MIDLAND "COFFIN". From E. H. Cooper, *Economic Geography*, U.T.P.

machinery tends to be made in numerous small factories in market towns in agricultural areas, near the customers. Lincoln and Ipswich are important centres.

The Chemical Industry

This is another industry, with a wide variety of products, that has expanded very greatly in recent years. Overall output is now about four or five times that of 1938. It employs about half a million people and contributes about £600 million to our exports—besides providing a vast range of products for use in other industries.

Chemical industry includes the manufacture of sulphuric acid, sodium carbonate, lime, cement, and glass, the processing of vegetable fats and oils for the preparation of soap, glycerine, and margarine, the refining of petroleum (see p. 259), the manufacture of fertilisers, pesticides, synthetic plasters, and explosives, and the preparation of fine chemicals, dyestuffs, paints and varnishes, bleaches, drugs and pharmaceutical preparations, and cosmetics.

Heavy chemical industries and especially those depending on imported materials, *e.g.* the manufacture of soap and margarine and petroleum refining, are usually near ports or estuaries. About half of our sulphuric acid (3 million tons a year) is made from imported sulphur, so many of these plants are also on or near the coast. Salt is an important raw material for certain chemical processes and the salt deposits of Cheshire have helped in the development of chemical industries in Flint and the estuaries of the Dee and Mersey. The great I.C.I. works at Billingham-on-Tees are also close to salt deposits. The manufacture of dyes and bleaches are often found in textile areas, *e.g.* the Glasgow region, and, especially, in south-east Lancashire. The location of works making drugs and fine chemicals is largely influenced by the availability of labour and the nearness of local markets.

Heavy chemical industries are important in Cheshire, the Wirral, and the Manchester Ship Canal districts, in Flint, Clydeside, the estuaries of north-east England, and in London.

Building and Contracting

This is one of our largest industries, employing over $1\frac{1}{2}$ million men. It differs, however, from those we have considered above in that it is not a factory industry. Although there are many large firms engaged mainly in public works construction, the great majority of workers are employed by small firms in almost every town and village in the country. The big firms often undertake the planning and supervision of work overseas, payment for which is an "invisible export" (see p. 260).

Services

The agricultural and industrial occupations referred to above account for less than half our total employed. The remainder, nearly fifty-five per cent. of the whole, are engaged in a wide variety of occupations, which, while they do not produce goods, are essential to the smooth and satisfactory running of our life.

Some three million people are employed in the distributive trades, wholesale and retail shops and warehouses, which enable the mass-produced goods of a manufacturer to be available, often at great distances, to the customers who want them.

Transport, sea, river, rail, road, and air, accounts for another one and a half million workers. Transport brings food and raw materials from a distance, even sometimes from another hemisphere, and enables the products of manufacture to be sent just as far. Transport also enables the modern worker to live at a distance from his place of work, *commuting* every day by rail or road between his home and his office or factory.

Getting on for a million and a half are employed on central and local government, but the largest figure for services is for the group "Professional and Financial Services" which accounts for no less than five and a half million.

Financial Services include banking, insurance, and accountancy. The Health Services cover doctors, dentists, nurses, opticians, pharmacists, and a wide range of medical auxiliaries. Education includes half a million teachers. Scientists, lawyers, surveyors, and a wide range of other occupations are all examples of Professional Services.

CHAPTER 5

THE WESTERN PENINSULAS

(1) THE SOUTH-WEST PENINSULA

On the west of Great Britain are three peninsulas:—

    (a) Cornwall, Devon, and Somerset.

    (b) Wales.

    (c) The Cumbrian peninsula.

These three peninsulas have many points in common, for they all contain high moorland areas, experience heavy rainfall, and enjoy equable climates. As they are on the west they are regions to which the early inhabitants of Britain were driven by the successive invaders in the early days of British history from pre-Roman times onwards. They all contain interesting historical monuments, such as stone circles and monuments. Often a similarity in place-names can be seen, e.g. *Pen*rith (Cumberland), *Pen*maenmawr (Wales), and *Pen*zance (Cornwall), and in all these regions there are interesting survivals of ancient customs.

DEVON AND CORNWALL

This part of England is bounded on the east by the line of the Jurassic limestone escarpment which passes east of the Mendips southwards to the coast of Dorset at Lyme Regis on the Devon-Dorset boundary.

Although the climate and products of Somerset are very similar to those of Cornwall and Devon as a result of similar climatic conditions, the former county is so different in structure that it will be described separately. The eastern boundary of Devon is a N.W. to S.E. line running from a point just east of the Foreland to Lyme Regis. The River Tamar may be taken as the dividing line between Cornwall and Devon.

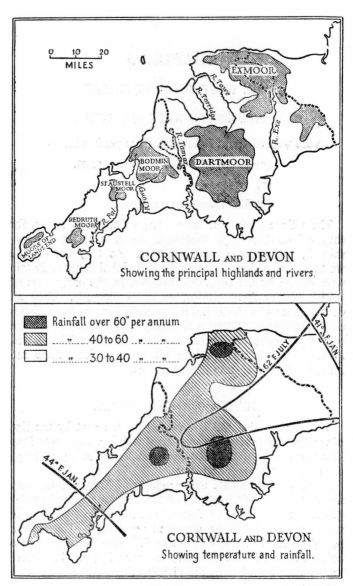

Fig. 26 (*a*).

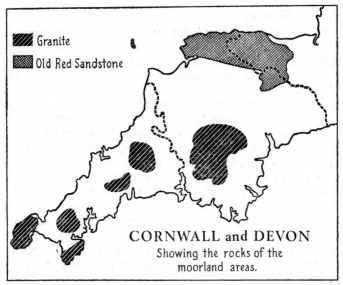

Granite

Old Red Sandstone

CORNWALL and DEVON
Showing the rocks of the
moorland areas.

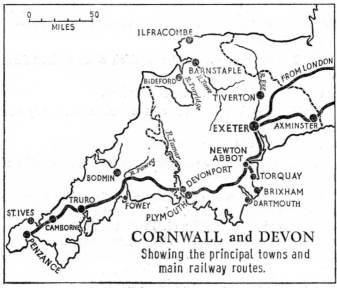

0   50
MILES

ILFRACOMBE

BARNSTAPLE

BIDEFORD

R.Towe

R.Torridge

R.Exe

FROM LONDON

TIVERTON

EXETER

AXMINSTER

R.Tamar

R.Fowey

NEWTON
ABBOT

BODMIN

DEVONPORT

TORQUAY

TRURO

FOWEY

BRIXHAM

PLYMOUTH

DARTMOUTH

ST.IVES

CAMBORNE

PENZANCE

CORNWALL and DEVON
Showing the principal towns and
main railway routes.

Fig. 26 (*b*).   (For railways see also page 63.)

Physical Features

In the north of Devon is the western portion of Exmoor, a plateau of rounded moorlands composed of Old Red Sandstone. Exmoor drops steeply to the north Devon coast, but falls more gently southwards to the plain of Devon. This plain is drained by the rivers Taw and Torridge northwards to Barnstaple Bay, and by the River Exe (which rises in Exmoor) southwards to Exeter.

In the southern "bulge" of Devonshire a great mass of granite rises to form the extensive moorlands known as Dartmoor, a wild, bleak, rainy, heather-clad region, which is very attractive to tourists. From it the River Dart and tributaries of the other Devonshire streams drain rapidly. Rising above the general level (1,200 ft) of the moorlands are huge masses of bare granite known as "tors", the chief of which are Yes Tor and Great Links Tor (see plate facing page 16). Large areas of Dartmoor are occupied by bogs due to the clay formed by the decomposition of granite under the action of rain.

Dartmoor (see plate facing page 16) is a good illustration of the scenery of a granite region which is characterised by:—

(*a*) Wide, open, valleys.

(*b*) The marshy valley bottoms which when drained form rich cattle pastures.

(*c*) Rounded hills with smooth outlines.

(*d*) The thin infertile soils of the moorlands, sandy and gritty in texture.

(*e*) "Tors" of bare granite crowning the uplands.

(*f*) Many springs and streams due to the impermeability of the rock.

West and south-west of Dartmoor are four similar granite moorlands of smaller area. They are the Bodmin moors, culminating in Brown Willy (1,375 ft), the St Austell moors, the Redruth moors, and the low moorlands near Land's End. Thirty miles beyond Land's End are the Scilly Isles, also composed of granite. The Cornish plains surrounding the granite moorlands are of Old Red Sandstone which weathers into a rich red soil. The chief rivers of Cornwall are the Fal,

Camel, and Fowey. On the low watershed separating the last two is Bodmin, the county town.

An important characteristic of the coast is the large number of drowned valleys or "rias", which provide good harbours (see plate facing page 48). The most notable is the large branching estuary of the Tamar known as Plymouth Sound. Similar in shape and size is Falmouth Harbour. Other large estuaries are those of the Dart, Exe, and Taw. Elsewhere the quaint little coves and harbours and the impressive grandeur of the rugged cliffs have made the coastal scenery of Cornwall and Devon famous for its beauty, and in the past renowned for its "sea dogs" and smugglers.

Climate

Because Cornwall and Devon is a peninsula open to the south-west winds from the Atlantic it is characterised by warm winters (6°-7° C., *42°-45° F.*), cool summers (16°-17° C., *60°-62° F.*), and a good average rainfall. An isotherm map of Europe reveals the fact that its winter temperatures are practically the same as those of the French Riviera. This will serve to emphasise the extreme mildness of the Cornish winters, but it must be remembered that Cornwall is much cloudier than the south of France, and also that in the south of France the insolation is greater and the winter days longer. Because of the mild winters, palms, aloes, and other semi-tropical plants will grow out of doors (see plate facing page 33).

Occupations

Many people in Cornwall and Devon are engaged in some kind of agriculture, and the type of farming is largely determined by the climatic conditions.

The rich pastures, resulting from the fertile soils of the lowlands, the equable temperatures, and the rainfall, have given rise to cattle rearing and an important dairying industry. Because these regions are so remote from densely-populated industrial areas they specialise in the production of butter and cheese, rather than in the sale of fresh milk. There is, however, a condensing depot at Lostwithiel to which the farmers of that district sell their milk direct.

Another industry which owes its importance to the mildness of the winters is the growing of early vegetables such as broccoli, peas, and beans for the northern markets. The growing of early flowers, both in Cornwall and the Scilly Isles, is due to the same cause, for frosts rarely occur. In Cornwall the flower fields are mostly to be found in sheltered valleys, while in the Scilly Isles stone walls surround the fields and serve as a protection against the wind.

Fruit-growing, too, is largely the result of the warm winters and sunny summers. Devon produces large quantities of "cider" apples, and cider is manufactured, *e.g.* at Whimple.

The variety of the scenery, the wide open moorlands, the winding Devon lanes and pleasant villages, the rugged grandeur of the coast, and the luxuriant vegetation all add to the attractions of the peninsula. Thus Cornwall and Devon are very popular holiday centres and their most important industry is the "Tourist Industry". On Saturdays in summer there are frequently traffic jams on the road bottle-necks at Exeter and Taunton. All around the coast are famous resorts such as Torquay, Looe, Newquay, and Ilfracombe. Because of the warm winter climate tourists visit Cornwall and Devon in winter as well as in summer, and for this reason it is known as the "English Riviera".

The close association of all parts of the peninsula with the sea has also had a great influence on the lives of the people. Standing on Bodmin moor it is possible, on a clear day, to see the sea both to the north and south of Cornwall. There is, here, a familiarity with the ocean in all its moods, and the people have developed a natural love of the sea. The sheltered harbours each have a tiny fishing fleet. A great variety of fish is caught (notably pilchards). The most important fishing centres are Newlyn, Plymouth, Brixham, Mevagissey, St Ives, and Looe. But the fisheries of the south-west are now of only minor importance, partly because both the fleets and harbours are small, partly because the region is so distant from the centres of dense population, and partly because the fishing grounds are not as productive as those of the North Sea (see also page 44).

Because of their close association with the sea, large numbers of men join the Navy, and Devonport on Plymouth Sound is a naval centre.

Quarrying and mining must also be included in the list of occupations. Granite is quarried in many localities for building purposes; slates are quarried at Penryn; and limestone near Torquay. The most important mineral is kaolin or china clay, which is formed by the decomposition of granite. The chief source of kaolin is the St Austell moorland. The clay is shipped from Fowey and Par, and is taken to the Mersey, whence it is dispatched to North Staffordshire for the manufacture of pottery, and to Lancashire for use in paper making, and also for "dressing" cotton fabrics. Tin ore has been mined in Cornwall for over 2,000 years, since the time when Phoenician traders sought it in exchange for purple cloth. To-day the Cornish mines are almost exhausted. Their annual output in recent years has been about 1,000 tons compared with a total world production of over 150,000 tons.

Great Britain imports annually about 25,000 tons of tin (as concentrates) for her tin-plating and other industries.

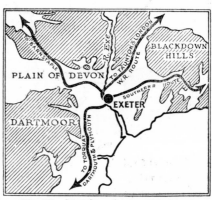

Fig. 27. THE POSITION OF EXETER.

Communications

The peninsula is served by two main railway lines, whose routes well illustrate the nature of Dartmoor as a barrier to communication. One route approaches Exeter from Axminster, and then strikes round the north of Dartmoor to Barnstaple. The other route approaches Exeter from Taunton by a more northerly route than the former, and then follows the southern coastal plain to Plymouth, whence the line proceeds to Penzance [Fig. 26 (b)].

Chief Towns

Exeter (95,000), the county town of Devonshire, is an old Roman station, situated at the lowest point of bridging of the

River Exe. From here the famous Roman Road, the Fosse Way, struck north-eastwards. It is a great market centre for east Devon. Its University was founded in 1955.

Torquay is the most famous of the sea-side resorts. It is situated on a sheltered bay on the "lee" side of Dartmoor, so that it is well sheltered from westerly gales and has a maximum of sunshine. With Brixham and Paignton, Torquay is now part of the new County Borough of Torbay (100,000).

Plymouth (250,000), at the mouth of the River Plym, stands at the entrance to a fine natural harbour known as Plymouth Sound. This position, and the fact that it is at the western end of the English Channel guarding the approach to the

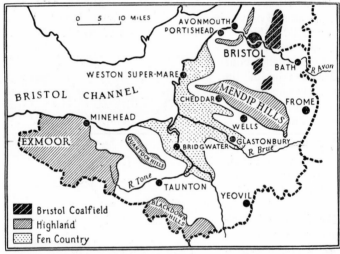

Fig. 28. THE NATURAL DIVISIONS OF SOMERSET.

"Narrow Seas" from the west, made it an important naval station in Elizabethan days (see Fig. 97). Devonport, adjoining it on the west, is the modern naval centre. Plymouth is the natural focus of routes from both Devon and Cornwall [see Figs. 26 (*a*) and (*b*)] and has light engineering industries.

Barnstaple (16,000), at the lowest bridging point of the River Taw, is the market centre for the north-western portion of the plain of Devon. Another market centre is Bideford, near the mouth of the River Torridge.

Above: The Pass of Llanberis, typical of Snowdonia. In the distance is Llanberis Lake. Note the swiftly-flowing stream in the lower left-hand corner; the stone walls; the boulder-strewn hillsides; and the scantiness of vegetation except in the valley bottom. (*B.R.*)

Below: A mining valley in South Wales. Note the road, the railway, with its coal trucks, and the stream, side by side, with the mountains in the background. (*Glyn Davies*.)

Above: A view of the melting shop at the steelworks at Margam, Port Talbot. (*The Steel Company of Wales Ltd.*)

Below: Oil refinery at Milford Haven. Tankers of up to 100,000 tons can unload at the berths. (*ESSO Petroleum Company.*)

SOMERSET

Somerset may be divided into four distinct areas (Fig. 28):—

(1) The highland areas of the south-west, including most of Exmoor, the Quantock Hills, and the Blackdown Hills.

(2) An extensive lowland drained by the rivers Parret, Axe, and Brue.

(3) The Mendip Hills.

(4) The lowland between the Mendips and the River Avon.

The Highland Areas of the South-West

This division includes part of Exmoor, the Blackdown Hills, and the Quantocks. The latter, like Exmoor, are composed of Old Red Sandstone. Between the Quantock Hills and the Blackdown Hills is the valley of the River Tone, a tributary of the River Parret.

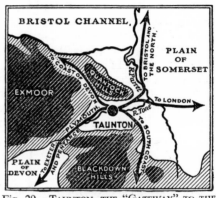

Fig. 29. Taunton, the "Gateway" to the South-West Peninsular.

Taunton, on the Tone (Fig. 29), situated about midway between the Bristol Channel and the English Channel, and controlling the route to the south-west, is one of the chief railroad foci of the western peninsula.

The Plain of Somerset

A careful comparison of the physical and geological maps shows that the plain of Somerset is composed of very new rocks. The plain is covered partly by alluvial and partly by peaty soils. It is uniformly low and flat except where "islands" of harder rock rise slightly above the general level. As in the Fens of Eastern England, this region has been drained by the cutting of innumerable ditches, and rivers have been straightened in order to increase their rate of flow, so that they can more easily drain away the surplus water. In olden days the firm islands within the marsh were refuges, *e.g.* King Alfred took refuge on the "Isle" of Athelney, and on these "islands", too, settlements grew up, *e.g.* Glastonbury. The coastline of this part of Somerset is straight, being composed of sand dunes 20-30 ft high, which rise above the level of the plain behind them. The plain is drained by sluggish streams, such as the Parret, Axe, and Brue.

Like Cornwall and Devon, Somerset is open to the influence of the westerly winds, which moderate the temperature and bring an ample, well-distributed rainfall. Because of the climatic conditions the reclaimed and drained land is used for rearing dairy cattle and for apple orchards. Cheddar, in the north of the plain, and Yeovil, in the south, are both noted for cheese. Bridgwater (28,000), at the lowest point of bridging of the Parret, has a famous cattle market. On the east the plain is bounded by the low limestone hills of the Dorset-Somerset border, part of the main limestone escarpment. On the coast, at Hinckley Point is a nuclear power station capable of producing at full load over 2 per cent. of our present consumption of electricity.

The Mendip Hills

The Mendips are really a limestone plateau nearly 1000 ft in average elevation. The limestone is an older type than the Oolitic Limestone, and is similar to that found in the Pennines. The scenery is of the "karst" type with caverns, and steep-sided gorges (*e.g.* Cheddar). As the limestone supports only short grass, sheep rearing is important, but dairy cattle are increasing where soils have been artificially improved.

To the east of the Mendips, and extending over the Wiltshire border, is a region famous for its woollen industry. The chief towns are Bradford-on-Avon, Frome, Trowbridge, and Westbury, all quite small. Before the Industrial Revolution this region, with the Cotswold area to the north, was the most important woollen manufacturing region in England, and is known as the "West of England woollen region" (Fig. 30). It originated because:—

(1) Sheep were reared on the limestone hills;

(2) There were good supplies of water;

(3) There was present in the limestone rocks supplies of fuller's earth, a soapy clay which was used to remove grease from the wool.

The competition of the woollen manufacturers of the West Riding of Yorkshire led to a decline in the West of England woollen industry. Though less important than formerly, it has survived because it has specialised in the manufacture of materials such as broadcloth, whipcords, and blankets. These woollen towns are all small, old, and picturesque, with quaint stone mills by the river side. They offer a complete contrast to the modern and often ugly industrial cities of the north.

The Lowland North of the Mendips

To the north of the Mendips is the lower basin of the Avon, which contains the Bristol coalfield. The Avon, after passing through the oolitic escarpment between Bradford and Bath, flows westward in great meanders, and

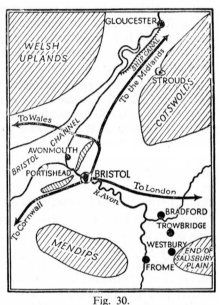

Fig. 30.

THE POSITION OF BRISTOL AND THE WOOLLEN TOWNS OF THE "WEST OF ENGLAND".

then crosses a small limestone plateau by means of a deep, steep-sided gorge at Clifton. Bristol (430,000) stands to the east of the gorge, and is thus sheltered by the plateau. Before the Industrial Revolution the south of England was the most densely-populated part of the country, and Bristol was the western focus of the trade of the English lowlands. It was the largest port on the west coast, and ranked second only to London. Now it takes tenth place. Its trade was originally with Ireland, but, with the colonisation of America and the growth of settlements on the west coast of Africa, its trade rapidly increased. Slaves obtained from Africa were exchanged for typical West Indian products, such as tobacco, sugar, cocoa, which formed the return cargo. It imports similar West Indian products to-day, as well as large quantities of petroleum, of aluminium, and of fruit, such as bananas and pineapples. The city has a number of industries based on its characteristic imports, viz. sugar refining, cigarette manufacture, and cocoa and chocolate works, and paper making; while, in recent years, it has become an important centre of the aircraft industry, and is now attracting a large petroleum chemical industry. A 78-mile pipe-line has been built from Fawley to Severnside, near Bristol.

A relatively easy route connects Bristol with London. This route follows the Avon Valley at first, then goes through the chalk uplands and follows the River Kennet to its junction with the Thames at Reading, and so along the Thames to London. This route (A4) is being supplemented by a new motorway (M4) more or less parallel to it (see Fig. 99). This motorway extends westwards of Bristol to Newport, crossing the Severn by the new bridge at Aust, which avoids the detour northwards to Gloucester to cross the river.

Two hundred years ago, Bristol was the great port of the west coast, while Liverpool was only a fishing village. To-day Bristol is certainly larger than formerly, but Liverpool is twice as large as Bristol. This is primarily due to industrialisation of Northern England. Ships, too, have grown larger, and Bristol now has two outports, Avonmouth and Portishead, at the mouth of the Avon. These outports handle shipping too large to be able to make their way up-river to Bristol docks. The ports handle considerable coastal traffic and their hinterland extends as far as the Midland industrial areas, as is shown by their chief exports, which are cars and engineering goods. Avonmouth has the largest zinc-smelting plant in the world.

Bath (85,000) was founded by the Romans on the site of hot mineral springs. It is still a spa and has engineering and other industries.

CHAPTER 6

THE WESTERN PENINSULAS

(2) WALES AND THE WELSH BORDERLANDS

The boundary between England and Wales is a north to south line which deviates little from longitude 3° W. Except in south Shropshire, where part of the plateau extends eastward into England, the boundary of Wales approximates very closely to the edge of the highland.

Physical Features

The greater part of Wales is composed of a plateau of old rocks, surrounded by narrow plains. This plateau has been deeply dissected by rivers such as the Dee, Severn, Wye, Teifi, Tawe, Conway, etc.

The mountains of Wales may be considered in three sections:—(1) North Wales; (2) Central Wales; (3) South Wales.

(1) NORTH WALES. This northern mountainous region, lying north of the valleys of the upper Severn and the Dovey, is divided into two sections by the valleys of the Dee and Mawddach. The southern portion is known as the Berwyn mountains, and the mass culminates westward in Cader Idris (2,927 ft). The mountain block north of the Dee is deeply dissected by the northward-flowing rivers, Conway and Clwyd. The highest peaks are in Snowdonia in the north-west, Snowdon (3,571 ft) being the highest mountain in England and Wales. The whole of the mountains of North Wales have been heavily glaciated. The hills are rounded, the rocks polished, and there are deep, steep-sided valleys (*e.g.* the lower Conway and Glaslyn), cirques, mountain tarns, and waterfalls (see plates facing pages 64 and 80).

(2) CENTRAL WALES. The region lying south of the upper Severn Valley and north of the Usk Valley consists of a series of north-east to south-west mountain ridges, Mynedd Bach, Mynedd Epynt, etc., whose western slopes are steeper than

their eastern slopes. Between these ridges flow the rivers Teifi and Towy. The River Wye (rising in Plynlimmon, 2,485 ft) cuts south-eastwards across these ridges by a series of picturesque transverse valleys.

(3) SOUTH WALES. South of the River Usk are the Brecknock Beacons, steep on the north and dropping more gently southwards to the coastal plains. The Brecknock Beacons consist of Old Red Sandstone, but the mountains to the south of them are composed of the carboniferous rocks of the South Wales coalfield. The mountains of South Wales are drained by two sets of rivers: (a) the Tawe and Neath which flow S.W. towards Swansea, and (b) the Taff, Rhymney, and Ebbw which flow S.E. towards Cardiff and Newport.

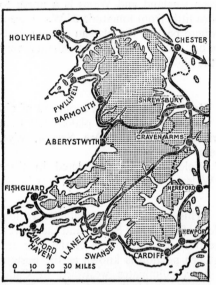

Fig. 31. To Show the Control of Relief on Railway Routes in Wales.—Note: (a) the coastal routes; (b) the east to west routes of North Wales; (c) the parallel N.E. to S.W. routes of Central Wales; (d) the "border" junctions; (e) the accessibility of Shrewsbury from North, Central, and South Wales.

Wales has little lowland. Apart from the river valleys, the chief lowlands are the plains of Gwent and Pembroke in the south, and the lowlands of Anglesey and the Lleyn Peninsula in the north-west.

The Influence of Relief on Communications

The large areas of highland and the steep gradients limit the railways of Wales to the coastal plains and river valleys (Fig. 31). The two most important railway routes follow the coastal plains, viz.:—

(1) The London Midland Region route from Chester to Holyhead.

(2) The Western Region route from Cardiff to Fishguard.

Holyhead and Fishguard are ferry ports from which steamers sail to Dun Laoghaire (Kingstown) and Rosslare. In North Wales another railway route from Shrewsbury to Aberystwyth follows the Severn and Dovey valleys. A single line coastal route follows the coast from Aberystwyth northwards to Pwllheli. In Central Wales there are four parallel N.E. to S.W. routes following the valleys between the scarped ridges. From west to east they are:—

(1) An unimportant route between Aberystwyth and Carmarthen following the Teifi Valley.

(2) A route from the north of England, which from Craven Arms in Shropshire strikes S.W. along the valleys of tributaries of the Wye, and the valley of the Towy to Swansea.

(3) A route from Hereford through Brecon to Swansea. This follows part of the Wye Valley, and, passing north of the Brecknock Beacons, follows the Tawe Valley to Swansea.

(4) An important line from Hereford to Newport and Cardiff.

In the South Wales coalfield there are numerous railways serving the villages of the mining valleys. Each valley has its own railway, and sometimes two lines, one on each side of the stream (see plate facing p. 64). These are engaged mainly in the transport of goods, especially coal.

Because of the mountainous nature of Wales and the consequent difficulty of communication between various parts of the country, there is no one centre which is easily accessible from all parts. It is for this reason that so many Welsh meetings are held in Shrewsbury, which is more accessible to the people of North, Central, and South Wales than is the capital of the country, Cardiff (290,000).

Distribution of Population and Industries

The distribution of population in Wales (Fig. 32), according to density per square mile, may best be considered in four sections:—

(1) The almost uninhabited area of the mountain plateau with less than one person per square mile.

(2) The river valleys and agricultural lowlands with a population up to 200 per square mile.

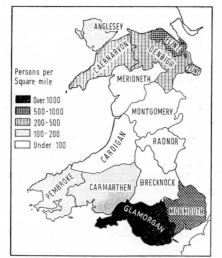

Persons per Square mile

- Over 1000
- 500-1000
- 200-500
- 100-200
- Under 100

(3) The narrow northern coastal plain and the Plain of Gwent, with a population density up to 500 per square mile.

(4) The densely-populated regions of the North Wales and South Wales coal-fields.

(1) THE MOUNTAIN REGION. On the highest parts of the Welsh uplands there are few people because the resources are meagre. The

Fig. 32. THE DISTRIBUTION OF POPULATION IN WALES AND MONMOUTHSHIRE IN 1961 ACCORDING TO COUNTIES.

damp climate, the low temperatures due to altitude, the thin soil, and the difficulty of access make sheep rearing the chief occupation. It is possible to travel several miles over the Central Welsh uplands without seeing a single inhabited house. Ruined cottages there are, evidence of the movement of people from these "poverty spots" to the cities of England and Wales. There are more Welsh people in London than Cardiff, an appreciable percentage of the dairy-men and drapers of the capital city being of Welsh descent.

Owing to the depression in the South Wales coalfield between the two World Wars this movement of Welsh people to England was accelerated and is still continuing.

(2) THE RIVER VALLEYS AND LOWLANDS. In the more accessible river valleys, where soils are deeper and richer, and the temperatures higher, mixed farming is practised, and this supports more people in scattered farms and villages.

In the upper Severn Valley there was formerly a flourishing woollen industry at Newtown and Welshpool. This has suffered through the lack of coal and the competition of such areas as the West Riding of Yorkshire. To-day, this industry is confined to Newtown, and the output is small. There are, however, a number of mills on the south-east side of the Teifi valley but the largest single centre is at Holywell in Flintshire.

(3) THE NORTHERN PLAIN AND PLAIN OF GWENT. On the plains of Pembroke, Lleyn, and Anglesey, important for cattle rearing, the density of population is greater than in the river valleys, partly because of the greater accessibility.

The Plain of Gwent, with its rich red soils, is a region of intensive farming, for it supplies the industrial areas of the coalfield. Dairying is an important occupation of the district, and there are a number of larger market towns such as Cowbridge, Llandaff, and Bridgend.

On the coast of North Wales the density of population is increased by the presence of a large number of holiday resorts, such as Llandudno, Rhyl, Colwyn Bay, etc. The combination of sea and mountain scenery, and the ease of accessibility from the English industrial areas, make this a popular holiday region. The opening of the Mersey Tunnel for road traffic greatly increased the importance of North Wales in this respect. In the north-west of Wales quarrying is an important occupation. There are many large quarries for road metal (granite) at Penmaenmawr. At Bethesda, Festiniog, and Llanberis and Nantlle there are slate quarries (see plate facing page 64). The slates of Festiniog are exported to all parts of the world. But slate is now much less used than formerly, its place for roofing being largely taken by tiles.

(4) THE COALFIELDS. The population is concentrated around the two coalfield areas in the north and south.

(a) *The North Wales Coalfield.* In the north-east of Wales, in the counties of Flint and Denbigh, is the North Wales coalfield (Fig. 33). It is neither so large nor important as the South Wales coalfield, but the mining of coal and the industries of the coalfield provide occupation for more people than any other part of Wales except the south and the population is increasing rapidly, especially in Flintshire. The coalfield extends from the Point of Air at the north of the Dee estuary, along the hill slopes through Flint and Mold southwards to Wrexham (40,000) and Ruabon. The greatest output of coal comes from the district around Gresford. There are a large variety of industries connected with this coalfield, viz. integrated iron and steel works as at Brymbo and Shotton, the last-named at the mouth of the Dee; chemical works in the neighbourhood

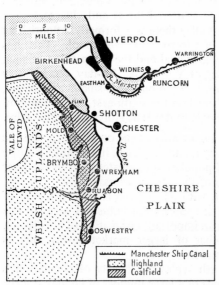

Fig. 33. THE NORTH WALES COALFIELD AND THE MERSEY ESTUARY.—Warrington—the original lowest point of bridging; Runcorn-Widnes formerly connected by transporter bridge; Liverpool-Birkenhead connected by tunnels and ferries. Note the effect of the Mersey road tunnel on communication between Liverpool and North Wales.

of Flint; rayon works and paper mills at Flint (15,000), Ruabon, Mold, and elsewhere; engineering works and brick kilns at Ruabon. The former small ports of Connah's Quay and Queensferry are now closed, and iron ore for Shotton is imported via Birkenhead by rail and that for Brymbo from the Banbury area. Limestone for smelting and for use in the chemical industries is available in the Flintshire hills.

(*b*) *The South Wales Coalfield.* The South Wales coalfield extends from the River Usk in Monmouthshire westwards through northern Glamorganshire to Llanelli (Fig. 34). There is also a narrow western extension of this coalfield in the

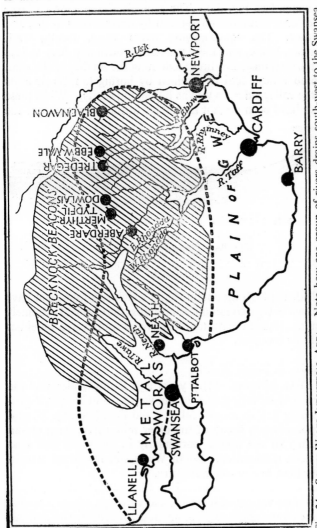

Fig. 34. SOUTH WALES INDUSTRIAL AREA.—Note how one group of rivers drains south-west to the Swansea area, and the other group to the Cardiff and Newport area. The valleys lying east of the Rhondda Valley all contain a railway—sometimes two. The heavy dotted line encloses the coal measures.

neighbourhood of St Brides Bay in Pembroke. Except for the western portion in Pembroke, this coalfield is a highland area for it lies entirely in the mountainous country south of the Brecknock Beacons. Structurally the coalfield is a basin or syncline (see Fig. 35). The geological map shows a large area of coal measures surrounded by narrow rims of grit and limestone. The south-flowing rivers Tawe, Neath, Taff, Rhymney, Ebbw, and their tributaries, have cut deep valleys into the coal measures thus facilitating the mining of the coal. In some valleys coal is obtained by boring tunnels or adits into the valley sides, as well as by sinking shafts. While these valleys have been a great advantage in the opening up of the

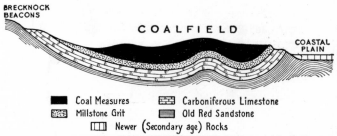

Fig. 35. SECTION FROM NORTH TO SOUTH ACROSS THE SOUTH WALES COALFIELD.

coalfield, the high mountain ridges which separate them have made east to west communication across the coalfield extremely difficult. Hence the routes all converge southwards on either Cardiff or Swansea.

Industries in South Wales

(i) COAL MINING. Fifty years ago South Wales was the largest coal-exporting area in the world. But to-day it produces only half as much coal as it did then (see Fig. 37, and also pp. 259-60). Some of the older mines have been closed but many of the others, particularly in the south and west have been mechanised. South Wales still has more men in mining than in any other industry.

The South Wales coalfield is famous for the quantity, quality, and variety of its coals, and there are ample reserves. On the east and south edges bituminous, or ordinary household, coal is mined. Further west the coal is known as "steam coal", for, while it burns with little flame or smoke, it gives great heat, and so is valuable for steamships. North of Swansea, and over the western half of the coalfield, the coal mined is an extremely hard coal known as anthracite. The relative importance of the leading British coalfields in 1965 is shown in Figs. 36 and 105.

France, Italy, and Germany were at one time Britain's principal markets for coal but this trade has gone. In Europe, Poland, the U.S.S.R., and the U.S.A. are all serious competitors. In Britain and in many other countries there has been in recent years a marked change-over from coal to oil and natural gas, both for power and for heating, thus reducing the demand for coal.

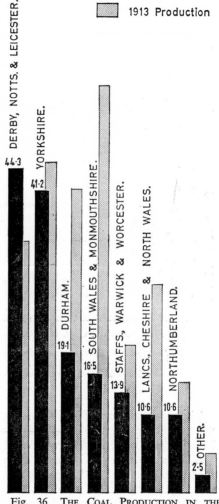

Fig. 36. THE COAL PRODUCTION IN THE COALFIELDS OF ENGLAND AND WALES IN MILLIONS OF TONS, 1965. (See also Fig. 105.)

Our present small exports, about 3 million tons a year, go mainly to Western Germany, Norway, and the Netherlands.

(ii) THE IRON AND STEEL INDUSTRIES. Along the northern edge of the South Wales coalfield near to the rim of limestone (see Fig. 35) iron ores were found. These ores, coupled with the available coal and limestone, gave rise to an iron smelting industry in a line of towns extending from Aberdare (40,000), through Merthyr Tydfil (27,000), Dowlais, Tredegar, and Ebbw Vale (27,000) to Blaenavon. To-day, these supplies of ore are nearly exhausted, but the smelting industry still continues at Ebbw Vale by obtaining ores from Banbury and from abroad.

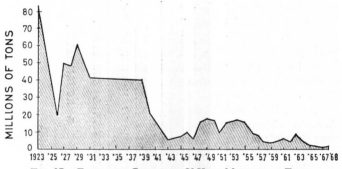

FIG. 37. EXPORT OF COAL FROM U.K. IN MILLIONS OF TONS.

N.B.—(1) 1926 was a year of Industrial Unrest.
      (2) 1939-45. Effect of War on Export Trade.
      (3) 1947. Fuel Crisis in U.K.

The easy transport of coal downhill has led to the development of a second group of smelting centres along the coast at Newport (112,000), Cardiff, Port Talbot, Swansea, and Llanelli, and these use iron ore imported from Sweden, Canada, and West Africa. The vast Margam plant at Port Talbot (51,000) (see plate facing page 65) produces more than one-twelfth of all Britain's steel. The South Wales industrial area is Britain's largest steel-producing district, and accounts for one-quarter of all our crude steel. Britain produces over 27 million tons of steel a year. Nearly one-quarter of this is exported in the form of plates, billets, bars, and girders, and another quarter is exported indirectly in manufactured articles such as vehicles and machinery.

(iii) OTHER METAL INDUSTRIES. Around Swansea (170,000) and Llanelli (30,000) is one of the greatest metal-smelting centres in the world, particularly of tin, zinc, nickel, and copper.

The tin-plating industry (*i.e.* the covering of sheets of iron with a thin layer of tin to prevent rusting) is the most famous of the metal industries of this district. Tin ore is imported from Bolivia and Nigeria. Large modern tin-plate plants have been opened at Trostre, near Llanelli, and at Velindre, and there is also a new mill at Ebbw Vale. Palm oil, into which the sheets are dipped to spread the tin evenly over the surface, is imported both at Liverpool and Swansea. The marked extension in the canning industry brought about by the ever increasing canning of food products has caused a great demand for tin plate which South Wales exports to countries all over the world. Welsh output is about one million tons.

Near Swansea, also, are the Mond Nickel Works, the greatest nickel works in the world. Zinc ores are smelted and iron sheets coated with a thin layer of zinc to form "galvanised iron", which as "corrugated iron" is exported in immense quantities for building purposes in hot countries, where it is more durable than wood. Swansea is also important for the refining of copper, and, together with Newport and Neath, engages in the working (although not the primary smelting) of aluminium. It should be noted that South Wales is generally more important for smelting and refining than for the manufacture of metal articles. Much of the refined metal is despatched to Birmingham, Sheffield, and Northamptonshire for manufacture.

(iv) OTHER INDUSTRIES. Other industries and occupations in South Wales are:—

(1) Sheep rearing on the highlands.
(2) Dairying and mixed farming on the coastal plains.
(3) Fishing, *e.g.* Milford, Cardiff, and Swansea.
(4) Some shipbuilding and repairing at Cardiff and Swansea.
(5) Oil refining at Llandarcy, near Swansea, and at Milford

Haven. Since Swansea docks cannot handle large modern tankers, crude oil is shipped to a deep-water oil terminal also at Milford Haven and then pumped to Llandarcy by a 60-mile pipe-line. Milford Haven is developing rapidly as a port and as an industrial area.

(6) Much of our nylon fibre is made at Pontypool (40,000).

(7) The manufacture of plastics and synthetic chemicals, *e.g.* at Barry (42,000), Newport, and Pontypridd (35,000).

(8) Light engineering at Merthyr Tydfil, Llanelli, Cardiff, and Swansea.

There are well-known seaside resorts on the coast, *e.g.* Tenby.

Links with Industrial England

Wales has three very important links with the industrial districts of England. Firstly, South Wales supplies much of the refined metals for the English metallurgical centres. Secondly, Wales provides a "playground" for the holiday-makers from industrial areas. Thirdly, it helps to supply some of our large cities with water. Owing to the heavy rainfall and large catchment areas of rivers, reservoirs have been constructed in the remote highland districts. Lake Vyrnwy in the Berwyn Mountains is a reservoir which supplies Liverpool with water, and the Birmingham Corporation have constructed three reservoirs in Central Wales, near Rhayader in the valley of the River Elan, a tributary of the upper Wye. Lake Celyn also supplies water to Liverpool and Lake Clywedog to other English areas.

The Welsh Borderlands

The Welsh borderlands fall naturally into four divisions:—

(*a*) The plains of Cheshire and North Shropshire, which are rich agricultural areas (see Chapter 13).

(*b*) The hills of South Shropshire, including the Longmynd, Wenlock Edge, the Clee Hills, and the Wrekin. This district is structurally an eastward extension of the Welsh Uplands. The chief occupations are sheep rearing on the hills and mixed farming in the valleys. The Clee Hills yield good road metal, and limestone is quarried along Wenlock Edge. The western half of this upland area is very picturesque, with large areas of open moorland. Still relatively remote and unspoiled, it is a region rich in traditions, folk lore, and the survival of quaint customs.

(*c*) The Plain of Hereford, composed of Old Red Sandstone and drained by the River Wye. On its eastern side the high granite Malvern Hills, crowned by the remains of a British Camp, separate this lowland from the plains of the lower Severn. The rich sandstone soils give rise to excellent pasture, and Hereford is famous for its cattle. Sheltered by the Welsh mountains on the west, Herefordshire does not have excessive rainfall, and for Britain, has a relatively high

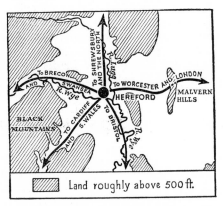

Fig. 38. Hereford, to Show its Central Position in the Hereford Plain and its Importance as a Route-Centre.

average of sunshine. It is therefore important for the growing of fruit, especially apples and pears. In fact, Herefordshire has a greater percentage of its area devoted to orchards than any other county. Like Devonshire, it specialises in the manufacture of cider and perry. It is the second English county for hop production, though the total yield is only about one-third that of Kent. The chief town and market centre is Hereford (Fig. 38), which controls routes:—

(1) Westwards via the Wye Valley into Wales.
(2) Northwards via a gap in the South Shropshire Hills to Shrewsbury and the north.

(3) Eastwards via tunnels through the Malverns to Worcester and London.

(4) Southwards via the Wye Valley and the Severn Tunnel to Bristol, and via the Usk Valley to Newport and Cardiff.

(*d*) Monmouthshire, which is divided into two very different sections by the north to south valley of the River Usk. West of the river is a coal-mining region (part of the South Wales coalfield), characteristically Welsh in outlook and relief. In contrast, between the Usk and the Wye on the eastern border of the county, is a region of lower land devoted to agriculture and more similar to the English plains in its development.

The Welsh border is crossed by a number of rivers which, rising in Wales and flowing east, provide valleys through which run the main roads and railways into Wales. From north to south these are the Dee, Severn, Teme, Wye, and Usk.

The Welsh border, too, is noted for its wealth of castles, which, in past history, guarded the valley routes into Wales. Among them are those at Chester, Chirk, Shrewsbury, Stokesay, Bishop's Castle, Clun, Ludlow, Wigmore, and Chepstow.

CHAPTER 7

THE WESTERN PENINSULAS

(3) THE LAKE DISTRICT

The third of the western peninsulas is the Lake District, lying between Morecambe Bay and Solway Firth. It extends through the counties of Cumberland, Westmorland, and a detached northern portion of Lancashire known as Furness.

It consists of (*a*) the Cumbrian Mountains, a central mass of granite, and old hard rocks, surrounded on all sides, except the S.E., by (*b*) lowlands of newer rocks (Fig. 39). On the S.E. the Lake District is linked with the Pennines by the highland known as Shap Fell, the chief physical obstacle of the west coast route to Carlisle. The highest peaks of the Lake District are Scafell Pike (3,210 ft), Scafell (3,162 ft), Helvellyn (3,118 ft), and Skiddaw (3,054 ft).

The Cumbrian Mountains

The central mountain mass is a dome-shaped highland from which the rivers drain radially like the spokes of a wheel. The river valleys were deepened considerably during the Ice Age, and now contain beautiful, long, narrow lakes. Sometimes these lie in hollows eroded by the glaciers, and sometimes they have been formed by morainic deposits acting as dams across the river valleys, as in the case of Windermere. In some valleys the lakes have been split into two parts by the silt carried into the lake by lateral mountain streams. For instance, Derwentwater and Bassenthwaite are separated by a "deltaic" lowland, and so are Buttermere and Crummock Water (see plate facing page 80). As a result of the radial arrangement of the valleys, communications in the Lake District are very difficult, there being only two railways and few good motor roads. Many of the valleys are connected by high and difficult passes along which wind narrow footpaths. Thus, it is only by walking that the beauties of the

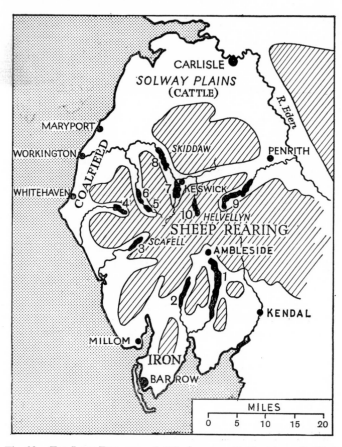

Fig. 39. THE LAKE DISTRICT.—1. Windermere. 2. Coniston. 3. Wastwater. 4. Ennerdale. 5. Buttermere. 6. Crummock Water. 7. Derwentwater. 8. Bassenthwaite. 9. Ullswater. 10. Thirlmere.

wildest and most remote parts of the "Lakes" may be enjoyed. The most important route is the first class road running northwards from Windermere over a low pass to Keswick via Thirlmere.

The combination of beautiful lake and mountain scenery attracts many holiday-makers, so that the towns of the high-land area are tourist centres, viz. Bowness, Windermere, Keswick, Ambleside, and Penrith.

Apart from the tourist industry the chief occupation is sheep rearing. The mountain "fells" are used as sheep runs by the farmers of the valleys. In these valleys mixed farming and dairying are practised.

There is also some quarrying and mining. The rocks of the Lake District yield slate and granite. The green slates of Westmorland are well known. Graphite is a form of carbon, the "black lead" used for pencils. At Keswick there is a small pencil-making industry which began because of the local supplies of graphite in Borrowdale, the valley to the south of Derwentwater. These local supplies are now exhausted, but the industry continues (an example of "industrial inertia") using supplies of graphite imported from Ceylon.

Thirlmere is a reservoir supplying Manchester with water, as is Haweswater. Wet Sladdale is a new reservoir just south of Haweswater.

The importance of the Lake District, with its glorious scenery and unpolluted atmosphere, as a holiday centre cannot be over-estimated, and already many large areas are in the hands of the National Trust, safeguarded for ever from the encroachments of industrialism.

The Surrounding Plains

The plains surrounding the Cumbrian Mountains fall into three economic divisions (see Fig. 39), viz:—

(1) The north Cumberland plain and the valley of the River Eden.

(2) The Cumberland coalfield.

(3) Furness and the Kent Valley.

(1) NORTH CUMBERLAND. The plain of North Cumberland extends along the north of the mountain core and south-eastward along the Eden Valley, which is bounded on the eastern side by the very steep mountain wall of the western

Pennines. This escarpment occurs along a fault-line known as the Eden Fault (a continuation of this fault can be traced along practically the whole of the western Pennines as far south as Cheshire).

These northern lowlands are composed of New Red Sandstone, overlain everywhere by glacial clays and sands. In the southern half of the Eden Valley these glacial deposits are in the form of drumlins, long hogback-shaped mounds of glacial debris, which, lying parallel to one another give the plain a "rippled" appearance.

As these plains lie on the west of England they have the characteristic equable and damp climate similar to that of the other western plains. Hence they are cattle-rearing regions and milk is sent as far as Newcastle and Liverpool. The arable farming is also that typical of the western plains; barley, wheat, oats, and root crops being grown and used for the feeding of animals. The sandy

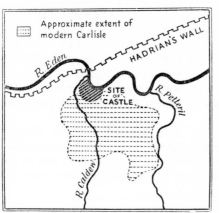

Fig. 40. (*a*). THE *SITE* OF CARLISLE TO SHOW HOW IT WAS SUITABLE FOR DEFENCE AS A BORDER FORTRESS IN EARLY HISTORY.

grass-covered flats bordering Solway Firth are used as winter pastures for the sheep from the mountain fells. This movement of sheep from summer to winter pastures is known as "transhumance". Transhumance is also practised in North Wales and in Kent, but in the latter county the sheep are moved from Romney Marsh inland and uphill to the Downs in winter.

The chief towns of the plain, such as Cockermouth, Appleby (2,000), and Carlisle (72,000), are all market towns.

Carlisle [Fig. 40 (*a*)], however, is an important railway centre, and has a number of industries, viz. biscuit-making, engineering, and cotton textiles. Its importance dates from

Roman times, when it was a fortress at the western end of Hadrian's Wall, which runs along the northern side of the Tyne Valley, to Wallsend, near Newcastle. The strength of its position was due to the fact that it was guarded on the west, north, and east by the streams Caldew, Eden, and Petteril, and that within this "moat", facing the Eden, was a steep and high river bank suitable for defence. It is the lowest point of bridging of the Eden and a border railway junction, "the Gateway to Scotland". The routes it controls are shown on Fig. 40 (*b*).

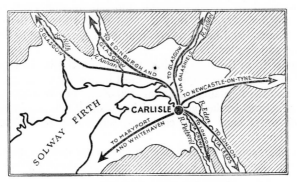

Fig. 40 (*b*). THE *SITUATION* OF CARLISLE IN RELATION TO THE SURROUNDING REGIONS.—To show its position in the centre of a plain and its control of natural routes. The line to Glasgow via Galashiels has now been closed.

(2) THE CUMBERLAND COALFIELD. This small coalfield lies on the coastal plain north of St Bee's Head and workings extend for some miles under the sea. Output is less than one million tons a year. Coal was formerly exported through the ports of Maryport, Workington, and Whitehaven to Ireland. This trade has now ceased and Maryport is no longer a port.

A small amount of iron ore is obtained at Egremont and Cleator Moor, and this, together with available limestone for use as a "flux", has given rise to an important industry at Workington; while new light industries have been established to provide alternative forms of employment at both Workington (30,000) and Whitehaven (27,000) (cf. South Wales Coalfield). There is an atomic energy plant at Sellafield, producing plutonium, and nearby at Calder Hall is the first large-scale atomic power station in the world, which started to feed electricity into the National Grid in 1956.

(3) FURNESS AND THE KENT VALLEY.   The most important feature of the southern plains is the occurrence of deposits of hematite iron ore, although production is now much less than formerly (see Fig. 7).   This ore has a higher content of iron than any other mined in Britain, viz. up to 50 per cent. (cf. the 20 per cent. of iron in the Lincolnshire ores).   Barrow is sheltered by Walney Island, and has an important ship-building industry, but only a small proportion of the local iron is consumed here; a certain amount is exported to South Wales and Scotland.

Apart from the iron-mining, agriculture, similar in type to that of the Solway plains, is the most important occupation of the southern plains.   Kendal (20,000), in Westmorland, manufactures leather goods and has a small woollen industry which dates back many centuries, but which now depends mainly on imported wool and the supplies of soft water.   The pure water supply has also given rise to paper mills in the Kent Valley.   Kendal also has various light engineering industries.

THE ISLE OF MAN

The Isle of Man, situated in the middle of the Irish Sea, is composed of rocks similar to those of the Lake District.   The chief occupations of the island are agriculture and fishing.   It is also a popular holiday centre, the chief resorts being Douglas (20,000), Ramsey, and Peel.   The island is administered in accordance with its own laws by the Court of Tynwald, and it has its own parliament, known as the "House of Keys".

CHAPTER 8

NORTHERN ENGLAND

(1) THE PENNINES

Divisions of Northern England

The Pennines and their surrounding lowlands together cover most of Northern England. The whole region of Northern England may be divided into a number of smaller regions, viz (Fig. 41):—

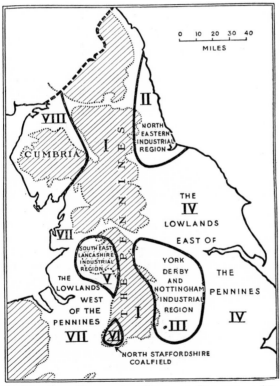

Fig. 41. NORTHERN ENGLAND TO SHOW THE SUBDIVISIONS (NUMBERED I TO VII) DESCRIBED IN CHAPTERS 8 TO 14.—Note that Cumbria was described in a preceding chapter.

(1) The Pennines.

(2) The Northumberland and Durham coalfield.

(3) The York, Derby, and Nottingham coalfield.

(4) The lowlands east of the Pennines.

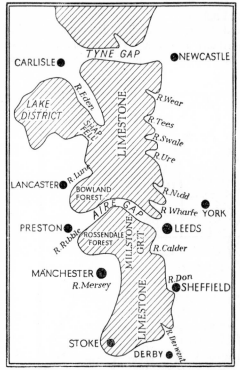

Fig. 42. THE PENNINES AND ITS GAPS.—River valleys indicated by name only.

(5) The South-East Lancashire coalfield.

(6) The North Staffordshire coalfield.

(7) The lowlands west of the Pennines.

(8) The north-western region of Cumbria, which was described in Chapter VI.

The Pennines: General

The Pennine Chain is not a range of mountains, but a dissected plateau with an average elevation approaching 2,000-3,000 ft, and with steep slopes on the east and west. It extends from the valley of the Tyne southwards to the Trent Valley in Derbyshire. Thus it is about one hundred and fifty miles long, but varies in width from twenty to forty miles. On the east side the 500-ft contour makes a fairly straight north to south line, broken only by the re-entrants of the river valleys (Fig. 42). From north to south these east-flowing rivers are:—

(1) Tyne, Wear, Tees, draining Northumberland and Durham.

(2) Swale, Ure, Nidd, Wharfe, Aire, Calder, and Don, which unite in the Vale of York to form the Yorkshire Ouse.

The western edge of the Pennines offers a strong contrast to the east. It consists of four "bulges", viz.:—

(1) The Cumbrian Mountains, joined to the Pennines by Shap Fell.

(2) Bowland Forest, which is mainly in Yorkshire as that county here approaches closely to the west coast.

(3) Rossendale Forest, between the valleys of the Ribble and Mersey in South Lancashire.

(4) A south-western spur, including part of North Staffordshire, where the Pennines gradually sink to the plains of Cheshire and North Shropshire.

The chief west-flowing streams, usually shorter than those flowing east, are the Kent, Lune, Ribble, Mersey, and the tributaries of the River Weaver.

The Pennine Gaps

Owing to its plateau character and the steep slopes on either side, the Pennine Chain is difficult to cross, and has always been a barrier between Yorkshire and Lancashire until the tunnelling for railways during the last century. There are three valley routes across the Pennines from east to west. These are:

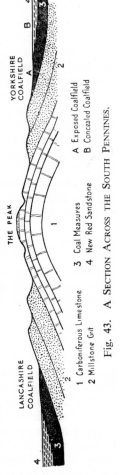

Fig. 43. A Section Across the South Pennines.

A Exposed Coalfield
B Concealed Coalfield

1 Carboniferous Limestone
2 Millstone Grit
3 Coal Measures
4 New Red Sandstone

(*a*) The Tyne Gap, between Newcastle-on-Tyne and Carlisle.

(*b*) The Stainmore Gap between the upper Tees and the upper Eden Valley, the most difficult and highest of the three.

(*c*) The Aire Gap, which links industrial Yorkshire with industrial Lancashire.

Both the Tyne and the Aire gaps are followed by road and railway, and the Aire Gap by the Leeds-Liverpool canal also.

Scenery and Occupations

The Pennine Chain was formed by the folding of the rocks of Northern England at the end of the Carboniferous Period. The top layers have been removed by various erosive agents, so that the Coal Measures, which once covered the Pennine upland, have been removed, and now exist only on the eastern and western flanks (Fig. 43).

In the Northern and Southern Pennines the Millstone Grit has also been removed, leaving large areas of Carboniferous Limestone exposed; but in the Central Pennines between Leeds and Manchester, Millstone Grit extends across the uplands from east to west. Millstone Grit is a coarse resistant sandstone which becomes black when exposed to the atmosphere, thus the central Pennine moorlands have a very dreary and bleak appearance. Wherever Millstone Grit is the surface rock the vegetation is of the moorland type, with bracken, cotton grass, heather, bilberries, and stiff grass. In these regions, too, are many peat moors and bogs. These moors are of little agricultural value, but the streams give an abundant supply of soft water (in contrast to the hard water of the limestone regions), and in the Central Pennines there are numbers of large reservoirs constructed to supply the industrial towns of Lancashire and Yorkshire with water (see plate facing page 80). Many of the hills on the "Grit" areas have sharp ridges and steep sides, and are known locally as "Edges". There are few trees, and walls of blackened grit replace the hedges of the lowlands.

The limestone areas of the North and South Pennines differ in many ways from the Grit regions of the Central Pennines. Many of the highest "peaks" of the limestone country are flat-topped, being capped with a residual layer of Millstone Grit (Fig. 43). These flat-topped hills of the "mesa" type are a characteristic feature of the Pennine scenery. The so-called "Peak" of Derbyshire is a high and relatively level

Above: The upper valley of the River Cocker in the Lake District. The lakes are Buttermere, Crummock Water, and Loweswater. This is a glaciated region with rounded hills and steep-sided, flat-bottomed valleys. The fertile valley bottom is used for mixed farming and the hillsides for sheep. *(G. P. Abraham.)*

Below: Ryeburn Reservoir in the Millstone Grit region of the eastern Pennines. *(Wakefield Corporation.)*

Above: Pen-y-ghent, a summit rising above the general level of the Pennine plateau, composed of Carboniferous Limestone with a "cap" of Millstone Grit, which can be detected by the change of slope near the top. Notice the bareness of the limestone plateau, the limestone walls and cottages. The fields are not cultivated but used almost entirely for sheep rearing. (*Fhotochrome Ltd.*)

Below: Staiths near Dunston, Co. Durham. Staiths are long pier-like structures by means of which the "export" of coal is facilitated. Trucks of coal are carried along the staiths and emptied into colliers alongside. (*Tyne Improvement Commission.*)

grit moorland. The same flat tops can be seen in Ingleborough and Pen-y-ghent (see plate facing p. 81).

The porous nature of the limestone gives rise to all the characteristics of "karst" scenery, viz. caverns, steep-sided valleys, dry valleys, disappearing streams, etc. The most famous of these underground streams is the Aire which now emerges at the foot of Malham Cove. There are famous caves at Ingleton in North-West Yorkshire and at Castleton in North Derbyshire. One of the latter is the famous "Blue John" mine, worked in the days of the Romans for its beautiful blue stone.

The limestone areas do not produce the same type of vegetation as the Grit, but are usually grass-covered and used extensively for sheep rearing. There are few people living in these regions. The scattered houses are built of limestone, as are the walls dividing the fields (see plate facing p. 81). The villages are situated in the more fertile valleys.

Apart from sheep rearing and mixed agriculture in the valleys, the Pennines are of little economic importance. Lead is mined in a few places, principally on Alston moor on the Cumberland-Northumberland borders, and in North Derbyshire. Some of these mines were probably worked in Roman times.

On the flanks of the Central and Southern Pennines are coalfields which, in contrast to the other portions of the Pennines, support a large industrial population. These coalfields will be considered in the following chapters.

CHAPTER 9

NORTHERN ENGLAND

(2) THE NORTHUMBERLAND AND DURHAM COALFIELD

Position

This coalfield lies in the counties of Northumberland and Durham, but a small portion of North-East Yorkshire must be included because of its economic relations with the region to the north.

The north-west of Northumberland and the west of County Durham are occupied by high moorlands (the Cheviot Hills and a portion of the Eastern Pennines). These areas are of little economic importance, and support only a scanty population. Between the mountains and the coast are lowlands drained by the rivers Coquet, Wansbeck, Tyne, Wear, and Tees. The River Tees is the boundary-line between Durham and Yorkshire.

On the lowland to the east of the Pennines is the Northumberland and Durham coalfield. The exposed coalfield (see Fig. 44) extends from the hills eastward to a line from

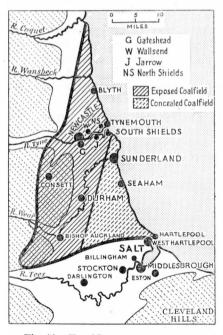

Fig. 44. The Northumberland and Durham Coalfield.

South Shields to Bishop Auckland. It reaches the coast from the mouth of the River Tyne northwards to the mouth of the River Coquet. South-east of the South Shields–Bishop Auckland line, coal measures lie under the surface rocks of Magnesian Limestone. This is a "concealed coalfield". Borings show the concealed coal measures do not extend south of a line from Bishop Auckland to Hartlepool. The lower valley of the River Tees is composed of New Red Sandstone, in which there are salt deposits (cf. Cheshire, page 129). To the south of the River Tees along the northern edge of the Cleveland hills are deposits of Jurassic iron ores.

Development of the Coal and Shipbuilding Industries

The importance of this coalfield dates back to the fourteenth century, when coal was exported by sea to London for domestic use. This coal was known as "Sea coal". At first coal was only exported from the seams which came to the surface near the coast. As these supplies were worked out coal was carried from the inland areas on pack horse to the coast, and also by coal barges along the rivers, but this mode of transport was expensive and difficult. Later, wooden tracks were laid and rails were used, down which the wagons travelled by gravity. Wooden staiths were built jutting out over the banks of the river, so that these wagons could be unloaded directly into the sea-going vessels (see plate facing page 81). But our export trade in coal to other countries has become very small (see Fig. 37), and even the coastwise export from coalfields to other parts of the United Kingdom has also greatly decreased. Tyne ports now handle about 4 million tons of coal a year, less than one-fifth the amount handled forty years ago. Much of the coastwise shipment is to the Thames district.

With the railway-building era, the Stockton and Darlington railway was constructed in 1825 for the primary purpose of carrying coal to the coast. Thus developed the great coal-exporting trade of the north-east. Nearly all the ports of the region share the trade in coal, viz. Blyth, the Tyne ports, Seaham, Sunderland, and the Hartlepools. The coalfield has a variety of good quality coals. North of the Tyne are seams of hard steam coal, while the coals of the south of the coalfield are among the best coking coals in Great Britain. The need for vessels to carry the coal gave rise to a shipbuilding industry. At first the vessels were made of wood, and, as English sources of the timber were exhausted, supplies were imported from Scandinavia. To-day the shipbuilding industries of this north-eastern region are as important as those of the Clyde.

Iron, Steel, and Chemical Industries

In 1850 deposits of iron ore were discovered at Eston Moor, and later the abundant deposits a few miles further south in the Cleveland Hills, and this together with the advantages mentioned below led to the development of iron smelting. Local supplies of iron ore are now exhausted.

Teesside has a unique position as an iron-smelting and manufacturing region due to:—

(1) The excellent coking coal of South Durham.

(2) Limestone from the Pennines and the Wear Valley.

(3) Nearness to the sea, helping the export of bulky goods.

(4) The possibility of importing high-grade ores cheaply by sea from Sweden and elsewhere.

Middlesbrough, on the Tees estuary, is remarkable for its rapid growth, due to the discovery of the Cleveland ores, and the development of the smelting and engineering industries. In 1830 it was a small village, and to-day its population is nearly 170,000. Middlesbrough has recently been united with Stockton, Billingham, Eston, Redcar, and Thornaby to form the new County Borough of Teesside.

Teesside imports iron ore from Sweden, North Africa, and Spain, and also obtains supplies from Cumberland and Northamptonshire. Some of the iron and steel produced is used in the shipbuilding industries, and much is exported to the Continent. The vast I.C.I. factory at Wilton, near Middlesbrough, makes polythene and synthetic rubber, and synthetic textile fibres such as "Terylene" from petroleum refinery by-products (see plate facing page 108). Middlesbrough imports petroleum and iron ore and scrap iron. Its exports consist of manufactured iron and steel, and chemicals and fertilisers.

In the Tees Valley the salt and anhydrite deposits are worked (the latter for the manufacture of sulphuric acid), and Billingham is noted for the large-scale production of heavy chemicals from oil and coal (see plate facing page 108). The Billingham works uses 5,000 tons of coal a day and has large railway sidings to handle this traffic. Other important towns of the Tees Valley are Darlington, with its railway engineering-works; Stockton, an iron smelting centre; and the Hartlepools. Hartlepool is the old port, and West Hartlepool is the much newer industrial port. A large oil refinery has recently been opened on Teesside.

Shipbuilding along the Tyneside

The estuaries of the Tyne and Wear are the great centres of the shipbuilding industry, and vessels of all sizes, ranging from transatlantic liners to small coasting vessels, are built there. At one time Britain built more than half the world's shipping, but our share is now down

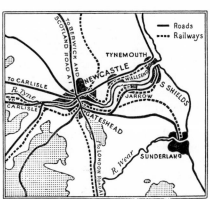

Fig. 45. NEWCASTLE-ON-TYNE, SHOWING HOW THE ROUTES CONVERGE ON THE LOWEST BRIDGING POINT OF THE RIVER.

to about five per cent. and our production in 1969 was only one-ninth that of Japan, and less than that of Germany or Sweden. Our export trade in ships has been lost to these competitors; Britain is now a net importer of new ships, *i.e.* more shipping is built abroad for British owners than is built in Britain for foreign buyers. Nevertheless, shipbuilding is still one of our very important heavy industries, using large quantities of steel. It is an assembly industry and gives employment outside the shipyards to twice as many people as in them, for ships require large amounts of equipment, fittings, machinery, boilers, paint, etc.

About 40 per cent. of our new construction is built on the Tyne, Tees, and Wear, another 30 per cent. on the Clyde, and the remainder mainly at Belfast and Liverpool. The Tyne, Tees, and Wear shipyards specialise in tankers and "tramp" vessels.

From Newcastle to the sea, a distance of about fourteen miles, the banks of the Tyne are lined with shipbuilding yards. The towns occur in pairs (see Fig. 45), one on the north and one on the south bank. Travelling seawards three pairs of towns are Newcastle and Gateshead; Wallsend and Jarrow; Tynemouth and South Shields.

Newcastle is at the lowest bridging point of the Tyne, and is the premier city and port of the whole region. It is still a considerable coal-shipping centre and the largest ship-repairing port. In addition to shipbuilding there are many other industries, including various kinds of marine engineering, the construction of bridges, as well as the manufacture of ropes, glass, paper, chemicals, the refining of sugar, the milling of flour, and the smelting of lead.

DURHAM. In this great industrial area one city stands apart, viz. Durham, which was originally a border stronghold, built on a hill within a meander of the River Wear. Thus its position was ideal for defence. It has a famous cathedral and a university, and, with a population of only 27,000 and its old traditions, is a great contrast to the newer, larger, and busier cities of the region.

Communications

Tyneside has direct communication with the west coast by the Tyne Gap, and the Tees Basin has a route to the west via the Tees Valley and the Stainmore Gap. The main route of the area is the railway route running north from Darlington to Durham, Newcastle, Berwick-on-Tweed, and Scotland.

This route, which is also the route of the Great North Road, is controlled by the Ferryhill Gap to the south of Durham, the north-south section of the valley of the Wear, the lowest bridging point of the Tyne at Newcastle, and the narrow coastal plain between the Cheviots and the sea.

CHAPTER 10

NORTHERN ENGLAND

(3) THE YORKS, DERBY, AND NOTTINGHAM
COALFIELD

Position

On the eastern flanks of the South Pennines and partly on the eastern lowlands, is the largest British coalfield, raising, at the moment, nearly half our total production. It extends from the Aire Valley near Leeds and Bradford southwards almost to the Trent and for administrative purposes is divided by the National Coal Board into two: (i) Yorks and (ii) Derby and Nottingham. Thus the northern half of the coalfield (*i.e.* north of Sheffield) is in the West Riding of Yorkshire, and the southern half occupies the eastern portion of Derbyshire and almost the whole of Nottinghamshire.

The Coal Mining Industry

The coalfield is about seventy miles long, and varies in width from ten to twenty miles. Eastward of the exposed coalfield the coal measures dip gently below layers of Magnesian Limestone and New Red Sandstones (see Fig. 43). Borings have been made through the overlying rocks, and coal is mined over a vast concealed coalfield which extends eastward almost to the Trent. The most easterly working is at Thorne, where coal is mined at a depth of 2,670 ft. The concealed coalfield is of greater extent than the exposed field (Fig. 46), so that the whole region is by far the most productive coal-mining region in Britain (see Fig. 36), yielding over one-third of the total coal output of the country. The thick and unbroken seams make coal mining profitable even at the greater depth. The collieries are larger, as a rule, than those of the exposed coalfield. Peaceful agricultural villages of eastern Nottinghamshire have become mining centres (see plate facing page 109). The most important development of the concealed coalfield has taken place around Doncaster. Coal is now exported mainly through Grimsby and Hull, largely to Scandinavia, Denmark, and the Baltic countries, the return imports being timber, wood pulp, iron ore, and dairy produce, and Immingham has also been developed by the National Coal Board as a modern coal-exporting port.

The eastward extension of coal-working has another aspect in that the coal supplies are within easy reach of the iron ore

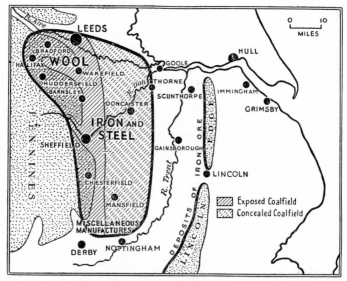

Fig. 46. The York, Derby, and Nottingham Coalfield. Showing: (*a*) The principal Industries and Towns. (*b*) Its relation to the Jurassic Iron Ores. (*c*) Its relation to the Coast and Sea Ports.

deposits along the western edge of the limestone escarpment (Lincoln Edge). The ores are mined at (*a*) Scunthorpe, (*b*) south of Lincoln, and (*c*) in the neighbourhood of Grantham. Because of the nearness of the coal supplies and the low percentage of iron in these Jurassic ores, the coal is being carried to the iron mines instead of vice versa as formerly. Scunthorpe, although away from the actual coalfield, is now one of the largest iron and steel producing areas in the country and accounts for nearly one-sixth of our total output. The population of Scunthorpe (71,000 in 1968) has more than doubled in the last thirty years.

There is a large variety of other industries associated with this vast coalfield, but three areas stand out for special consideration. They are:—

(1) The West Riding woollen industry in the north of the coalfield.

(2) The iron and steel industries of the Sheffield region in the centre of the coalfield.

(3) The miscellaneous industries of the Derby-Nottingham region in the south of the coalfield.

The West Riding Woollen Industry

The West Riding woollen industry is centred round the valleys of the rivers Aire, Calder, and Colne in the north of the York, Derby, and Nottingham coalfield, and its output of woollen goods is greater than that of all the other woollen manufacturing regions added together.

The weaving and spinning of wool is an old industry which was practised in Britain before the Norman Conquest. After 1066 it increased in importance, and weaving guilds were formed in many towns, such as Lincoln. Then came a period when most of the English wool was exported to Europe, and the English people imported cloth from Flanders in return.

Thus there was a danger of the English weaving industry falling into decay. Edward II encouraged Flemish weavers to settle in England, and in 1331 John Kempe, a weaver, settled in Norwich and later went to Kendal in Westmorland, where he manufactured cloth called "Kendal Green". Gradually more foreign weavers settled, until England became famous all over Europe for the quality of her woollen cloths. Woollen goods were manufactured in numbers of market towns in the southern portion of England, but some districts were more important than others, viz.:—

(1) The East Anglian area with woollen industries at Lincoln, Norwich, and Ipswich.

(2) The "West of England", an area including the southern Cotswolds and the western slopes of Salisbury Plain.

(3) East Devonshire, around Exeter and Tiverton.

(4) South Lancashire.

(5) West Riding of Yorkshire.

(6) The Tweed Valley of the Southern Uplands.

With the Industrial Revolution, the discovery of the use of coal, and the invention of machinery, dating from about 1760, a great change took place in the woollen industry. Large factories were built, and one or two of the woollen areas, particularly the West Riding of Yorkshire, gained rapidly in importance. In some of the old woollen areas, which were remote from the newly-developed coalfields, the industry almost disappeared or only managed to survive in a small way by specialisation in a particular branch of the industry, *e.g.* blankets at Witney (Oxfordshire), whipcords at Chipping Norton (Oxfordshire).

The most important woollen areas to-day are:—

(1) The West Riding of Yorkshire.

(2) The Tweed Valley and Ayrshire in Scotland (see Fig. 101).

(3) The "West of England" (see Fig. 30).

(4) Leicestershire.

(5) Scattered areas mainly in the mountainous regions. The woollen industry of the eastern counties has virtually disappeared.

The early weavers first settled in the Aire and Calder valleys because of the abundant supplies of wool from the Pennine sheep. Wool is naturally greasy, and must be washed before it can be manufactured, hence good supplies of soft water are desirable. The streams of the Central Pennines drain from the Millstone Grit moorlands, and the water is soft in contrast to the waters of the streams from the limestone moorlands further north and further south. This is one of the principal reasons for the location of the woollen industry on the eastern slopes of the Central Pennines.

Many of the earlier mills were built well up in the dales in order to use the power of the swift Pennine streams. In journeying across the Pennines to-day these old mills can be seen standing derelict. With the increased use of steam power the new mills were built further down stream on the coalfield at the foot of the hills. The coalfield also used to yield good supplies of iron ore for the manufacture of machinery, but these are now exhausted (see Fig. 7).

The bulk of the wool used to-day is imported from Australia and New Zealand, and it is imported principally at London, where the wool market, a heritage of the trade with Europe in the Middle Ages, is world-famous.

The chief city of the region is Leeds, which, situated on the Aire where it emerges from the hills, commands an easy route to the west coast, via the Aire Gap (Fig. 47). Leeds is the centre of the ready-made clothing industry, and has important engineering and chemical industries—dyes, glass, soap, and leather.

Bradford, situated on a small south-bank tributary of the Aire, ranks as the second town in importance, and is the chief wool market of the district.

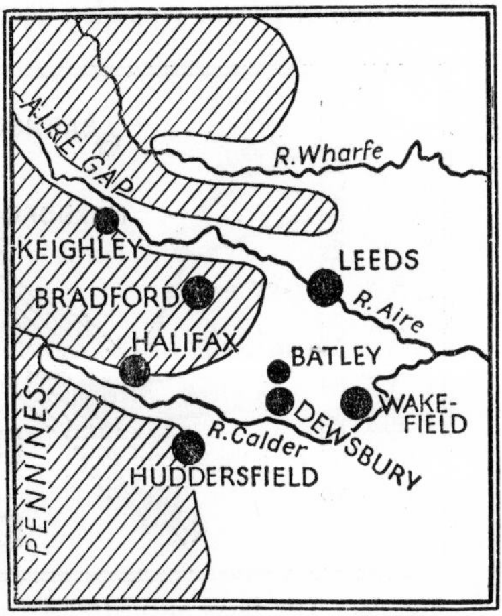

Other woollen towns are Huddersfield, Halifax, Wakefield, Dewsbury, and Batley. Halifax specialises

Fig. 47. THE WOOLLEN TOWNS OF YORKSHIRE.—Notice the position of Leeds at the entrance to the Aire Gap.

in the manufacture of carpets, and Dewsbury and Batley in "shoddy", *i.e.* material made from waste woollen fabrics. Huddersfield is also important for the manufacture of dye-stuffs.

The towns of the north-western half of the woollen area manufacture worsteds, which are made from the finest wools, and are so called because they were first made at the village of Worstead near Norwich. The south-eastern towns make "woollens" from wool of somewhat coarser quality.

The area south of the woollen towns is a very important coal-mining district, the chief centre being Barnsley.

The Iron and Steel Industry of the Don Valley

Like the woollen industries of the West Riding, the iron and steel industries of the Sheffield region are old-established. Knives were made here as long ago as the fourteenth century. Local iron ore was smelted with charcoal obtained by burning wood from the forests of the Don Valley. In order to secure a good "draught" most of the small furnaces were situated on the moors. Later the craftsmen moved to the valleys, where the streams were dammed to form small ponds ("hammer ponds"), the water from which was used to work bellows. This source of power was also used to turn the grindstones for

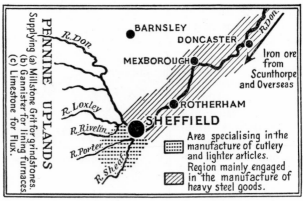

Fig. 48. THE IRON AND STEEL DISTRICT OF SOUTH YORKSHIRE.

sharpening the cutlery. To the west of Sheffield are five small streams all converging on the city, and to-day the ruins of many old mills and dams can be seen in these valleys. As the industry grew, foreign ore was imported from Sweden for special steels, but in those days the costs of importation were very high. Eventually the timber reserves were seriously depleted. Coke replaced charcoal for smelting, and there were ample supplies of coking coal. The rocks of the Pennine Chain provided not only the millstones for grinding, but also supplies of gannister, a hard rock used for lining the blast furnaces. Limestone, for use as a flux, was also obtained from the Pennines. The great factor in the pre-eminence of the Sheffield steel industry is the inherited tradition of craftsmanship.

To-day the Don Valley between Sheffield and Doncaster is a great steel-working region. In the plains to the east of Sheffield the manufactures are of the heavier type. Cutlery and light articles are made in Sheffield and to the west and south-west of the city (Fig. 48).

Steel is a combination of iron and carbon. In recent times there has been a great advance in the manufacture of "alloy steels". Various metals are mixed with ordinary steel to produce alloys possessing special qualities. Manganese is

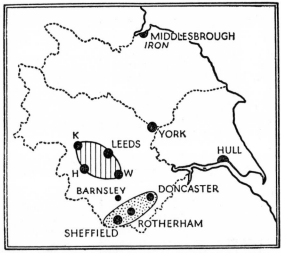

Fig. 49. YORKSHIRE.—Shows the areas engaged in the Woollen and Steel Industries. Note what a small part of the West Riding these areas occupy. *Vertical line shading* = Woollen Manufactures. *Dotted shading* = Steel Manufactures.

added to produce a tough non-magnetic steel, tungsten for hard tool steel, vanadium for spring steel, and chromium for stainless steel. All these metals have to be imported. Nearly all our special steels are made at Sheffield.

The Industries of the Derby and Nottingham Area

Near the southern end of the Yorks, Derby, and Nottingham coalfield there is a miscellany of industries. The two great centres are Derby and Nottingham, neither of which is actually on the coalfield, though one railway linking the two cities passes through a mining area around Ilkeston.

Most of the industries in this region are those which use cotton, wool, silk, linen, and rayon for the manufacture of a host of articles. The most important single manufacture is probably that of lace. Lace-making was originally a domestic industry. It was not until the end of the eighteenth century that lace was produced by machinery, and then only plain net could be made.

The invention of the Jacquard loom made it possible to

weave patterns on net, and from 1834 onwards the lace-making industry extended rapidly. One-third of the lace-makers of Britain have their factories in Nottingham, but lace-making is important over the whole of the triangular area enclosed by lines joining Lough-borough, Derby, and Southwell (Fig. 50).

Fig. 50. THE LACE TRIANGLE OF THE EAST MIDLANDS.

Another very important industry is the manufacture of hosiery. This industry is distributed over the whole region from Leicester northwards to Mansfield. Hosiery includes not only stockings and socks, but all kinds of "knit wear": jumpers, bathing suits, knitted costumes, etc., and in this trade all types of fibre are used. Of special note is the increase in the use of rayon and newer synthetic fibres such as nylon, "Terylene," etc. Leicester is the largest centre, making every kind of knitted goods. Nottingham, Hinckley, Lough-borough, and Mansfield are other hosiery centres.

Nottingham (1948) and Leicester (1957) both have new universities.

The small-ware industry is concerned with the manufacture of tapes, braids, shoe laces, elastic, fringes, and a vast range of other similar articles. Derby is one of the chief centres of this industry, but it is scattered throughout nearly all the towns and villages of the district.

Nottingham owes its origin to its defensible site. The Trent in this district meanders over flat plains liable to extensive flooding. By the side of the Trent, and rising above the flood plains, is a sandstone hill, close to a point where the river could be easily crossed. This hill is the site of Nottingham castle, around which the city has grown. Centuries ago the blacksmiths of Nottingham smelted ore with the charcoal from Sherwood Forest to the north. To-day Nottingham has important engineering industries and is the main centre for the manufacture of cycles. The tobacco and pharmaceutical manufactures are world - famous. Standing between

Fig. 51. THE POSITION OF DERBY.—(*a*) At the edge of the highland. (*b*) At the bend of the River Derwent. (*c*) As a route centre.

the coalfield to the north and the agricultural lands of the Trent to the south, Nottingham is a great market centre, and the oaks of Sherwood Forest and the hides of the cattle of the Midlands gave rise to a leather tanning industry.

Two or three small oilfields in Nottinghamshire produce a total of less than 100,000 tons of oil a year as against imports of 100 million tons a year.

Derby (Fig. 51) is situated at a sharp bend of the River Derwent where it leaves the south Pennines for the Trent plains. The position of Derby was of great strategic importance during the struggle between the Danes and the English for mastery of the Midlands (note the Danish suffix "by", cf. Grimsby), and like many other old strategic towns it is now a great route centre.   For this reason it became the headquarters of the Midland Railway engineering works, and it is also noted for the manufacture of motor cars and especially of aero engines.   Up to 1800, silk manufacturing was the principal industry of Derby, but it is now unimportant, though the manufacture of rayon and of paper is noteworthy.   Derby also has a famous, though small, pottery industry, the lead for glazing being obtained from the hills of North Derbyshire.

Above: Part of the I.C.I. Chemical Works at Wilton near Billingham-on-Tees, show the ethylene gas separation and petroleum refining plant.   (*I.C.I.*)

Below: Stripping the overburden in the iron ore mines at Corby, Northamptonsh The smaller digger in the foreground loads ore into trucks.   The dragline, the larges the world, is capable of removing up to 100 ft of overburden.   As the shallower deposits are gradually exhausted, underground mining may be necessary.   (*Stewart Lloyds Ltd.*)

Above: An older coal mine.   *Below:* A new modern mine, Killoch Colliery, Ayrshire.
(*National Coal Board.*)

CHAPTER 11

NORTHERN ENGLAND

(4) THE LOWLANDS EAST OF THE PENNINES

That part of England which lies between the Pennines and the North Sea falls into three natural divisions, viz.:—

(I) The Vale of York.

(II) The scarplands and vales of Eastern Yorkshire.

(III) The scarplands and vales of Lincolnshire.

The Vale of York

Lying immediately to the east of the Pennines is a low plain never rising to 200 ft above sea-level. It extends from north to south through Yorkshire, and varies in width from over thirty miles in the south to ten miles in the north. It is the northward continuation of the Trent lowlands, and so is part of the route to Scotland, which has been important since the days when Roman legions marched northwards against the Picts. The foundation of the plain is New Red Sandstone, but this is covered almost everywhere by alluvium or by glacial deposits. Much of the alluvial land around the head of the Humber was once fen country, but it has been drained and is now rich agricultural land. The northern half of the Vale is covered with morainic soils, and a terminal moraine, stretching across the Vale from the Yorkshire Wolds to the Pennines, formed in early times an important east-west route slightly raised above the lower land.

Being on the sheltered lee side of the Pennines, and having a variety of rich soils, the Vale of York is an important agricultural area. It is the most northerly region of extensive wheat-farming in England. Barley, oats, and root crops are cultivated, and in addition, there is much market gardening for the supply of vegetables, etc., to the towns of the Yorkshire coalfield. To the east of Leeds acres of rhubarb are a notable feature of the cultivation.

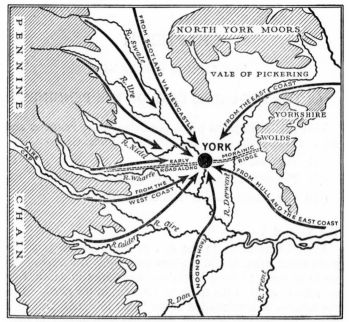

Fig. 52. The Position of York, Showing the Importance as a Route Centre and Its Relation to the Ouse Basin.

The population is centred in villages and market towns. Many of the latter are situated where the Pennine tributaries of the Ouse leave the hills for the plains so that they act as market centres for both the people of the Yorkshire Dales and the Vale. Such are Richmond, Ripon, Knaresborough, and Wetherby.

The greatest centre of the Vale is York, an ancient city dating back to Roman times (Fig. 52). It owes its importance to a number of factors, viz.:—

(1) It stands in the middle of the Vale at the crossing of the north-south river route by the east-west road route along the morainic ridge.

(2) In olden days York was the limit of the tides, so that small sea-going vessels could reach York.

(3) York was the first point upstream at which there was firm ground raised above flood level.

(4) It is a great focus of natural routes, for not only does it stand on the north to south lowland "way", but on it converge routes from the dales to the west (*i.e.* of the Swale, Ure, Nidd, Wharfe, and Aire) and from the east coast via the Vale of Pickering.

(5) Its great historical importance is due primarily to its position on the great north route. Hence, as Eboracum, it was the principal Roman military station of northern England. It is still the ecclesiastical capital of northern England.

(6) To-day it is not only a great market centre, but, because of its historical remains, a great "show" city. It has recently become the home of a new university.

(7) It also has important industries such as the manufacture of agricultural implements, leather, gloves, and chocolate.

York is no longer the largest city in Yorkshire, for to-day the newer industrial cities (Leeds, Bradford, Huddersfield, Sheffield, Middlesbrough, and Hull) have larger populations.

The Scarps and Vales of East Yorkshire

This region lies between the Vale of York and the east coast, and structurally is similar to the scarps and vales of South-East England. From the mouth of the Tees to the Humber there are four distinct regions, viz. (*a*) The North York Moors. (*b*) The Vale of Pickering. (*c*) The Yorkshire Wolds. (*d*) The plains of Holderness.

(*a*) THE NORTH YORK MOORS. These moors are composed of oolitic (Jurassic) limestone, the Cleveland and Hambleton Hills forming the steep northern and western edges. On the east there are picturesque cliffs (*e.g.* at Whitby and Robin Hood's Bay). On the south the moorland limestones dip gently under the clays of the Vale of Pickering.

The moorland is deeply dissected by such valleys as Eskdale and Newtondale. In the vales mixed agriculture is practised, but the high moorland is covered with heather and coarse grass suitable only for rough grazing. The former importance of the iron ores of Cleveland on the northern edge of the moors has already been discussed (page 96), and extensive deposits of potassium salts, suitable for making fertilisers, have recently been found in Eskdale, near Whitby, at a depth of about 4,000 ft. Very promising finds of natural gas have been made at Lockton and nearby in Eskdale. The gas is trapped in porous magnesian limestone rocks a little more recent than the sandstones in which gas has already been found off-shore under the North Sea.

Population is scanty on the moorlands, and the area is served by the market towns in the marginal lowlands. The largest town in the region is Whitby, market town, seaside resort, and fishing centre, with a population of only 12,000.

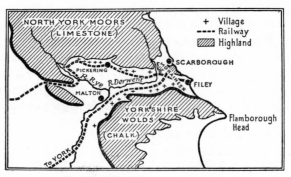

Fig. 53. THE VALE OF PICKERING.

(*b*) THE VALE OF PICKERING. The flat-floored, poorly-drained Vale of Pickering lies between the Yorkshire Moors and the Yorkshire Wolds (Fig. 53). To-day it is drained by the westward-flowing Derwent, a tributary of the Yorkshire Ouse, but there is evidence that it was formerly drained by an east-flowing stream to Filey. During the Ice Age moraines were deposited near the coast, blocking the outlet of this old river. The water rose, forming a great lake (known to geologists as Lake Pickering), which eventually overflowed south-westward across the low watershed near Malton. At this point the river cut a gorge, and gradually the lake was drained, leaving the muds of the lake bottom exposed. The flat lands of the centre of the Vale are still liable to extensive flooding, and for this reason the villages are located around the edge of the Vale on land above flood level. Thus there

Above: Preston. The picture shows a cotton mill surrounded by workers' houses. Note the crowding of these houses; the straight streets set at right angles; the absence of gardens. (*Aerofilms Ltd.*)

Below: Port Sunlight. Part of Messrs Lever Bros Soap Works and of the modern garden city built for their workers. Note the wide streets, open spaces, and picturesque lay-out. (*E. N. Hemmings.*)

Above: Shrewsbury, an ancient market town, the principal part of which lies within river loop (in the background the river follows the line of the trees). The arched bridge carries the road to Wales. The railway station is built partly on another bridge. Compare carefully with the diagram on p. 138. (*Aerofilms Ltd.*)

Below: In the foreground the Eastham Locks at the entrance to the Manchester Ship Canal. In the centre the Queen Elizabeth II Dock for oil tankers, opened in 1954 and capable of handling four 30,000 ton tankers at once. (*Manchester Ship Canal Company*)

are two lines of villages linked by two east to west main roads, one along the northern side of the Vale and one along the southern side. Parallel to these main roads are two railway routes which link the seaside resorts of Scarborough and Filey with the interior. Roads, railways, and villages all avoid the riverine marshes.

The rich water meadows are famous for their cattle, while the better-drained lands away from the river are used for arable farming. There are no large towns in the Vale, Pickering and Malton being small market towns.

(c) THE YORKSHIRE WOLDS. These are the most northerly portion of the chalk escarpments. Never rising to more than 800 ft, the Wolds drop steeply to the Vale of Pickering on the north and gently to the plains of Holderness on the south. Eastwards they terminate in the bold promontory of Flamborough Head. Formerly they were wide expanses of unfenced grassland used as sheep runs, but to-day, although the Wolds are still important for sheep rearing, the method of farming has changed. Much of the land is now ploughed, barley and wheat being grown, as well as root crops on which the sheep are fed. The relatively modern fertility of the Wolds is the result of scientific farming and manuring.

(d) HOLDERNESS. The foundation of Holderness, a low plain lying between the Wolds and the Humber, is chalk, on top of which are deposits of glacial clays and alluvium. The River Hull flows southward over a flat badly-drained area, noted for its cattle, but on account of its marshiness almost devoid of villages (cf. the Vale of Pickering).

The coast between Flamborough Head and Spurn Head is crumbling very quickly, because the sea cliffs are composed of soft clays and loose sands. It is estimated that the coastline is receding at an average rate of 5 ft to 7 ft per year, and that a strip of land roughly two to three miles wide has been submerged since Roman times. This is the region of "drowned villages", and many farms and villages are to-day threatened with destruction. Much of the material worn from this coast is carried by tidal currents up the Humber where it is redeposited, so that villages once situated on the sea coast are now some miles inland (e.g. Beverley). The towns of

Holderness are either small market towns (Beverley, Driffield) or seaside resorts (Hornsea, Withernsea).

Hull alone, dominating the Humber, and the third port of the United Kingdom, stands out as a great city. More correctly designated Kingston-on-Hull, this port is situated on the north bank of the Humber, where a small river (the River Hull) enters the estuary (Fig. 54). The seaport

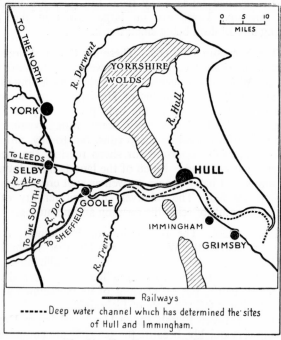

Fig. 54. The Position of Hull.

originated in the sheltered creek of the River Hull, and for centuries served only its immediate hinterland. The prosperity of the port rapidly increased with the development of the wool and iron industries of the West Riding and the canalisation of the Aire, Calder, and Don. Thus Hull was linked by water with such centres as Leeds, Wakefield, and Sheffield. Though road and rail transport have replaced canal transport, there is still a fair amount of barge traffic for bulky articles (*e.g.* coal). The great disadvantage of the position of Hull is the lack of direct easy communication southward. Railways strike westward to cross the river at Goole, and here also is the last road-bridge between Selby and the sea.

Its chief imports are dairy produce and timber (especially pit props) from the Baltic countries, wool from Australia, Argentina, and London, grain and flour, oil seeds, and mineral ores. Oil refineries express the oil and compress the residue of the seeds into "cake" for feeding live stock. There are also saw mills and paint works.

Its principal exports are iron and steel goods from the West Riding, and coal, but the hinterland of Hull includes also the cotton manufacturing region of South Lancashire and the industrial areas of North Staffordshire and the Midlands (Fig. 55). Hull is one of the world's largest fishing ports, due to its nearness to the fishing grounds of

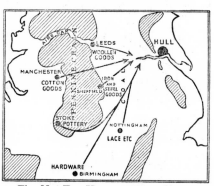

Fig. 55. THE HINTERLAND OF HULL.

the North Sea, and more than one-fifth of all our fish is landed here. Greatly increased industrialisation of the area is likely if the recent finds of natural gas off-shore lead to the exploitation of an important gas-field.

Goole, at the head of the Humber, is a smaller port than Hull, with similar imports and exports.

The Scarps and Vales of Lincolnshire

Like East Yorkshire, Lincolnshire is structurally similar to South-East England, and consists of five regions which, from east to west, are:—

(1) A coastal plain known as the Lincoln marsh.

(2) A north-south belt of chalk downs.

(3) A clay vale.

(4) A north-south low and narrow ridge of oolitic limestone.

(5) Part of the Trent lowlands in the north-west.

(6) An extensive fenland area bordering the Wash in the south and south-east.

The east to west alternation of plains and scarped ridges is due to the tilting of the strata as shown in the section (Fig. 56), and to its subsequent erosion.

Fig. 56. SECTION SHOWING THE PRINCIPAL DIVISIONS OF LINCOLNSHIRE.

(1) The coastal plain is a flat region of silts and clays between the Lincoln Wolds and the sea. When drained these lowlands form excellent pasture land. The sandy shores of the coast have given rise to a number of seaside resorts, viz. Skegness, Mablethorpe, Cleethorpes.

(2) The chalk Wolds, averaging 300 to 500 ft in height, are almost everywhere covered with glacial soils. Like the Yorkshire Wolds, they were once extensive sheep runs, but have been brought under cultivation by the adoption of scientific methods of farming. A fourfold system of crops is usually adopted, wheat or oats being followed by roots, barley, and clover in turn. Sheep are fed on the turnip fields by a system of "folding". By this method far more sheep can be grazed per acre, and the Lincolnshire breeds of sheep are world famous.

(3) The clay vale of Lincolnshire is narrow in the north and widens southwards, where it is drained to the Wash by the River Witham. The farming of this lowland is partly pastoral and partly arable. The cultivation of sugar-beet is important, and there are sugar factories at Spalding, Bardney, and Brigg.

(4) The limestone ridge (L i n c o l n Heights or Edge) is both narrower and lower than the chalk upland. In the north of the county it rises to less than 200 ft, but reaches 450 ft in the south. Like the Wolds, its surface is covered with glacial deposits, and agriculture is similar, sheep rearing being important. Immediately to the west of the limestone ridge are deposits of Jurassic iron ore. These are worked extensively around Scunthorpe, where, because of the nearness of coal in Nottinghamshire, large blast furnaces

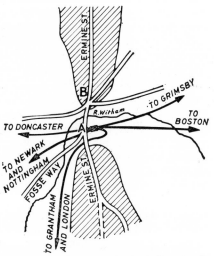

Fig. 57. LINCOLN.—The shaded portion is the Lincoln Edge (limestone) through which the River Witham cuts a gap. Double lines are roads, and single lines are railways. Note how the old Roman road, Ermine Street, keeps to the unforested hill tops. The old part of Lincoln with its cathedral, markets, etc., are in the area B. Railway station and factories are in lower region A.

have been established, making Scunthorpe one of the premier smelting centres in the kingdom (page 100).

An interesting point about the limestone ridge is that an old Roman road, Ermine Street, follows its crest from the north to the south of the county.

(5) West of the limestone ridge extend the Trent plains, rich grazing lands for cattle. In the north-west of Lincolnshire is an isolated fenland area, the Isle of Axholme, so called

because it is practically surrounded by the rivers Trent, Don, and Idle. This land has been drained, and produces good crops of potatoes, turnips, etc.

(6) The fenland area is described in Chapter XV.

Lincoln (Fig. 56), the county town, stands in a water gap, where the Witham flows through the limestone ridge. The details of its position are shown in Fig. 57. Lincoln is the great market centre for the plains to the east and west.

Lincoln is famous for the manufacture of agricultural implements and, of more recent development, the manufacture of excavating apparatus. Iron was originally brought from the Sheffield region by canal, but now can be obtained more easily from Scunthorpe. The eastward extension of coal-mining in Nottinghamshire has lessened the cost of transport for fuel.

Gainsborough and Grantham, both to the west of the limestone ridge, manufacture agricultural implements, an industry not surprising in view of the great agricultural development of Lincolnshire and the consequent demand for ploughs, harvesting machines, harrows, rakes, tractors, etc.

Grimsby, sheltered from north-easterly gales by Spurn Head, is a great fishing port, handling one-fifth of all the fish landed in this country, and from it there is a system of railways by which fish can be transported quickly to the industrial areas. Wood-pulp, timber, and foodstuffs are imported, coal, iron and steel manufactures, rayon and chemicals are exported.

Immingham, a few miles to the north of Grimsby, was built in 1912 at a point where the swing of the current provided deeper water than at Grimsby (see Fig. 54). It is essentially a port developed by the railway, and handles about five times the tonnage of Grimsby. Crude petroleum, iron ore (for the Scunthorpe and Rotherham furnaces), fertilisers, timber, and pit props are imported. Coal from the York, Derby, and Nottingham coalfield is the chief export, followed by petroleum products, building materials, and chemicals.

A large-scale map of Lincolnshire shows that a large number of towns end in the syllable "by". This is a Danish suffix (meaning village), and its prevalence indicates the extent to which the Danes settled in this area in the pre-Norman period.

CHAPTER 12

NORTHERN ENGLAND

(5) THE SOUTH-EAST LANCASHIRE COALFIELD

Position

The coalfield of South-East Lancashire lies between the rivers Ribble and Mersey, and is partly on the flanks of the Pennines and the moorlands of Rossendale Forest, and partly on the surrounding lowlands. There is no concealed coalfield as in the Northumberland and Durham and the York, Derby, and Nottingham coalfields, for the western edge of the coalfield is limited by "faults", beyond which the coal measures are at too great a depth to be worked. To the south of this coalfield the coal measures dip steeply under the Cheshire plains, but they are again too deep to be worked.

Development of the Cotton Industry

The South Lancashire coalfield is best known for its cotton industry, although this industry employs fewer workers than engineering even in the cotton area.

South Lancashire was originally an important woollen industry area, dependent on the sheep of the Pennine moorlands and the soft water of the Central Pennines. Hence there arose in this area a population skilled in the art of spinning and weaving, not cotton, but wool. This is very important, because, when the new fibre, cotton, was first imported from the countries of the Eastern Mediterranean about the sixteenth century, it was taken to an area where the population knew how to spin and weave. At first the introduction of the new fibre into England was viewed with suspicion, for it was feared that it might have an adverse effect on the woollen and linen industries of the country. In South Lancashire, the woollen "guilds" were not as powerful as in other districts, and so there was less opposition to the introduction of cotton. Thus the manufacture of cotton goods was established in Lancashire before the Industrial Revolution, and the woollen industry was gradually ousted.

It was not until about 1770 that the rapid growth of the cotton industry really began. One of the most important reasons for its immense growth was the number of inventions of machinery for cotton manufacture mainly by Lancashire men. Hargreave's spinning "jenny", Arkwright's spinning frame, and Crompton's mule, all invented during the eighteenth century, revolutionised cotton manufacture and contributed enormously to its growth.

There are numerous swift streams flowing from the moorlands which, before the use of steam, were an important source of power for driving machinery, and the later development of the coalfield and of its deposits of iron ore was a great asset. The dampness of the Lancashire atmosphere, too, must be taken into account, for if cotton is spun in a dry atmosphere, the threads snap. To-day the air of factories can be moistened by artificial means, so that dryness of the atmosphere is no longer a serious drawback.

Finally, one must not forget the inborn perseverance and thriftiness of the Pennine peoples, and the foresight and initiative of those citizens who conceived and carried out the great schemes of the Manchester Ship Canal, and the building of Lancashire's great port, Liverpool.

The Cotton Industry To-day

The cotton industry extends over the Lancashire boundary into Derbyshire (Glossop) and into Cheshire (Stockport, Stalybridge, and Hyde), and into Yorkshire (Todmorden and Skipton).

The cotton towns fall into two groups. Firstly, there is a northern group of weaving towns, including Preston (see plate facing page 112), Blackburn, Accrington, and Burnley. These towns are all in the Ribble Valley, and, with the exception of Preston, at the mouth of the river, are situated on the edge of the hills in the southern half of the valley.

Secondly, there is a southern group of towns engaged mainly in spinning, including Bolton, Bury, Rochdale, Oldham, Ashton, Stalybridge, Hyde, and Stockport. These towns form a semicircle around Manchester, the great cotton metropolis (Fig. 58), and are situated at the foot of the moorland, usually at a point where a valley opens out and a stream leaves the hills for the plains (*e.g.* Rochdale on the River Roch).

Manchester, on the River Irwell, a tributary of the Mersey, is thus in a very central position, and all valley routes from the north, east, and south-east lead to it. Therefore it has become the collecting centre, not only for the raw cotton for dispatch to the various towns, but also for finished goods, exported either via the Ship Canal or Liverpool. Manchester is, by virtue of the Ship Canal, the seventh port in Great Britain but

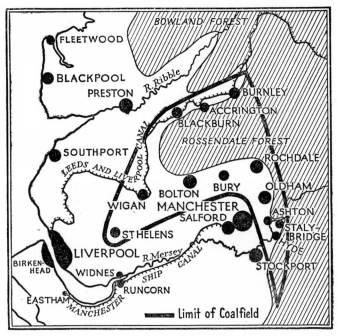

Fig. 58. THE TOWNS OF SOUTH LANCASHIRE.

handles less than one-quarter of the trade of Liverpool (see plate facing page 113). Petroleum is the chief cargo handled.

Raw cotton is imported via Liverpool or Manchester. The United States supplies a quarter; the Sudan, Brazil, Iran, and Turkey each supply about one-twelfth. The remainder comes from Peru, Argentina, Mexico, Egypt, and many other countries.

Weaving and spinning are by no means the only processes of cotton manufacture. After the cloth has been woven it has to pass through many processes before it is finished, including bleaching, printing, and dyeing. In these processes the soft water of the Pennines is again valuable.

Eighty years ago Lancashire produced nearly four-fifths of all the world's cotton goods. To-day we import more cotton cloth than we export. The decline in Lancashire cotton was to a great extent due to the rise of cotton manufacture in Japan and China and later in India and Hong-Kong. By 1933 Japan's export of cotton goods exceeded that of Great Britain. Japanese cotton goods found an increasing market in India, once the greatest market for English cotton fabrics.

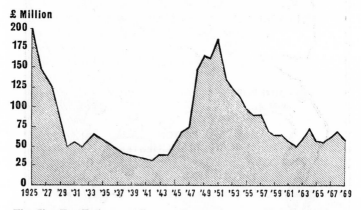

Fig. 59. THE EXPORT OF COTTON GOODS FROM THE UNITED KINGDOM, 1925-69. RAYON EXPORTS ARE NOW CONSIDERABLY GREATER THAN THOSE OF COTTON. (In interpreting this graph it should be borne in mind that present prices are about five times those of 1939.)

In 1959-60 the Lancashire cotton industry was reorganised. Some 400 old-fashioned mills were closed, reducing the number of spindles and looms to less than half. Other factories were re-equipped with up-to-date machinery similar to that in the more recently built mills of its overseas competitors. This enables the industry to produce more cheaply but requires a smaller labour force. Many mills were re-equipped and converted to manufacture rayon and other synthetic fibres, *e.g.* at Preston.

As in some other industries where foreign competition is severe Britain tends to specialise in the production of the finer qualities, where experience and skilled labour are more important.

Other Industries

The greatness of the cotton industry has hitherto somewhat overshadowed the other industries of South-East Lancashire, which is also one of the most important electrical and heavy

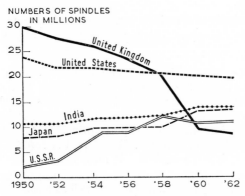

Fig. 60. NUMBER OF COTTON SPINDLES IN UNITED KINGDOM, UNITED STATES, JAPAN, AND INDIA.
(The reorganisation of the Lancashire mills in 1959-60 has reduced the number of U.K. spindles by over 12 million.)

engineering districts in the world. The manufacture of machinery for the textile industries takes first place, and dates back to the period of inventions at the end of the eighteenth century. Almost every large town of the coalfields is engaged in this branch of the iron industry, making machinery not only for the Lancashire mills, but for the ever-growing cotton industries in many other parts of the world, *e.g.* Japan, India, China, Brazil, etc.

South Lancashire is also famous for electrical engineering, and many world-famous firms have their works in this region. Other branches of engineering work include the manufacture of heavy road vehicles (in the Chorley-Leyland area), railway engines, gas and oil engines, steam hammers, and a vast range of machinery connected with industries such as flour milling, mining, paper-making, chemicals, etc.

Paper-making is another of Lancashire's many activities. For this industry the following conditions are needed:—

(1) An abundant supply of pure water.

(2) Fuel.

(3) Easily imported supplies of wood pulp, esparto grass, or waste rags.

(4) A supply of chemicals, *e.g.* caustic soda (from Cheshire).

(5) A variety of substances for dressing paper, such as glue, china clay, resins, etc.

In Lancashire the streams from the great moorlands supply pure water; coal is at hand on the coalfields; raw materials are imported through Liverpool and Manchester; chemicals are easily obtained from the Cheshire salt district; and china clay comes into the Mersey ports primarily to supply the pottery industry of North Staffordshire, but some is diverted northwards into Lancashire. It must not be forgotten that Manchester is a great northern "news" centre, publishing well-known daily papers, and this, as well as business activities and the need for paper for packing, creates a great demand for paper. The paper-making centres are ranged round Rossendale Forest, and include such towns as Burnley, Chorley, and Darwen.

Manchester is also the centre of one of the greatest rubber manufacturing districts of Britain. The north-eastern suburbs of the city, *e.g.* Ancoats and Clayton, are specially important. Rubber manufacture is also carried on in other Lancashire towns, *e.g.* Leyland.

The manufacture of asbestos boarding is an industry of recent growth for which this district is becoming noted. Asbestos is imported from Quebec, and the chemicals necessary for the industry are near at hand.

There is a large petroleum refinery at Stanlow on Merseyside, and the manufacture of dyes and chemicals is also important in this area. Halewood and Ellesmere Port have vehicle works.

CHAPTER 13

NORTHERN ENGLAND

(6) THE NORTH STAFFORDSHIRE COALFIELD

Position

On the south-west corner of the Pennines, around the headstreams of the Trent, on the North Staffordshire coalfield is the industrial area known as "The Potteries" (Fig. 61).

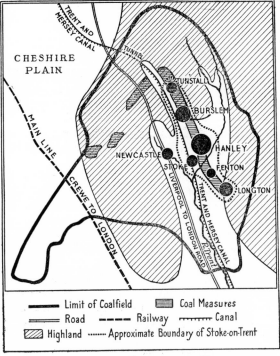

Fig. 61. THE NORTH STAFFORDSHIRE COALFIELD.

It is by nature a bleak, undulating upland, rising steeply from the Cheshire Plain on the west, whilst the Pennine folds sink more gradually southwards and eastwards beneath the sediments of the New Red Plain (p. 128) of Central England. Communication was therefore difficult westwards and easy towards the south and east, a fact which had a marked influence upon the development of communications in the days of turnpike roads, canals, and the early railways. The coalfield is triangular in shape, but the coal is worked only on the eastern and western sides. It is along the eastern limb of the coalfield that the pottery towns, Tunstall, Burslem, Hanley, Stoke, Fenton, and Longton, now federated into the city of Stoke-on-Trent, stand. To the west is Newcastle-under-Lyme, the ancient market town of the district, cn a strip of agricultural land in the middle of the coalfield. It holds aloof from the neighbouring industries, and is important mainly as a residential area.

The Pottery Industry

The making of pottery is a very old industry, and in early times almost any district which had suitable clay manufactured pots of some kind. The North Staffordshire area, because of its altitude and poor soils, did not provide rich farming land, and many of the farmers using local clay and brushwood for firing, made pottery in their spare time for sale in the neighbouring market towns, *e.g.* Uttoxeter. Thus was developed the traditional skill which is the basis of the modern industry. The great variety of local clays and the easily won coal, especially in the eastern section of the coalfield, provided resources for the infant industry such as probably no other coalfield could offer. Whilst for the making of pottery local clays have now largely been superseded by white clays obtained from Southern England, there is still a very large quantity of this local clay used in the making of saggars, the vessels in which the fine ware is baked, and for such articles as drain pipes and chimney pots. Now large quantities of Cornish and Dorset clays, flint, and china stone are imported.

The Trent and Mersey Canal

The modern development of the industry, and the pre-eminence which it has attained are due in no small measure to the inventive skill and business ability of Josiah Wedgwood. He studied carefully the needs of the industry, imported china clay from Cornwall, and showed how good quality pottery could be made cheaply and in large quantities. As there were no railways in those days, and the clay was brought from small Cornish ports, such as Fowey, to the Mersey estuary, as it still is, because of the cheapness of water transport. The clay was then taken up the River Weaver to a point near Northwich, loaded on pack animals, and thus carried across Cheshire to the coalfield. This latter part of the journey was so tedious and expensive that it made the cheap production of pottery almost impossible. It also limited the amount of clay that could be obtained, and such a journey was obviously not suited to the export of fragile ware. Wedgwood realised these difficulties, and was the pioneer of the Trent and Mersey canal, which was cut about 1770. This canal crosses Cheshire and passes under the Pennine slopes by a tunnel near Kidsgrove. After reaching Stoke it continues eastwards down the Trent Valley and joins the river near Nottingham, so that there is a continuous waterway from the Mersey to the Humber. Thus North Staffordshire was given cheap transport for the importation of kaolin and the exportation of pottery, and since it had already coal, coarse clay, and a population of skilled potters, the area has grown to be one of great importance. To-day it is the chief pottery area in the world, employing nearly 80,000 workers, but the china clay now comes by rail and road.

The Pottery Towns

It is interesting to note that with the passage of time the towns have tended to specialise on different types of ware. Thus white earthenware is manufactured in the northern towns from Stoke to Tunstall, whilst the production of china is centred chiefly in Longton, Fenton, and Stoke. Local clay is still used in Burslem and Tunstall for the manufacture of tea-pots, whilst the coarse wares, such as drain pipes and tiles, are the products chiefly of the western section of the coalfield. The smoke and grime of the Potteries has been greatly reduced in recent years by the rapid growth of the use of gas-fired and electrically fired kilns. To-day, the Potteries are a "smokeless zone".

CHAPTER 14

NORTHERN ENGLAND

(7) THE LOWLANDS WEST OF THE PENNINES

To the west of the Pennine Chain lie (1) the plains of Lancashire, viz. the lowlands of Lancashire between the Pennines and the Irish Sea; and (2) the lowlands of Cheshire and North Shropshire between the Pennines and the Welsh Uplands (Fig. 62).

Structure and Soils

Structurally, the Lancashire plains are composed of New Red Sandstones and New Red Clays, but these are almost everywhere covered by glacial deposits, varying from clays too heavy to plough, as in South Cheshire where 95 per cent. of the land is permanent pasture, to light sandy soils (e.g. *Sand*bach). In a few elevated regions the sandstones rise above the glacial deposits of the lowlands. Where this occurs there are picturesque red scarps and pine-covered hills or heath lands as in

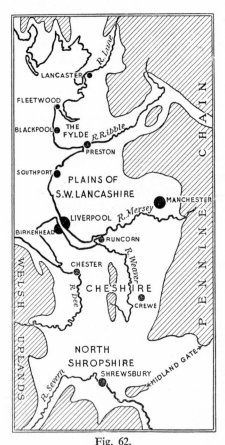

Fig. 62.
THE LOWLANDS WEST OF THE PENNINES.

Above: Oxford, the University city. (*Aerofilms Ltd.*)

elow: Oxford, the industrial town—the Morris Motor Works in the suburb of Cowley.
(*Nuffield Organisation.*)

Above: Goring Lock. There are many of these locks between Oxford and the sea to rai
the level of the water and so make the river more navigable for large river steamer
To-day, the river is used mainly as a "playground". (*B.R.*)

Below: The Thames at London. In the centre is St Paul's Cathedral. (*Aerofilms Ltd*

(1) the Wirral, (2) on the Central Cheshire ridge, (3) on the Shropshire-Staffordshire borders, and (4) in the isolated hills of North Shropshire. There are also large areas of peaty soils as in Chat Moss on the Lancashire-Cheshire border, and in South-West Cheshire. These latter soils are particularly valuable for growing potatoes.

Dairying and Agriculture

Lancashire and Cheshire have more cattle per 100 acres than any other English counties. The equable temperature, the well-distributed rainfall, and the demand for milk, butter, and cheese in the neighbouring industrial areas have led to the development of a great dairying industry. North of the Ribble a larger proportion of cattle are reared for meat.

Despite the undoubted pre-eminence of cattle rearing and dairying, other forms of agriculture are important. The Fylde peninsula between the rivers Ribble and Lune is noted for pig and poultry rearing. In the western lowlands of Lancashire between the Mersey and the Ribble there is much arable land, potatoes and wheat are extensively grown on peaty and lighter soils. Other agricultural activities are the cultivation of strawberries in the Dee Valley and the growing of sugar-beet and considerable quantities of barley in North Shropshire. In parts of eastern Cheshire rye is grown, and the rye straw sent to the Potteries, where it is used for packing china.

Salt, Chemical, and Silk Industries

The plains west of the Pennines are not, however, entirely dependent on agriculture. In the New Red Clays, which lie underneath the glacial soils of eastern Cheshire, there are extensive deposits of salt, extending from the Mersey southwards into Shropshire. Salt is worked principally in the middle Weaver Valley around Northwich, Middlewich, Winsford, and Sandbach (Fig. 63). There is to-day only one salt mine (at Winsford). Elsewhere borings are made and water is pumped into the salt layers. The brine is then raised to the surface and evaporated. This method of obtaining salt has led to extensive subsidence in the salt regions, *e.g.* at

Northwich, and many such subsidences can be seen near the main railway line north of Crewe. Salt is prepared for domestic use, and large quantities are exported to the fishing centres of Nova Scotia and Newfoundland, and to tropical countries where starchy foods are the basis of the diet, viz. India, Central Africa. Annual production is about three million tons, of which two-thirds is used in our chemical industries.

The greatest importance of the salt industry is in its relation to the chemical industry, now one of our most important industries. This is carried on at Northwich in Mid-Cheshire, and Runcorn and Widnes, on opposite shores of the Mersey. The chemical industry of North Cheshire supplies chemicals for use in the cotton industry (bleaching agents, etc.); for the glass manufactures of St Helens; for the soap manufactures of Port Sunlight (see plate facing page 112) and Warrington, as well as for the tanneries of Warrington. The two latter industries have also some connection with cattle rearing. The leather industry began because of the local supplies of hides, though to-day large quantities are imported. The soap industry, too, could formerly obtain the necessary fats locally, but now a large variety of vegetable oils are imported via the Mersey estuary.

On the eastern borders of Cheshire are three important silk-manufacturing towns, viz. Macclesfield and Congleton in Cheshire and Leek in Staffordshire. The supplies of pure soft water have been important in localising the industry because of its suitability for dyeing processes.

The Manchester Ship Canal

The completion in 1894 of the Manchester Ship Canal, which gives a thirty-six-mile waterway between Eastham (on the south bank of the Mersey estuary) and Manchester, opened up large tracts of country hitherto of little industrial importance. The canal is 30 ft deep and 120 ft wide. Because of the easy transport facilities factories are springing up all along the canal banks, viz. oil refineries, breweries, etc., and in particular there has been a great expansion of both factories and residential areas for workpeople in the Trafford Park area immediately to the west of Manchester. The tonnage passing through the canal has doubled since 1938.

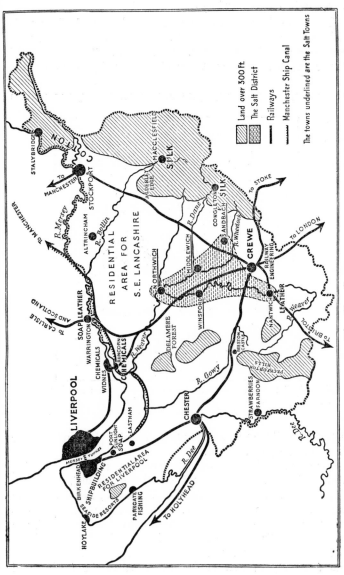

Fig. 63. CHESHIRE.

Liverpool: History and Development

The natural outlet of the Lancashire plains and of the coal-field further inland is Liverpool.   Liverpool is situated at the mouth of the Mersey estuary.   Because of its "bottle-necked" shape and the consequent strength of the tidal currents, the estuary is at this point deeper and freer from sandbanks than elsewhere, though dredging is constantly necessary to maintain

Fig. 64. THE HINTERLAND OF LIVERPOOL.—Tunnels enable goods from Yorkshire to be exported across the Pennines, and the Mersey tunnel gives more direct communication with North Wales.

a sufficient depth of water for large vessels.   Its foreign trade is second only to London.

Two hundred years ago Liverpool was a small fishing village situated round a creek called the "Pool".   In those days there was a little trade with Ireland, but it was mainly carried on through Chester, and Northern England was so scantily populated that there was little need for a great port.   Then there came an increase in trade associated with the famous "Trade Triangle" which was fostered by the discovery of new lands.   Ships sailed from Liverpool laden with guns, ammunition, trinkets, etc., which were sold to native chiefs in West Africa. There, slaves were collected for transport to the West Indies, whence the ships returned to Liverpool with cargoes of cotton, sugar, and tobacco.

With the coming of the Industrial Revolution and the development of the cotton industry, the need for a good port was realised, and Liverpool became the great importing centre for raw cotton. Miles of docks line the north bank of the Mersey. Liverpool exports much of the products of the industrial North and Midlands and also has an appreciable re-export trade.

The hinterland of Liverpool (Fig. 64) was originally merely the South Lancashire lowland. With the extension of roads and railways and the cutting of the Pennine tunnels the sphere of the trading activities of Liverpool rapidly expanded, and the hinterland is now no longer confined to South Lancashire. Liverpool exports woollen and steel goods from Yorkshire; pottery from North Staffordshire; hardware from South Staffordshire; chemicals from Cheshire; and in fact a variety of goods from all parts of England. Her imports are not confined to cotton, but include wool for Yorkshire from Australia and Argentina; dairy produce from Ireland, tin ore from Bolivia; and a vast range of products from the Americas, such as wheat, tobacco, sugar, timber, wood pulp, and hides, etc.

Though Liverpool has lost some of its passenger traffic to Southampton, it still retains about one-quarter of the passenger traffic of Great Britain. Despite the cutting of the Ship Canal, Liverpool still imports three times as much raw cotton as Manchester, and only in the case of very few commodities, *e.g.* crude oil and aluminium, does the amount imported by Manchester exceed that of Liverpool.

The industries of the city are, as in many ports, based on the imports. Thus in Liverpool there are flour mills, sugar refineries, and factories for the manufacture of cattle foods, chemicals, soap, and margarine. There are also shipbuilding yards, metal refineries, especially for tin, and electrical engineering and vehicle works. The Mersey tunnel has solved a great transport problem, not only easing connections between

Liverpool and Birkenhead, but between Liverpool and Chester and North Wales. Liverpool has regular air and water connections with Ireland and the Isle of Man.

Other Towns

BIRKENHEAD. On the opposite shore of the Mersey is Birkenhead, the twin port of Liverpool. It has a famous shipbuilding yard, and imports large numbers of live cattle from Ireland. Communication between Liverpool and

Fig. 65. THE POSITION OF LANCASTER.—(*a*) Where the western lowland is narrow. (*b*) At lowest bridging point of River Lune. (*c*) At a route centre.

the Wirral is by ferry-boat, or by electric train service, or by the Mersey tunnel roadway. Communication between Liverpool and Birkenhead is chiefly by ferry-boat or by road through the Mersey tunnel.

LANCASTER. This old Roman fortress (Fig. 65) is situated at the lowest bridging point of the River Lune. Here the Pennine uplands come closer to the west coast than elsewhere, so that west coast routes to Scotland had, perforce, to pass through Lancaster. At the same time there was easy communication via the Aire Gap with York, the Roman fortress of the east. Hence it was of great strategic importance in Roman times. To-day it stands on the main Midland Region route to the North. Its manufactures of linoleum are of some importance, and it has a new university.

CHESTER. At the lowest point of bridging of the Dee, Chester (Fig. 66), another Roman fortress, guarded the route to North Wales, as Lancaster guarded the route to Scotland.

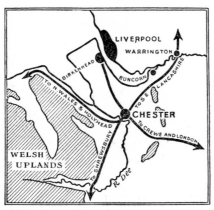

Fig. 66. THE POSITION OF CHESTER.—(*a*) Original lowest bridging point of River Dee. (*b*) Within a loop of the river. (*c*) Controlling the narrow north coastal plain route into Wales.

THE PORTS OF THE DEE-MERSEY REGION.—(*a*) Chester. Roman and medieval port—note canalisation of Dee below Chester. (*b*) At Latchford (Warrington). Roman port, the original lowest bridging point of the Mersey. (*c*) Liverpool, Birkenhead, Runcorn, modern ports. Runcorn now lowest bridging point.

Like York, it is a "show" city, having a fine cathedral and completely preserved walls. At one time Chester was an important port, but the silting of the Dee, the increased size of ships, and the competition of Liverpool led to its decline. An attempt to revive its importance was made by straightening and canalising the Dee between Chester and the estuary, but its trade to-day is insignificant.

WARRINGTON. Originally the lowest bridging point of the Mersey, Warrington was a port of some importance in Roman

times. To-day it is the point at which the west coast route
(L.M.R.) to Scotland crosses the Mersey. It has important
industries of soap making, tanning, etc., and also metal
industries. A bridge crosses the Mersey and the Ship Canal
some miles nearer the sea at Runcorn.

CREWE. Crewe (Figs. 67 and 68), unlike the neighbouring
market towns of Nantwich and Sandbach, is entirely of

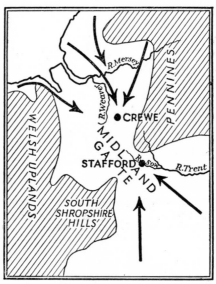

Fig. 67. CREWE AND STAFFORD.—Showing their positions in relation
to the Midland Gate.

modern origin. Nor is it a road centre, for the main road
between Manchester, Liverpool, and London passes some
miles to the north-east of the town. A little more than a
century ago its site was occupied only by a few scattered farm
houses. When railways were first developed across the
Cheshire Plain it was the point upon which the lines from
Birmingham, Manchester, and Liverpool converged, and
when these and other small railway companies combined to
form the old London and North Western Railway, now
absorbed in the Midland Region, it soon became the principal

engineering centre of the system. Its central position relative to London, Carlisle, Holyhead, etc., should be noted.

The cheapness of the heavy clay land, which was of low agricultural value, the nearness to the North Staffordshire coalfield, and the ease with which its commanding position in the Midland Gate enabled it to be developed as a focus of railway routes, all contributed to its rapid growth.

Fig. 68. CREWE. Showing its central position in relation to the old L. and N.W.R. system.

The fortunes of the town have been closely connected with the prosperity of the railway which finds employment for the majority of the men. The female labour is utilised in the local clothing and shirt factories. Recently motor works have been established, thus extending the engineering activities of the town.

SHREWSBURY. At the extreme south of the North Shropshire Plain, Shrewsbury [Fig. 69 (*b*)] is near to the most

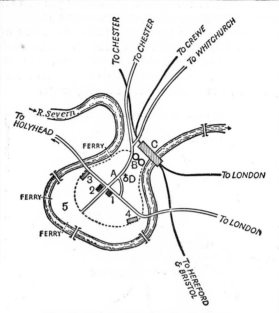

Fig. 69 (a). THE SITE OF SHREWSBURY.

The dotted lines represent the position of the old Walls. A. The original Market Place near the Church. B. The Castle guarding the "Neck". C. The Railway Station—built over the river because of lack of room. D. The principal Church on the highest point of the town.

1. Market Square, second position of market }
2. Present Market, third position of market. } near main cross roads.

3. Priory.   4. Friary.   5. Low land — originally marshy — now a park.

Note the number of bridges and ferries necessary.

northerly bend of the Severn, and is almost surrounded by one of its meanders (see plate facing page 113). It is the great market centre of the district, placed between the highlands of South Shropshire and the plains of North Shropshire.

It commands (1) the Severn route into Wales; (2) a southerly route via the Church Stretton Gap to Hereford and Bristol; and (3) is on the main road route between London and Holyhead.

In Roman times it was a fortified British stronghold, known

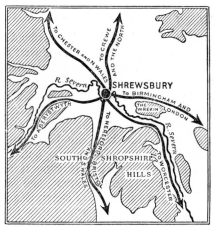

Fig. 69 (*b*). THE SITUATION OF SHREWSBURY.

as Pengwerne (the hill among the alders), and four miles to the east was the Roman city of Uriconium. Thus, though Shrewsbury with its wealth of half-timbered houses and historical associations is a "show" town, it lacks the Roman walls characteristic of Chester and York. To-day it is an important railway junction.

CHAPTER 15

THE CENTRAL PLAIN OF ENGLAND

Position and Relief

In the Midlands of England there is a lowland area roughly triangular in shape. It is bounded on the west by the Welsh mountains, on the north by the Pennine uplands, and the south-east by the limestone escarpment (Fig. 70). Flowing roughly parallel to the three sides of the triangle are the rivers Severn on the west, Trent on the north, and the Avon (tributary to the Severn) and the Soar (tributary to the Trent) on the south-east and east. The rivers are thus marginal to the central area and no large river flows through it. This absence of large rivers has been one of the greatest disadvantages with which the region has had to contend, and was one of the main reasons for its great network of canals (see Fig. 71).

Structurally, this plain is composed of New Red Sandstone and Clays, and is part of the great Y-shaped sandstone plain (often known as the Great Red Plain) which borders the Pennines on the west, south, and east, and extends south-westwards to the Severn estuary.

Rising above the general level of the plain are hilly districts, "islands" of harder rock, the sources of small streams which drain to the marginal rivers. The chief of these hilly districts are:—

(*a*) Charnwood Forest, a region of very old rocks with granitic intrusions, in Leicestershire.

(*b*) The hills known as Cannock Chase in South Staffordshire.

(*c*) The Clent and Lickey Hills of North Worcestershire.

(*d*) The Wrekin and the other hills of East Shropshire.

All these districts are the natural "playgrounds" for the industrial workers of the Midland cities.

In the neighbourhood of each of these upland areas are outcrops of coal measures, forming:—

(1) The Leicestershire coalfield.

(2) The Warwickshire coalfield.

(3) The South Staffordshire coalfield.

(4) The East Shropshire coalfield, which is linked southward with the unimportant coal measures of the Forest of Wyre.

Agricultural Activities

Climatically and agriculturally the Midland plains may be considered as transitional between the equable and rainy

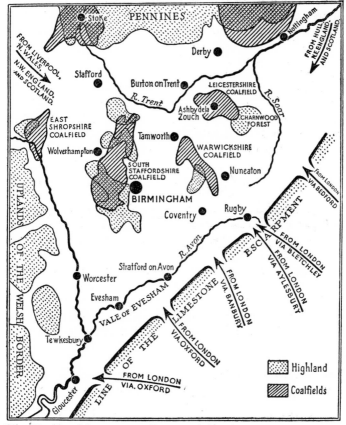

Fig. 70. The Midlands of England.—Showing—I. The triangular arrangement of the bordering uplands and rivers. II. The relation of the coalfields to the hilly country.

dairying lands of the western, and the more extreme and drier arable lands of the eastern, plains. The soils derived from the New Red Sandstones and Clays support excellent pastures and a high percentage of the land is devoted to permanent pasture for cattle rearing. To the west, in central Staffordshire, dairying is important, but stock rearing for meat increases eastward, being specially important in the neighbourhood of Melton Mowbray and Market Harborough. In general, it may be said that the percentage of dairy cattle decreases eastward and the percentage of "beef" cattle increases eastwards. Everywhere, however, in the neighbourhood of the coalfields and large cities, dairying plays an important part in the farming activities. The amount of arable land is greater in the east of the region where wheat, barley, oats, root crops, and sugar-beet are cultivated. The eastern half of Leicestershire is noted for sheep rearing.

In the south of the plain in the valley of the Stratford Avon and in Worcestershire is a very important fruit-growing and market-gardening region. While all types of small fruits and orchard fruits are grown, plums are of especial importance, particularly around Evesham. This region is open to the mild west winds which penetrate inland through the lowland "gate" between the Cotswold Hills and the Welsh mountains. It is particularly due to its good climate, partly due to its rich loamy soils, and partly to the demands of the industrial cities of the Midlands for fresh vegetables and fruit that this region has become so important. Further west, Worcestershire grows sugar-beet which is refined at Kidderminster.

Though farming is undoubtedly an essential part of the economic life of the Midlands, far greater importance must be attached to the development of the coalfields and their attendant industries.

The Midland Coalfields

The Midland coalfields are not important to-day for the amount of coal they yield. The total output of the four coalfields is less than one-tenth of the coal mined in Great Britain, and of this the South Staffordshire coalfield produces most (see Fig. 36).

THE EAST SHROPSHIRE COALFIELD. This region is unimportant to-day both for its output of coal and for its industrial activities, but it is of interest because it once ranked among the premier iron-working districts of Britain, and Shropshire formerly contained more forges than any other district except the Weald (see page 180).

The East Shropshire coalfield is now an industrial "backwater". The famous centre was Coalbrookdale, the home of Abraham Darby, a great pioneer of the iron industry. It was he who developed the possibilities of using coke instead of charcoal for smelting iron ore. Two miles from Coalbrookdale the first iron bridge was erected in 1779 over the Severn, and the town which has grown up around the bridge is called Ironbridge. It was here, too, that Wilkinson, another great ironmaster, launched the first iron barge, which was used to carry goods on the Severn. Iron rails were first made at Coalbrookdale, and were in great demand during the early days of railway building. The Coalbrookdale ironworks still exist, and a variety of iron goods are made in the neighbouring villages of Madeley, Horsehay, etc. There are only a few small coal mines now in operation, and none employs more than a score of miners.

Tiles and bricks are manufactured in the neighbourhood.

THE SOUTH STAFFORDSHIRE COALFIELD. This coalfield extends from the outskirts of Birmingham northwards through Wolverhampton and Walsall along Cannock Chase to within ten miles of Stafford. Within the lines joining Wolverhampton, Walsall, Birmingham, and Dudley is an immense conglomeration of towns with a total population of nearly four million. Over one million people live in Birmingham, the second largest city in Great Britain. (Note that Birmingham is not in Staffordshire but in the extreme north of Warwickshire.) Other towns of the industrial district are Willenhall, Darlaston, Wednesbury, West Bromwich, Bilston, and Tipton. The region is generally known as the "Black Country" because of the unsightliness of its factories and pit-heaps, its almost continuous urban areas, and its scarcity of green fields and open spaces.

In this coalfield there were formerly large deposits of black-band iron ore which gave rise to an important smelting industry, for in 1860 there were 180 blast furnaces producing about 15 per cent. of the pig-iron of Great Britain. The smelting industry has declined to such an extent that there were in 1965 only six furnaces in the four counties of Staffordshire, Warwickshire, Worcestershire, and Shropshire, producing between them only about 3 per cent. of the pig-iron of Great Britain. It must be remembered, however, that one modern furnace has a much greater output than the small furnace of a century ago. To-day, instead of producing pig-iron, South Staffordshire imports it from South Wales, Northamptonshire, and Scunthorpe, and uses it as the raw material for an immense variety of metal manufactures. The reasons for the decline in the smelting of iron ore are:—

(1) The exhaustion of supplies of local ores and the consequent expense of the transport of such a bulky commodity, in view of the inland position of the coalfield.

(2) The decrease in the output of coal and the fact that local coals are not good coking coals.

To-day the South Staffordshire coalfield is primarily important for its hardware manufactures. The region is said to make anything from "a pin to a steam engine", but more surprising than the variety of articles it manufactures is the variety of metals it uses.

Though its manufacturing industries were originally based on iron, it now manufactures goods made of zinc, copper, nickel, lead, aluminium, and many alloys such as brass and bronze. Birmingham also uses the precious metals, viz. gold, silver, and platinum, in its jewellery workshops. In fact, as a metal, and particularly non-ferrous metal, manufacturing region, South Staffordshire is probably unequalled by any other similar district in the world.

The inland position of this industrial area, away from navigable rivers and from the sea coast, has had a great influence on the nature of the articles it manufactures. Because of the expense of overland transport the district has specialised in the manufacture of goods requiring relatively little raw material but a high degree of skilled workmanship, *e.g.* watches, rifles, sewing machines, scientific apparatus, and jewellery. Many of the towns specialise in the manufacture of one particular class of goods, viz. Dudley makes chains, Wolverhampton locks and keys, and West Bromwich springs and weighing machines. Associated with the Birmingham, Coventry, and Solihull car factories is the rubber industry centred at Wolverhampton and Birmingham. Rayon is made at Wolverhampton. Other manufactures are the "luxury" industries associated with many large cities, viz. chocolate, silk, furniture, etc.

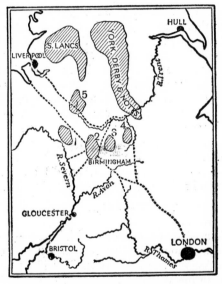

Fig. 71. The Relation of the Midland Coalfields to the Rivers and Ports.—1. East Shropshire. 2. South Staffordshire. 3. Warwickshire. 4. Leicestershire. 5. North Staffordshire. Dotted lines are a diagrammatic representation of the canals, showing in particular how the Birmingham area is linked to four great ports by waterways which are now hardly used.

Birmingham is almost at the centre of the quadrilateral formed by joining the great ports of London, Bristol, Liverpool, and Hull. To facilitate the export of bulky goods and the import of metal ores, canals have been built, linking

Birmingham with the marginal rivers of the Midland Plain, thus giving easy and cheap access by water to the estuaries of the Thames, Severn, Mersey, and Humber and their corresponding ports (Fig. 71.) Within the Black Country itself there is an intricate network of canals in constant use. The disadvantage of this canal system is that neither in depth nor width are the canals suitable for large barges. Schemes for their improvement are often suggested, and already improvements are being made in the canal linking London and Birmingham.

THE WARWICKSHIRE COALFIELD. As far as the output of domestic coal is concerned this is the most important of the Midland coalfields, but it has not the great industrial development of South Staffordshire. Most of the coal is distributed for domestic use, large quantities being sent to London. The coalfield extends from Tamworth in the north to Nuneaton in the south, but there are no important towns on the coalfield itself.

Coventry, an industrial centre a few miles to the south, draws its supplies of coal from this area. It is famous for its motor car industry which arose out of an earlier manufacture of cycles. Coventry also manufactures hosiery, gloves, silk ribbons, and rayon, and is one of the most prosperous and rapidly growing towns in England.

THE LEICESTERSHIRE COALFIELD. This coalfield lies to the west of Charnwood Forest in the north-west of Leicestershire. Like the Warwickshire coalfield, it has not given rise to a group of large industrial centres. The chief coal-mining centres are Ashby-de-la-Zouch and Coalville, relatively small towns. As in the Warwickshire coalfield, most of the coal is distributed for domestic use, though some is used in the hosiery centres of Hinckley, Loughborough, etc.

The West Midlands industrial area centred on Birmingham is the only one of our conurbations that is still rapidly growing (see page 268).

Other Industries of the Midland Plain

The hosiery and small ware industry of Leicestershire and the districts to the north of it have already been discussed (page 106).

The cattle rearing of the Midlands has given rise in many places to the tanning of leather and the manufacture of boots and shoes, as at Leicester, the greatest centre, and Stafford. The boot and shoe making industry is also located south of the edge of the limestone escarpment at Northampton, Wellingborough, and Kettering.

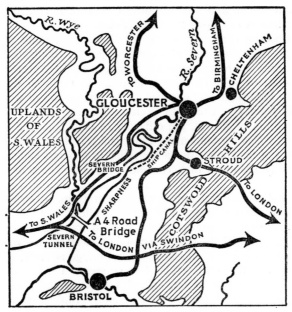

Fig. 72. GLOUCESTER.—As the lowest bridging point of the Severn, Gloucester controlled the routes from London to South Wales. The building of the Severn Bridge and the cutting of the Severn Tunnel each in turn reduced the distance by rail between London and South Wales.

Burton-on-Trent is famous for its breweries, largely because of the amount of barley grown on the sandstone plains, and because of its water supply for brewing.   To the north, *e.g.* at Tutbury, gypsum is mined and sent to Stoke-on-Trent for the manufacture of moulds for pottery making.   Stourbridge, to the south-west of Birmingham, specialises in "English Cut" glass.   At Droitwich and Stafford there are salt deposits in the underlying New Red Clays, cf. Cheshire and the lower

Tees Valley. The granites of Mount Sorrel in Charnwood Forest are quarried for road metal.

Rugby, an important railway junction, is a great centre for the manufacture of electrical equipment.

Worcester, situated at a point on the Severn where the river could easily be forded, is a market centre for the agricultural and fruit-growing areas of Worcestershire. It is of Roman origin, and was important because it controlled a route into Wales along the Teme Valley.

Gloucester (Fig. 72), at the lowest bridging point of the Severn, is another city of Roman origin. It controlled the most southerly route across the Severn to South Wales before the construction of the Severn Tunnel. In medieval times it was an important port engaged in the exportation of woollen goods from the Cotswold region. Largely owing to the competition of Bristol, the difficulty of navigating the lower Severn, which contains many sand banks, and the increase in the size of the ships, Gloucester failed to progress sufficiently rapidly to become a first-class modern port. The ship canal from Sharpness to Gloucester improved the approach to the port, but the construction of the Severn Tunnel diverted the South Wales rail traffic and affected Gloucester adversely. More recently the great increase in road transport has once more emphasised the importance of Gloucester as a bridge-town, but the effects of the new road bridge at Aust, thirty-five miles to the south, remains to be seen. The Gloucester Ship Canal is one of our inland waterways being further developed by the Transport Commission. Tanker barges use this canal to take some 600,000 tons of petroleum a year from the Bristol Channel ports to distributing centres at Gloucester, Worcester, and Stourport. Gloucester imports timber for the Midland coalfields, has ironworks and match factories, and also manufactures nylon.

Both Kidderminster and Bridgnorth in the extreme west of the Midland Plain have carpet factories. This industry is a survival of the old woollen industry based on the supplies of wool from the South Shropshire Hills and Wales.

CHAPTER 16

SOUTH-EAST ENGLAND

(1) THE BASIN OF THE WASH

General Division of South-East England

To the south and east of a line drawn from the mouth of the River Tees to the mouth of the River Exe is a region composed of scarped ridges alternating with clay vales and plains. Structurally, this part of England consists of younger rocks than the remainder of the country. The limestone and chalk, with their associated clays, are of Secondary age, while the clays of the London Basin and the Hampshire Basin are of Tertiary age. These rocks were subjected to slight tilting during the period of Alpine folding. The subsequent erosion of the softer clays has produced low plains and fertile vales, while the more resistant belts of chalk and limestone rise above the lowlands as scarped ridges.

The general arrangement of these ridges and vales in relation to the earth-folding is shown in Fig. 73. From A to B the rocks were folded into a shallow basin or syncline. From B to C the rocks were raised in an arch-shaped fold or anticline.

The general arrangement of the chalk and limestone hills and their associated vales is shown in Fig. 5 and described on pages 7 and 8.

The English lowlands (south of Lincolnshire, which was described in Chapter X) can be divided into the following regions:—

(1) The basins of rivers flowing into the Wash.

(2) East Anglia.

(3) The Thames Basin.

(4) South-East England, *i.e.* south of the lower Thames.

(5) The Hampshire Basin.

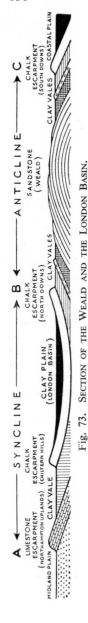

Fig. 73. Section of the Weald and the London Basin.

THE BASINS OF RIVERS FLOWING TO THE WASH

Extent

This region extends from the Wash south-westwards between the limestone and chalk ridges as far as Buckinghamshire, where a low watershed (less than 500 ft) separates the Wash drainage from that of the upper Thames (Fig. 74).

The rivers Welland, Nene, and Great Ouse all rise in the limestone ridge and flow in roughly parallel courses to the Wash. Within this region must also be included the lower valley of the River Witham, which rises on the west side of the limestone ridge in Lincolnshire, and, after flowing through the ridge at Lincoln, drains the clay vale and fenlands of Lincolnshire south-eastwards to the Wash.

The Wash drainage area may be conveniently subdivided into the three main sections which are dealt with below, viz. :—

(*a*) The dip slope of the limestone escarpment.

(*b*) The Fenlands.

(*c*) The higher plains to the south-west of the Fens.

Dip Slope of the Limestone Escarpment

This corresponds roughly to the county of Northamptonshire. Farming in this area varies in relation to the elevation and the quality of the soil. Sheep rearing is important on many of the higher portions of the Northampton Uplands, but on the lower hill slopes and in the river valleys arable farming and cattle rearing predominate.

The rearing of cattle has given rise to important leather industries at Northampton, Kettering, and Wellingborough.

The modern importance of this district is due to the exploitation of the Jurassic iron ores (see plate facing page 96) from Wellingborough, northwards to Corby (cf. Lincolnshire

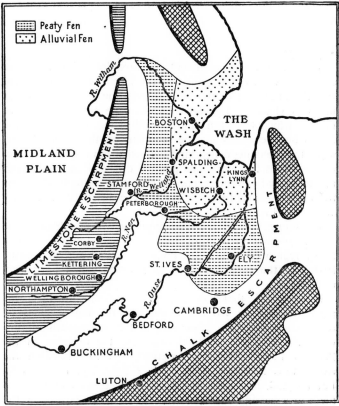

Fig. 74. The Basin of the Wash.

and North Yorkshire). This is a relatively recent development and there are now a large number of blast furnaces, since it is cheaper, because of the low iron content of the ore (20-30 per cent.), to bring coal to the iron ore rather than to take the iron ore to the coalfields. New settlements are developing around the old villages (*e.g.* at Corby, the population of which has increased from 1,600 in 1931 to 45,000 in 1969). Northamptonshire now produces more pig-iron than any other area in Britain except the north-eastern coastal districts of England. Some of this is converted into steel locally, but the bulk of the pig-iron produced is sent to South Staffordshire.

The Fenlands

The Fens is the name given to the area drained by the lower courses of the rivers flowing into the Wash. On the landward side the boundary of the Fens follows the fifty-foot contour line very closely. This lowland was once a shallow inlet of the sea which has been gradually filled in. Currents of the North Sea deposited marine sediment on the seaward side, while the rivers deposited land-derived silt in the lagoons and marshes thus formed. The gradual decay of the marshland plants formed extensive deposits of peat, varying in thickness from a few inches to several feet. The distribution of peaty and alluvial fens is shown in Fig. 74.

The conversion of the wild unproductive marshlands, the happy hunting ground of fishermen and fowlers, into a fertile region of plenty, the home of settled agriculturalists, is due to the extensive drainage schemes which have been undertaken.

It is probable that a portion of the Lincolnshire Fens was partly drained in Roman times, but the big schemes of reclamation had their beginning in the seventeenth century when the Duke of Bedford organised the draining of the Bedford Level. The chief method was to straighten the rivers, thus increasing their rate of flow, *e.g.* the Bedford Level Canal, and then to cut tributary ditches draining to them in a herring-bone pattern. Most atlas maps show the two straight parallel cuts which divert the waters of the Ouse; the region between these channels, known as the Wash, collects surplus or flood water. Water is also pumped into the drainage channels. This was first done by hand, later by windmills, and to-day by steam pumps. Little of the original fenland now remains. The fenland region, because of its flatness, sluggish rivers, bulb fields, dykes, and windmills is reminiscent of Holland (see plate facing page 32). Many of the rivers by the deposition of sediment have raised their beds slightly above the level of the surrounding country, which in the peaty areas has also been lowered by shrinkage of the peat as a result of improved artificial drainage.

The climate of the Fenlands is typical of the east coast, *i.e.* it tends to be somewhat "continental" in character with greater extremes and less rainfall than the west coast. Though the prevalent wind is south-westerly, the region is subject to dry east winds from the Continent and the average amount of sunshine is high. The Fens is one of the very few areas in the British Isles where there is any serious soil erosion problem. In dry spells, particularly in the spring, before there is a good plant cover, strong winds are apt to blow away the dry powdery soil in dust storms.

Conditions are particularly good for the cultivation of cereals, especially wheat. Oats and barley are also cultivated. In recent years there have been definite changes in Fenland agriculture. Potatoes are now by far the most important crop, and sugar-beet cultivation has made rapid strides. There are sugar-beet factories at Ely, King's Lynn, Peterborough, and Spalding. The district around Spalding is noted for growing bulbs, and around Wisbech there is an important fruit-growing area, chiefly specialising in the cultivation of strawberries. Much of the fruit is canned or deep frozen.

The towns of the Fen country fall into three groups:—

(1) Those on the fenland fringe, such as Cambridge, St Ives, Peterborough, and Stamford—all market towns. Besides having its ancient university, Cambridge is the regional administrative centre for East Anglia, and its light industries include printing, the manufacture of scientific instruments, and of radio and television equipment. Peterborough has railway and other engineering works and there is a sugar-beet factory. Local clay is used for brickmaking.

(2) Those situated on "islands" of firm ground, such as Ely, Wisbech, and Spalding. The origin of these towns dates back to the period before the reclamation of the Fens, when the slightly-elevated and better-drained sites were the only

possible places for settlement. Many of them provided safe refuge in times of political difficulty, *e.g.* the Isle of Ely (cf. the Isle of Athelney in Somerset).

(3) Those situated on or near the coast, such as Boston and King's Lynn, which have lost most of their former importance as a result of the increase in the size of the ships and the silting of the mouths of the rivers. Both export some of the pig-iron from the Wellingborough region, and Boston imports timber and has large canneries.

The Wash is still being filled up by the deposition of marine sediments. Eventually the whole of the inlet will be dry land. Meanwhile, proposals have been made for schemes to reclaim the Wash in a manner similar to that by which most of the former Zuyder Zee has been converted into fertile lowland.

The Higher Plains to the South-West of the Fens

Extending from the borders of the Fen country south-westwards to Buckinghamshire is a clay plain drained by the upper courses of the rivers Nene and Great Ouse. It rises in height south-westwards from 50 ft to 500 ft and in general includes Huntingdonshire, Southern Cambridgeshire, Bedfordshire, and Northern Buckinghamshire. In the eastern half of the district arable land predominates, and the crops are those typical of Eastern England, viz. wheat, barley, oats, clover, and roots. Around Sandy in the east of Bedfordshire is an old-established market-gardening district which sends fresh salads and vegetables to London. South-westwards, the percentage of permanent pasture increases, and dairying predominates. This is one of the important sources of London's milk supply. The towns, such as Bedford and Buckingham, are all market towns. On the southern margin of the region commanding a gap through the chalk ridge is Luton.

The clay of this district is very suitable for brickmaking and there are a number of large brickworks especially near Peterborough and Bedford, which produce nearly one-third of our bricks.

LUTON. Luton occupies a gap in the Chilterns, where the River Lea, near its source, breaks through on its way to the Thames. The river valley provides a relatively easy route through the chalk hills, which is followed by the main railway line from London to Leicester.

Luton has long been famous for the manufacture of hats, the raw materials for which were obtained locally. The clear colour and light weight of the straw grown on the chalky soils of the Chilterns made it very suitable for plaiting. Originally the industry was essentially of the domestic type, and was carried on in the villages of Southern Bedfordshire and the neighbouring parts of Hertfordshire and Buckinghamshire, but during the last hundred years the manufacture of hats has concentrated in Luton. The domestic features of the industry have disappeared and the principal supplies of raw material are now imported.

The manufacture of hats, which employs some 4,000 people, is now quite overshadowed by other newer industries which have developed during the last thirty years and have led to a great increase in the size and prosperity of the town. The manufacture of motor cars now employs five times, and engineering (vacuum cleaners, etc.) three times as many people as hat manufacture, and the aircraft industry also employs over 4,000 workers.

Luton is typical of many towns in Southern England, which have attracted new industries, particularly light engineering, including the manufacture of road vehicles, aircraft, and vacuum cleaners. Bedford, also, has attracted a number of small industries which have turned what was originally a market and educational centre into a mainly industrial town.

CHAPTER 17

SOUTH-EAST ENGLAND

(2) EAST ANGLIA

Physical Characteristics

East Anglia comprises the extreme north of Essex, Suffolk, and Norfolk, except for the north-west corner of Norfolk around King's Lynn, which is part of the Fenlands. It corresponds to the district which was the Angle kingdom of early history, bounded on the west by impassable marshes of the Fens and on the south by the forests which grew on the heavy clays of the London Basin. In the west is an arc-shaped ridge of chalk convex to the east coast, from which the land drops gently eastwards, and is drained by such rivers as the Wensum, Yare, Waveney, Orwell, and Stour. The chalk ridge is known as the East Anglian Heights in the southern half, where it runs south-west to north-east. It rises to about 400 ft, and presents a scarp face to the north-west. In this region, around Newmarket, the famous racing centre, there are still tracts of the open "down" country which have not been brought under the plough. In Western Norfolk the chalk lands, known as the Norfolk Heights, are neither so high nor so broad, but many

Fig. 75. EAST ANGLIA.

of the characteristic features of chalk lands, *i.e.* open downs and dry valleys, are evident. Between the chalk ridge and the sea, East Anglia is composed of deposits of Tertiary age, but these, as well as most of the chalk lands, have been everywhere covered with a thick mantle of glacial clays and sands, varying so much in texture as to produce regions of distinctive agricultural activities. The major variations of the soils of East Anglia are shown on Fig. 75. The soft and loose materials of the East Anglia coastlands are easily eroded by marine action. Like Holderness, this is a region of receding coastline and lost villages. In past time these coastal areas have also been partially submerged, as is proved by the drowned valleys (estuaries of the Stour, Orwell, Colne, etc.) of the Suffolk and Essex coast.

The shallow, peaceful, reed-bordered lakes, known as the Norfolk Broads, were formed in the thirteenth century, when owing to subsidence of the land the sea flooded very extensive peat-pits from which peat had been dug for centuries as fuel. The Broads are bordered by much reclaimed marshland.

Climatically, East Anglia, like all the eastern regions of Britain, is less equable, and drier, than the western regions. The warmth of the summers and the high average of sunshine duration are important factors in determining the type of agriculture. The total yearly rainfall is less than 25 in., and while most of the rain falls during the summer half of the year it is largely of the thunderstorm type, quickly over and followed by bright sunshine. Since less than twenty-five inches of rain is insufficient to give maximum yields with certain crops, many farmers find it profitable in dry years to make use of irrigation by overhead sprays.

Agricultural Activities

Though the climate of Britain is not really ideal for the cultivation of wheat, the nearest approach to the ideal conditions (see page 26) are found in East Anglia.

Wheat, barley, and root crops are grown throughout the region. Some localities, as a result of varying soil conditions, specialise more in the production of one crop than another. One important fact stands out, and that is that throughout

East Anglia, famous as this district may be for its wheat lands, a greater acreage is devoted to barley than to wheat.

The richest soils are the loams of Eastern Norfolk, and these were the first to be used for intensive agriculture. The extension of arable farming into the less fertile areas, particularly the sandy regions, was made possible by the system of crop rotation adopted in the eighteenth century.

Turnips were the real basis of the new agricultural system. Sheep which fed on the turnip fields trod and manured the soil, preparing it for the barley or wheat crop. Clover was also introduced as a fodder crop. These methods of cultivation were practised on the chalk downs, now having a higher percentage of arable and wheat land than any other section of East Anglia. Barley and turnips and sheep rearing are of most importance in the northern sandy area, and the sheep are removed in summer to the pastures of the coastal alluvial fringe.

Cattle rearing is specially important near King's Lynn and in the region of loamy soils north of Norwich. The permanent pasture lands of the Broadland region provide rich summer pastures for the cattle of East Norfolk.

The acreage under wheat is greatest on the chalk downland and on the boulder clay regions of the centre of East Anglia. A feature of present-day agriculture in East Anglia is the increasing importance of sugar-beet, of which the residual pulp can be used for stock feeding. While the sugar-beet is grown in all sections of East Anglia, it has become most important in the Breckland region, in those districts where the soil has been improved by special treatment. This region, lying between the Norfolk Heights and the East Anglian Heights, is a low chalky area covered with a thin layer of light sand, and is similar to the Geestland of Holland and the heath lands of western Denmark and the north German plain. Much of it is still open heath land or has been planted with trees. On its poor soil rye often replaces wheat. The sandy regions of the south-east also still have much heath land.

Industrial Activities

In the Middle Ages, East Anglia had important trade relations with Flanders, to which it exported wool for the Flemish woollen factories, barley for the Flemish breweries, and wheat for food for the Flemish people. Later, instead of exporting wool, the people of East Anglia used it for manufacturing, and the region of Norfolk between Norwich and the sea was formerly an "industrial" area of England.

The woollen industry, unable to survive the competition of Yorkshire, has disappeared. At Lowestoft there are small manufactures of net and sailcloth to supply the fishing fleets.

The most important industrial activities of East Anglia are related to agriculture; sugar-beet factories at Cantley, Bury St Edmunds, and Ipswich; the manufacture of agricultural machinery at Norwich and Ipswich; flour milling and malting at Ipswich, Colchester, and Chelmsford; the preparation of mustard and vinegar and the canning and freezing of food at Norwich; brewing in many of the market towns.

Many of the coastal towns are important fishing centres. The chief of these are Lowestoft and Yarmouth which are busy during the herring season (about October), when large quantities of herrings are cured or packed in salt for export to the Continent. These towns are near the North Sea fishing grounds, and have quick rail communication with London.

Harwich has long been a ferry port, from which passenger vessels sailed regularly to the Hook of Holland, Rotterdam, Flushing, and Antwerp, and more recently to Hamburg and elsewhere. In the last decade it has developed rapidly as a commercial port, thanks to our increasing trade with western Europe. In 1969 Harwich ranked as our fourth port, ahead of Southampton (see p. 174). Even more spectacular is the rise of Felixstowe, only four miles from Harwich which in 1969 was our sixth port, ahead of Manchester.

These rapidly developing ports have the most modern equipment and are prepared to adopt new methods, such as containerisation. Their efficiency is already attracting traffic from older ports, especially London. However the increasing traffic is beginning to cause a heavy strain on the main roads leading to these ports, especially those from the Midlands, which are having to carry an ever-increasing number of heavy vehicles.

Many of the coastal towns, such as King's Lynn, Ipswich, Yarmouth, Lowestoft, enjoyed considerable prosperity as ports during the Middle Ages, when they traded extensively with the Continent. Their trade declined because of the smallness of their harbours and the rapid increase in the size of their ships, so that now their importance as ports is purely local, although increasing again.

NORWICH. A city of Saxon origin, Norwich is situated on the River Wensum near its confluence with the River Yare (Fig. 76). It was of early importance as a fortress and an ecclesiastical centre (it has a castle and a cathedral), and in the Middle Ages was an important river port, trading largely in wool. The convergence of river valleys gave Norwich a high degree of nodality, so that it became an important road, and later a railway, centre. This nodality gave it preeminence as a market town for the whole of the Norfolk region. Its industries include the manufacture of agricultural implements, leather goods, fertilisers, mustard, starch, vinegar, beer, etc., all of which are connected with the agricultural activities of the region.

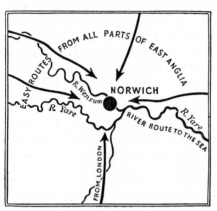

Fig. 76. THE POSITION OF NORWICH.

IPSWICH. The situation of Ipswich, at the tidal limit of the River Orwell, was important when roads were poor, for goods could be carried inland up the estuary. It is also at the lowest point where the river could be easily bridged. It was important as a wool port during the Middle Ages, and later was engaged in woollen manufactures. From the sixteenth to the eighteenth centuries it was a shipbuilding centre. Like Norwich, its industries are largely connected with agriculture, and include engineering, the manufacture of agricultural implements and fertilisers, flour milling, malting and brewing, the refining of sugar, and the canning and freezing of foods.

ove: Oast houses at a farm in Kent.   Hops are being brought in to dry.   (*Picture Post.*)

low: Rochester, the lowest bridging point of the Medway, with its road bridge and
railway bridges.   In the foreground are the ruins of the Norman Castle, with its keep
still nearly intact.   Note the shipping and the chalk quarry.   (*Aerofilms Ltd.*)

Above: Dover Harbour. Note the chalk cliffs. (*Aerofilms Ltd.*)
Below: Part of the "New Town" being built at Crawley, one of a number of such
relieve the congestion in the London area. (*Aerofilms Ltd.*)

CHAPTER 18

SOUTH-EAST ENGLAND

(3) THE THAMES BASIN

The Course of the Thames

The Thames rises in the south-western end of the Cotswold Hills and flows eastward along the Clay Vale, receiving a number of tributaries from the dip slope of the Cotswolds, viz. the Colne, Evenlode, Windrush, and Cherwell. After its confluence with the Cherwell at Oxford (the limit of navigation for river steamers), the river swings in great loops over the clay plains and then flows through a gap in the chalk ridge (the Goring Gap), (see plate facing page 129). On the east side of the gap at Reading the east-flowing Kennet joins the main stream, which proceeds to flow in a great northward bend towards the foot of the Chiltern Hills. The river then turns south-east and makes a large southward bend, receiving the tributaries Wey and Mole, which rise to the south of the North Downs. The river then meanders across the plain to the sea, receiving the River Lea on the north bank, and the Darent and Medway on the south bank.

The Thames Basin is divided into five regions (Fig. 77). They are:—

(1) The Cotswolds.

(2) The upper Thames Basin, which is part of the Clay Vale lying between the limestone and chalk ridges.

(3) The Chalk Hills.

(4) The London Basin, enclosed by chalk ridges on the north, west, and south.

(5) The region to the south of the North Downs, which is drained by the upper courses of the Wey, Mole, and Medway. (This region will be described in Chapter 20.)

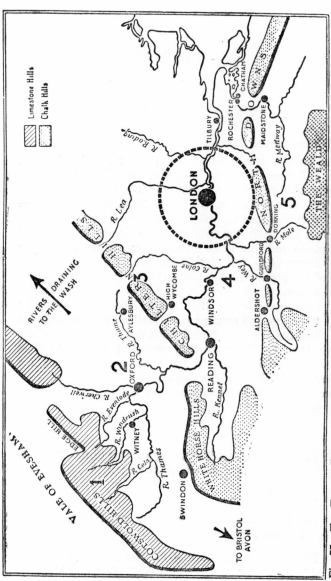

Fig. 77. THE THAMES BASIN, SHOWING TRIBUTARIES, CHIEF TOWNS, AND NATURAL DIVISIONS.—The circle around London denotes the approximate limits of "Greater London". 1. The Limestone Hills. 2. The Clay Vale. 3. The Chalk Hills. 4. The London Basin. 5. Vale of Holmesdale.

The Cotswolds

Rising in places to 1,000 ft, the Cotswolds are the highest and broadest portion of the limestone ridge. From their high western edge there are extensive views of the lower Severn plain and the Welsh hills beyond. The Cotswold villages, with their clear streams, beautiful Elizabethan manor houses, and stone cottages with their wealth of flowers growing even by the roadside, are among the most picturesque in England. Much of the higher land of the Cotswolds is still used extensively for sheep rearing, but there are few treeless open downs. Stone walls often enclose the fields, and there are beautiful woods of beech and pine.

The slopes facing south-east and the valleys of the Thames tributaries are farming regions of mixed agriculture. At one time there was an important woollen industry, but this survives

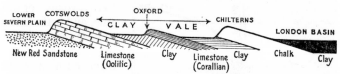

FIG. 78. SECTION OF THE OXFORD CLAY VALE.

in only a few places, notably at Witney (blankets), Chipping Norton (whipcords), and at Stroud on the eastern side of the Southern Cotswolds.

The Clay Vale

The upper Thames Basin is bordered on the north-west by the dip slope of the Cotswolds, and on the south and south-east by the scarp slopes of the White Horse Hills and the Chiltern Hills. The Clay Vale, often known as the Vale of Oxford, is a region of clay soils, largely used for permanent pasture and cattle rearing. Aylesbury, to the east of Oxford, is the centre of a rich dairying region. Much of the milk is sent to London, but some is used in local creameries and "patent food" factories. The lighter clays and loams of the south of the vale are among the most valuable farming lands in Britain, producing large crops of cereals. On the whole, throughout Southern England, there is a tendency to increase permanent pasture and dairying at the expense of arable land and cereal production. This is partly due to the competition of cheaper cereals from abroad, and partly to the dominance of London, with its immense population and increasing demands for fresh milk and dairy produce.

Running through the centre of the vale from north-east to south-west, and parallel to the limestone and chalk scarps, is a "miniature" scarp of Corallian limestone which forms low heights around Oxford (Fig. 79).

Oxford is situated in the centre of the Clay Vale, at the confluence of the Thames and Cherwell, and where the river flows through the Corallian ridge. Thus it stands at the "cross-roads" of the vale, and is the great market centre of the region. Its importance as a market centre is, however, masked by its importance as an industrial centre and as a university city (see plate facing page 128). The colleges of Oxford and Cambridge owe their foundation and endowment to the agricultural wealth of Southern England in the Middle Ages, in contrast to the newer universities (principally in the northern cities) which derive most of the endowments from industrial wealth. On the outskirts of Oxford, at Cowley, are the famous motor works, indicative of the modern tendency of manufacturing industries to concentrate in the old route centres of Southern England.

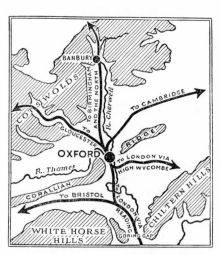

Fig. 79. THE POSITION OF OXFORD.—Showing its importance as a route centre.

West of Oxford, at the foot of the White Horse Hills, is Swindon, a town which, like Crewe (page 136) owes its origin and growth to a railway. A hundred years ago Swindon was a small village, to-day it is a large town and the chief engineering centre of the British Railways' Western Region. Like Crewe, it is centrally situated in relation to the railway system which it serves.

The Chalk Escarpment

Separating the upper and lower Thames Basin, the chalk escarpment is broken by the Thames Gap at Goring. West of the gap are the White Horse Hills and the Berkshire Downs, while to the east of the gap are the Chiltern Hills. The Chiltern Hills are broken by a series of gaps which are utilised by railways radiating north-westwards from London (see Fig. 84):—

(1) The Western Region uses the Thames Gap for its route from London to Oxford, Swindon, and South Wales.

(2) The Western Region main line to Birmingham uses the High Wycombe-Princes Risborough Gap.

(3) The London Midland Region route follows the Amersham-Wendover Gap to Aylesbury.

(4) Another London Midland Region route uses the Berkhamsted-Tring Gap.

(5) A third London Midland Region route uses the St Albans-Luton Gap.

A first glimpse of the forested slopes of the Chilterns serves to destroy all previous conceptions as to what the scenery of the chalk country should be, yet, a few miles further east, there is open chalk down country in the neighbourhood of Dunstable. In the chalk lands there is a variety of types of scenery and soil.

(1) Much of the chalk country provides good arable land, as in the East Anglian Heights.

(2) Where the chalk soils are not deep enough for ploughing, or where the gradients are too steep, the chalk is covered with short springy turf, which is good sheep pasture. This is the "down land" type of chalk land.

(3) There is sometimes a layer of gravel covering the chalk, and this produces a rough heathy land covered with bushes, such as gorse and hawthorn.

(4) Chalk land is sometimes covered with a layer of "clay with flints". Where this occurs there are extensive woodlands of oak and beech. When these woodlands are cleared the land provides good cattle pasture. The beech forests of the Chilterns were the reason for the origin of the chair-making industry at High Wycombe, which now also makes furniture of all kinds.

The Lower Thames Basin, or the London Basin

The London Basin is a V-shaped plain, tapering westwards to the Vale of Kennet. It is bounded on the south by the North Downs, and on the north by the Chilterns, and through it the lower Thames flows eastwards to the sea.

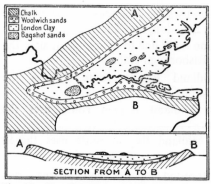

Fig. 80. THE ROCKS OF THE LONDON BASIN.

Structurally it is a basin or syncline of chalk (Fig. 80) filled with rocks of Tertiary age, the chief being London Clay. Between the London Clay and the chalk are pebbly and sandy soils known as Woolwich Sands, which appear at the surface around the edge of the clay and result in decided infertile areas such, for example, as the Blackheath Common.

Above the London Clay occur patches of sands (Bagshot Sands), which are of little agricultural value, and give rise to heath land and pine woods. Such regions are to be found at Hampstead and Harrow. Because they are higher than the surrounding land these sandy areas are being developed as residential centres. To the south-west of London is Bagshot Heath, on which are situated the military training centre of Aldershot, the Bisley rifle ranges, and the military colleges of Sandhurst, Wellington, and Camberley.

Except for these relatively infertile districts the rural areas of the London Basin are all primarily concerned with the provision of food for the capital. The clay lands are used for dairying, the lighter soils, as in Essex, for market gardening, and sheep are reared for their mutton on the surrounding chalk ridges.

West of London the Thames-side towns provide residential areas and "playgrounds" for the workers of the metropolis. This is specially so at Henley, Marlow, and Maidenhead, where the Thames cuts northwards into the chalk, and the river scenery is more picturesque than it is in the flat clay lands nearer London. At Windsor, the Thames cuts into a chalk bluff on which stands Windsor Castle.

Reading (Fig. 81), at the confluence of the Kennet and the Thames, is a great focus of routes, for it commands the routes eastwards to London; northwards to Oxford and the Midlands; westwards through the Vale of Kennet to Bath and Bristol; and southwards to Southampton. Because of its nodal position and the variety of products from the surround-

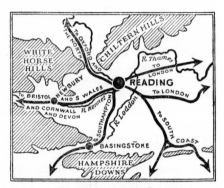

Fig. 81. THE POSITION OF READING AS A ROUTE CENTRE.

ing vales and downs it is an important market centre, and was of great strategic importance during the Civil Wars. Its two principal industries are seed-growing and biscuit-making.

Newbury, in the Vale of Kennet, is another market centre, and, because of the nearness of open chalk downland on the north and south, is well known as the centre of a district famous for the training of race-horses.

The dominating unit of the London Basin is London, and to it the roads, railways, agriculture, "playgrounds", dormitory towns, and industries are all tributary.

CHAPTER 19

SOUTH-EAST ENGLAND

(4) LONDON

London: Its Position and Origin

It is difficult to define exactly what is meant by London. The actual City of London is a very small area (less than 700 acres) lying north of the Thames near London Bridge. This is the business centre of the world, and though half a million people work within its limits by day, only about 10,000 reside there, often as night watchmen. Many of the city workers live as much as thirty miles from their employment, and travel daily from distant "suburbs". These "dormitories" extend to the forested hills of the Weald, and even to Brighton on the south; to Maidenhead on the west; to the Chiltern Hills on the north; and to Rochester and Chelmsford on the east.

Greater London, however, does not include, for administrative purposes these far-flung suburbs, and may be approximately limited by a circle of fifteen miles radius with its centre at London Bridge. This circle bounding Greater London passes through Watford, Epping, Erith, Epsom, Staines, and Uxbridge; within these limits live well over eight million people with an average density of 12,600 to the square mile (Fig. 82).

London probably originated as a Roman settlement, situated at a point where the river could be crossed with relative ease, possibly near Westminster, where there was a ford. The firm banks also, at a later date, made possible the building of a bridge near this point. Until the construction of Tower Bridge further downstream, London Bridge was the lowest point of bridging. It soon developed as a crossing place of the Thames, and therefore became an important road centre. The two low hills nearby, on which St Paul's and the Royal Exchange are now built, were suitable positions for the defence of this important bridge. The original settlement was roughly coincident with what is now termed "The City", *i.e.* it is the heart of London. From such

168

beginnings London grew. The phenomenal development and expansion of the city in late history is due to a number of causes, viz. :—

(1) Sea-going vessels, because of the high tides, can reach London Bridge in the heart of the city, hence it grew as a port.

(2) The main roads and railways from all parts of Britain were built to converge on London.

Fig. 82. LONDON.—Circles drawn at 10, 15, and 30 miles from the city. This diagram should be compared with the atlas and the towns near the 30-mile circle located.

(3) The Thames estuary is opposite the busiest region of the Continent, with which it has traded for centuries.

(4) London has a great, though diminishing, entrepôt trade, handling most of our re-exports.

(5) London is not only the capital of England, but has also for centuries had world-wide interests and connections.

(6) In more recent times the constant assemblage of a vast range of raw materials at London has caused a great industrial development.

(7) Finally, as London has grown, the immense market provided by its population, and the availability of labour there, has attracted, and is still attracting, numerous miscellaneous industries. These days these two factors are the most important in deciding the location of new and developing industries of nearly every type.

Water Supply

One of the most important necessities for the existence and health of the millions of people of this vast urban area is an adequate supply of pure water. About 85 per cent. of

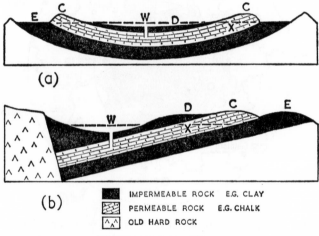

Fig. 83. ARTESIAN WELLS.

London's water supply of 50 gallons per head per day (*i.e.* 400,000,000 gallons daily) is obtained from the River Thames and purified. The remainder is obtained from a number of sources:—

(1) Three hundred years ago water was carried by wooden conduits from the upper course of the River Lea in Hertfordshire to supply London. This is now conveyed to London by more modern methods.

(2) The structure of the Thames Basin makes it possible to obtain water by boring artesian wells (Fig. 83). In this way water from the underlying layers of porous chalk is raised to the surface. Where the artesian water does not rise sufficiently high to reach the surface it has to be pumped, sometimes from a depth of 600 ft. There are hundreds of such wells. At the end of last century the number of private bores, made by manufacturers who used large quantities of water, rapidly increased. The reserves of subterranean water were diminishing so quickly that there were grave fears of a water shortage, and new schemes had to be formulated to increase the supply of water, and to avoid the danger of shortage in time of drought.

Communications and Trade

Although ridges of chalk hills surround the London Basin on three sides, they do not seriously interfere with communication between London and the provinces, for they are broken by a number of gaps (Fig. 84) which are used by the main railways converging on the metropolis (see also Fig. 98).

The Southern Region, with termini at Waterloo, Victoria, and Charing Cross, links London with all the south coast ports and seaside resorts from Weymouth eastwards to Dover.

The Eastern Region, with termini at Liverpool Street, King's Cross, and Marylebone, links London with the Eastern Counties and the Midlands, and with Scotland, via the North-Eastern Region route to Berwick and Edinburgh.

The Midland Region, with termini at St Pancras and Euston, links London with North Wales, the Midlands, the industrial areas of Lancashire and Yorkshire, and with all Northern Scotland via the west coast route through Crewe and Carlisle, or via the Midland route through Leeds and Carlisle.

The Western Region, with a terminus at Paddington, links London with Cornwall, and with South and Central Wales.

Not only do the main railways converge on London, but so do the great trunk roads. Some of these important roads are the Great North Road (A1) from Edinburgh; the Dover Road (A2); the Portsmouth Road (A3); the Bath Road (A4); the Holyhead Road (A5); and the road from Manchester and Carlisle (A6).

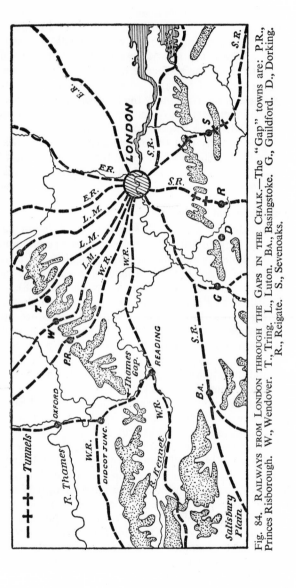

Fig. 84. Railways from London through the Gaps in the Chalk.—The "Gap" towns are: P.R., Princes Risborough. W., Wendover. T., Tring. L., Luton. BA., Basingstoke. G., Guildford. D., Dorking. R., Reigate. S., Sevenoaks.

In recent years London's road communications have been greatly improved by the construction of wide by-pass roads to avoid congested areas, *e.g.* the Kingston and Watford by-passes and by the new Motorways, to the Midlands (M1), to Dover (M2), and to South Wales (M4).

While railways and roads link London with all parts of Britain, important sea routes link her with all parts of the world.   Hence the port facilities are of great importance in connection with the maintenance of overseas routes.   The Port of London extends from London Bridge downstream to Tilbury, which might be termed the outport of London.

Since early times, London Bridge has been the limit of navigation for sea-going vessels.   Goods destined for points above London Bridge are carried by barges and lighters. The "reach" of the Thames between London Bridge and Tower Bridge, is known as the "Pool of London".

The sides of the Thames are now lined with docks and warehouses for ten miles from Tower Bridge to Woolwich. The building of the docks was facilitated by the soft nature of the soil and rocks, and much land, hitherto useless on account of its marshiness, became of great commercial value.   From Tilbury docks, opened in 1886, ocean liners depart for all parts of the world.

Finally, London is an important centre for transport by air. The airport at Heathrow, near Staines, is the largest and busiest in Europe, and handles both transatlantic and European traffic.   Gatwick, twenty-five miles south of London, is a relief airport, as is Stansted in Essex.   Heathrow is the busiest international airport in the world.   In 1969 it handled over 14 million passengers and nearly 1,000 tons of freight a day.   Over one-eighth of all our foreign trade is carried by air and almost all of this uses Heathrow.   Air transport is used only for goods of high value compared with its weight, such as complicated machinery and instruments, urgently needed spare parts, furs, and so on.   In 1969 imports and exports through Heathrow approached £M2,000, not far short of the sea-borne trade of Liverpool.

After much controversy it has now been decided to locate the new London relief airport on reclaimed land at Foulness in Essex.

Trade, Markets, and Industries

London is the greatest port in Britain (Fig. 85). It receives nearly 25 per cent. of our imports, and dispatches nearly 30 per cent. of our exports and also has an important, though diminishing, entrepôt trade. This latter accounted in 1969 for some £M57 of re-exports, more than half our total re-exports,

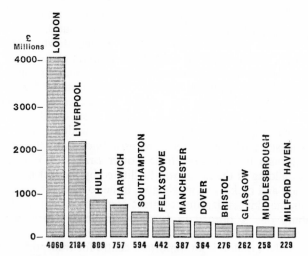

Fig. 85. Value of Imports and Exports of Leading Ports, 1969, in £ Millions.—The largest single import at most of our ports is Petroleum.

of which wool and tea were the largest single items. A striking feature of the imports is the high percentage of certain imported commodities which London handles, *e.g.*

Commodity	% of British Imports through London	Commodity	% of British Imports through London
Tea	80	Cheese	56
Coffee	67	Raw Sugar	50
Meat	60	Bacon	40

In addition to the above, London imports wheat, timber, metal ores, tobacco, vegetable oils, and a host of other commodities. More than half our very large export of vehicles is shipped from London.

The assembling in London of vast quantities of foodstuffs and raw materials has had a two-fold effect:—

(1) The growth of great markets, such as Smithfield for meat; Covent Garden for fruit, flowers, etc.; Billingsgate for fish; the Provision Exchange for bacon and dairy produce; and Leadenhall for poultry.

(2) The development of industries based on imported raw materials, partly because of the easy means of exporting the finished goods. The industrial development owes much to the network of communications and to the increased use of electric power, made possible by the "grid" system.

The industries of London fall into three groups:—

(*a*) The old-established industries, such as the silk manufacture of Spitalfields, the leather working of Bermondsey, and the bell-making of Stepney.

(*b*) The industries involving large quantities of bulky raw materials, such as oil refining (at Shellhaven and the Isle of Grain), flour milling, sugar refining, the manufacture of cement and paper, and many types of engineering. These industries are generally to be found in the "East End" of London, near the docks.

(*c*) The "new" industries, such as the manufacture of gramophone records, radio and television sets, electrical apparatus and electronics, patent foods, confectionery, motor vehicles, and so on. There is a great tendency for these industries to be established on the fringe of London, along the railways, and the main arterial roads.

During recent years there has been a great increase in manufacturing industries in South-East England. In the counties bordering London there are now more industrial workers than in the seven counties (Northumberland, Durham, Cumberland, Westmorland, Lancashire, Yorkshire, and Cheshire) of the so-called "industrial North".

London is our most important centre for the manufacture of clothing, furniture, glassware, plastics, pharmaceutical goods, of scientific apparatus, and for printing, and, except only for textiles, is one of the principal manufacturing areas for all our other leading industrial products.

CHAPTER 20

SOUTH-EAST ENGLAND

(5) KENT, SURREY, AND SUSSEX

Position and Relief

The extreme south-east of England comprises the counties of Kent, Surrey, and Sussex, and the eastern borders of Hampshire, the whole region lying south of the Thames and east of longitude 1° W.

Structurally, this region is an anticline, which has been eroded to expose alternate layers of hard and soft rock resulting in alternations of hilly ridges and flat plains (Fig. 86).

In the centre, on the borders of Kent, Surrey, and Sussex, is a hilly district of sandstones and sandy soils, rising to 800 ft, known as Ashdown Forest, which is bordered on the north and south by vales of Wealden Clay. These two vales and the intervening sandstone area are known as the Weald.* To the north and south of the Weald are low ridges of Greensand, well marked on the northern side, where the ridge is known as Ragstone Ridge, but low on the southern side. Beyond the Greensand ridges to the north and south are vales of Gault Clay—the Vale of Holmesdale in the north and the Vale of Sussex on the south. To the north and south respectively of these two vales are the chalk escarpments of the North and South Downs, with their steep slopes facing towards the Weald. On the north the North Downs sink gently to the plains of the Thames Valley, and in the south the South Downs slope gently to the coastal plains. On the map the bounding rims of chalk are somewhat similar to a wishbone in shape (Fig. 87).

The rivers of South-East England rise in the Weald to flow northwards through gaps in the North Downs to the Thames, *e.g.* Wey, Medway, or else southwards through gaps in the South Downs to the sea, *e.g.* Arun, Adur, Ouse.

* Authorities vary as to the exact definition of the Weald, as to whether it is bounded on the north and south by the chalk hills or the Greensand ridges.

Above: Chesil Beach, a spit of sand and gravel joining Portland to the mainland.
(*Valentine and Sons, Ltd.*)

Below: Southampton Docks, with railways coming down to the dock side, and the River Test in the background. Note the storage sheds, some of which are specially equipped to handle fruit. (*British Transport Docks Board.*)

Above: Ribbon development along a main road at Sanderstead, Surrey. Note the go
course. (*Aerofilms Ltd.*)

Below: London Airport. (*Aerofilms Ltd.*)

The broad flat valleys parallel to the ridges, and occupied by the east-and west-flowing tributaries, are called *longitudinal* valleys, *e.g.* Vale of Sussex and Vale of Holmesdale. Where the valleys are deep and narrow, and lie across the "grain" of the country, they are known as *transverse* valleys. The latter valleys are of great value for communications, since they facilitate transport between the regions on either side of the ridges.

The coastal features of South-East England reflect very clearly the structure of the region. Where the chalk ridges reach the sea there are bold headlands, *e.g.* North Foreland, the cliffs of Dover, and Beachy Head. Where the softer clays reach the sea the coastal regions are low. Dungeness, a prominent feature of the

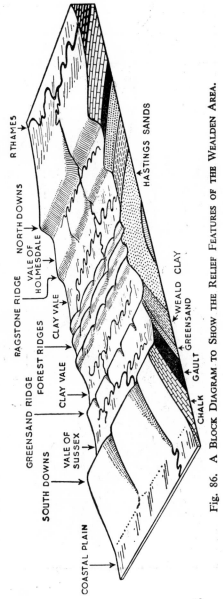

Fig. 86. A Block Diagram to Show the Relief Features of the Wealden Area.

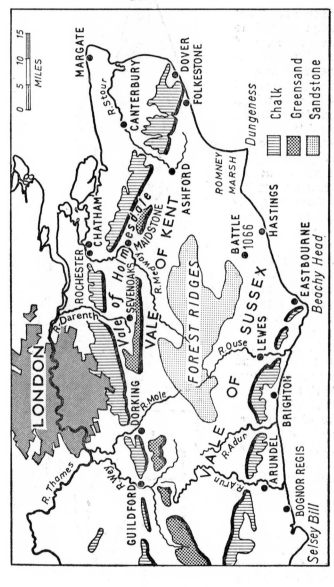

Fig. 87.   SOUTH-EAST ENGLAND—MAIN FEATURES.—Compare the arrangement of hills and vales carefully with that shown in Fig. 86.   Notice the position of "Gap" towns.   While the geological nature of the high ground has been indicated this is not a geological map and does not show the full extent of the various materials.

coast, is not a bold headland but an accumulation of silt and gravel behind a former sand spit. The low-lying area behind Dungeness is known as Romney Marsh.

Climate

This region approaches the Continent more closely than any other part of Britain. As in other parts of Eastern Britain, the climate is "semi-continental" in type, with hotter summers and colder winters than the average. Rainfall is low on the sheltered vales (25 in. to 30 in.), but is higher on the ridges (30 in. and over, rising to 40 in. in the west of the South Downs). A prominent climatic feature is the long duration of sunshine, particularly along the south coast. This has an important result on agriculture and on the popularity of the south coast resorts.

Agriculture

In general it may be said that agriculture in Kent, Surrey, and Sussex is determined not only by soil and climatic conditions, but also by insatiable demands of London. Because of this there has been in recent years, as in other parts of Southern England, an increase in the rearing of dairy cattle on permanent pasture at the expense of arable land. Not only milk, but fruit, vegetables, hops, and mutton find a ready market in London.

The sandy soils of the Wealden Heights are not fertile, and there is much uncleared woodland. In the surrounding clay vales dairying is the most important branch of farming, and large crops of hay are harvested.

On the fringes of these vales, where the clays are mixed with chalk on the one side, or with sands on the other, there are rich soils which are used for the cultivation of fruit (strawberries, raspberries, currants), hops, cereals, roots, and potatoes. In this part of England, in contrast to East Anglia, the cultivation of barley is less important than that of wheat.

Where the North and South Downs are capped with "clay with flints" there are large woodland areas, as on the South Downs west of Arundel. On exposed chalk areas the short springy turf makes excellent sheep pastures, principally on the South Downs. The lowlands of Romney Marsh are also used as summer pastures for sheep, but in the winter the flocks are transferred to the drier pastures of the Downs (cf. Norfolk Heights, page 158). The downland is also used for training race-horses, *e.g.* Goodwood, Epsom. The North Downs are being increasingly used as residential areas for London.

Because of the demand for mutton in London and the extent of downland and other sheep pastures, Kent has more sheep per 100 acres than any other English county. The important areas for fruit and hops are in East Sussex, mid-Kent, and on the northern side of the eastern half of the North Downs. Near Worthing there are many acres of glass-houses used for the cultivation of toma-toes.

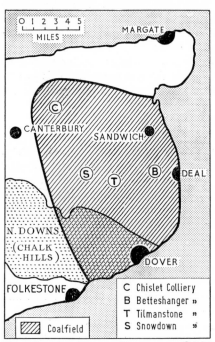

Fig. 88. THE DOVER COALFIELD.—Chislet Colliery has now been closed

Industries

An Ordnance map of the Wealden area reveals such names as Forge Farm, Iron River, etc. Such names date back to the time of the Wealden iron industry, which flourished for many centuries prior to the Industrial Revolution. The sandstones supplied the iron ore, whilst the charcoal for smelting came from the woods of the clay vales. The iron was forged and hammered out by hand, although occasionally power was here and there derived from the streams as the ruins of the water-driven forges show. This industry has now disappeared, for it could not survive in face of the competition of regions like South Staffordshire and Sheffield, with their abundant supplies of ore and newer methods of smelting with coke.

Suitable deposits of clay and chalk have led to the area around Dartford and Gravesend producing about one-third of the United Kingdom's cement.

In the south-east of this county, between Canterbury and Dover, is the most recently worked coalfield in the country (Fig. 88). The coalfield is entirely "concealed", and is therefore not shown on the geological map. Deposits of iron ore

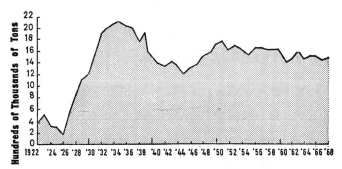

Fig. 89. COAL PRODUCTION IN THE KENT COALFIELD.

also occur in the south-west of the coalfield. An interesting feature of this region is that mining and its attendant industries has been developed in such a way that industrial "ugliness" does not mar the natural beauty. Output, after falling for some years, has now levelled out.

The industrial centre around Chatham, Rochester, and Gillingham may soon be amalgamated and given a new name. Chatham is a great naval port, originally established as part of the scheme of defence of the Narrow Seas and the Thames estuary (see Fig. 97). Rochester (see plate facing page 160), with ruins of a fine Norman castle which once guarded the Medway Gap, shares with Chatham a variety of industries,

viz. paper-making, oil refining, engineering, and the manufacture of cement made from chalk and river muds.

Other industries of South-East England are those connected
with agriculture, *e.g.* the making of steam tractors and thresh-
ing machines at Rochester, the manufacture of jam, and the
bottling of fruit and vegetables. Many of the coastal towns
are important for their fisheries, *e.g.* Whitstable for oysters.

Towns

Many important towns of this region are situated in gaps in
the chalk hills, *e.g.* Guildford, Dorking, Arundel, and Lewes,

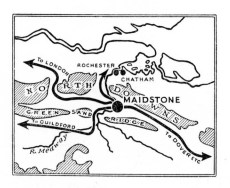

Fig. 90. THE POSITION OF MAIDSTONE.

or else they are so situated in the vales that they command the
routes through the neighbouring gaps, *e.g.* Maidstone (Fig. 90),
Ashford, Canterbury. All such towns are naturally great road
centres, and as such become great market centres. In olden
days castles defended the routes through the gaps, *e.g.* Arundel
and Rochester. To-day, many of the gap-towns have become
important railway centres, *e.g.* Ashford with its railway
engineering works.

Another important group of towns include the seaside
resorts. Within easy reach of London, especially in these
days of quick and cheap motor transport, they might all be
termed "London by the Sea". Among these are Margate,
Folkestone, Hastings, Brighton, Worthing, and Bognor Regis.

Residential towns for London are chiefly located on the higher lands of the central Weald and on the North Downs.

At Crawley (67,000) one of the numerous new towns planned to relieve the congestion in the inner metropolitan area has been built (see plate facing page 161).

Ferry Ports

The "ancestors" of the modern ferry port were the Cinque

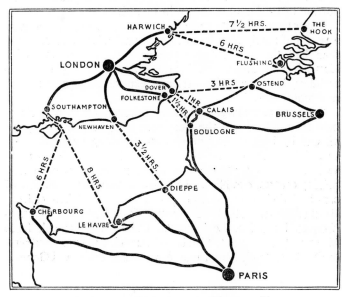

Fig. 91. THE FERRIES OF THE NARROW SEAS.

Ports. These five old ports, Sandwich, Dover, Hythe, Romney, and Hastings (and later Winchelsea and Rye were added), were established before the Conquest. In the Middle Ages they practically controlled the fishing industry and trade with the Continent. In return for special privileges they had to provide ships and men for the Navy. With the exception of Dover (see plate facing page 161), the Cinque Ports are now of little importance, for their harbours have gradually filled with silt.

Regular communication with the Continent is maintained through ferry ports. The south coast is served by a number of railways which used to belong to separate companies, later amalgamated as the Southern Railway. Each of these railway companies had its own ferry port to which it ran services of express trains. A train-ferry service operates between Dover and Dunkirk. The corresponding continental stations are similarly situated at the termini of quick main line routes to Paris or Brussels. The ferry ports of the south-eastern portion of England are shown in Fig. 91.

Dover handles nearly three million cross-Channel passengers a year and nearly four hundred thousand of their cars. Less than half this number of passengers use Folkestone, with Harwich and Newhaven in third and fourth places. In addition, Dover also imports and exports large numbers of new motor cars.

Of recent years large and increasing numbers of passengers between England and the Continent have been travelling by air and by 1961 slightly more were travelling by air than by sea. There are regular direct flights from London to the various European capitals and to other important cities and holiday centres, *e.g.* Nice. In addition, very large numbers of cars and their occupants are flown across the Channel from Hurn (Bournemouth) to Cherbourg, from Lydd (near Dungeness) to Deauville, Le Touquet, Calais, and Ostend, from Manston (Ramsgate) to Calais and Ostend, and from Southend to Calais, Ostend, Rotterdam, Strasbourg, Basle, and Geneva.

CHAPTER 21

SOUTH-EAST ENGLAND

(6) THE HAMPSHIRE BASIN

Position and Relief

The Hampshire Basin extends through Dorset, Hampshire, part of Wiltshire, and the south coast plains of Sussex, west of Brighton. It is similar in structure to the London Basin, that is, it is a syncline or downfold of chalk filled with Tertiary rocks, *e.g.* London Clays and Sands (Fig. 92). Just as chalk hills surround the London Basin, so they surround the Hampshire Basin, the steep faces of the ridges facing outwards. But the chalk "rim" of the Hampshire Basin is very wide (up to thirty miles) on the northern border, where it forms the chalk "plateau" of the Hampshire Downs and Salisbury Plain. This chalk plateau is separated from the scarped ridge of the White Horse Hills by the Vale of Pewsey and the Vale of Kennet, which together provide a great natural route for road and rail communication between London and Bristol. From Salisbury Plain the chalk lands strike south-west as the Western Downs, and then turn abruptly eastward parallel to the coast as the Purbeck Downs. Here the chalk has been breached by the sea, but it reappears in the chalk stacks of the Needles, and forms a west-east ridge across the Isle of Wight, ending at Culver Cliff. Within the chalk rim only a small percentage of the lowlands has exposures of London Clay, and these are principally around the margins. A much larger area is covered with sands (Bagshot Sands, cf. page 166) than in the London Basin, and these sandy soils are generally infertile and covered with extensive heaths and pine forests, *e.g.* the New Forest.

Rivers and Communications

Whereas the London Basin is drained by one main stream and its tributaries, the Hampshire Basin is drained by a series of streams arranged fanwise. From west to east they

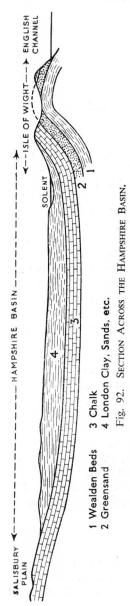

Fig. 92. SECTION ACROSS THE HAMPSHIRE BASIN.

1 Wealden Beds
2 Greensand
3 Chalk
4 London Clay, Sands, etc.

are the Frome, Stour, Avon, Test, and Itchen (Fig. 93). It is supposed that before submergence separated the Isle of Wight from the mainland, the Frome flowed eastward along the lowlands now occupied by Solent and Spithead, and that the other rivers of the Hampshire Basin were tributary to it.

Communications from the London Basin outward is facilitated by "gaps" in the chalk rim. The rivers of the Hampshire Basin and their tributaries have cut valleys in the encircling chalk rim, but, owing to its great width, these natural routes into the Hampshire Basin are "valley corridors" rather than gaps. Because of this, two lines of market towns and route centres have developed, one group on the outer rim and one on the inner rim of the chalk, and usually a pair of these towns lies on each important route. The most important routes are the two which link the Hampshire Basin with the London Basin, viz. from Southampton via Alton (the Itchen route), and from Southampton via Basingstoke (the Test route). Other routes follow the Avon and Wylye valleys from Salisbury to Warminster, the Stour Valley through Blandford, and the Frome Valley through Dorchester.

Agriculture

Agriculturally the chalk land has a variety of aspects. The upper chalk is porous and dry-surfaced, and is of little use other than for sheep rearing. In both the Hampshire Downs and the Salisbury Plain there are still wide tracts of unfenced downland, but visitors to this district are generally disappointed to find that the "wide open spaces" are neither so wide nor so open as they are expected to be. Below the hard porous chalk are layers of somewhat pebbly chalk, usually infertile—such as is usually associated with the military training grounds of Salisbury Plain. As in other chalk regions, chalk is sometimes covered with a layer of "clay with flints". Here, as elsewhere, these soils are associated with woodland, but if

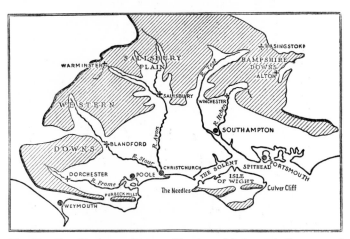

Fig. 93. THE HAMPSHIRE BASIN.—Showing: (*a*) the encircling zone of chalk upland; (*b*) the rivers; (*c*) the principal towns: "gateway" towns are marked with a cross.

cleared can be made into reasonably good arable land. The chalk of the lower slopes, somewhat marly in character, is extremely fertile, and is nearly everywhere used for the production of cereals. Twenty-five years ago there were three acres of permanent grass to every arable acre, but to-day there is more arable land than grassland, and the number of sheep pastured has fallen by a half. Near the streams of the lower valleys are rich water meadows associated with cattle rearing. The fame of Wiltshire bacon indicates an important side-line of the dairying industry.

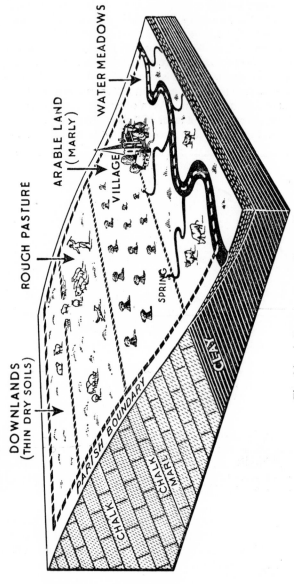

Fig. 94. A Parish in the Chalk Country.

Because of the varying quality of the upland and lowland soils, parishes in the chalk regions have a characteristic form and shape (Fig. 94). They are usually "strips" of land varying in width, one end on the valley stream and the other up on the chalk heights. Thus each parish had water meadows, arable land, rough pasture, and downland, and possibly timber, and could therefore be virtually self-supporting. The village centre of such parishes was usually placed part way up the hill slope where the lowland clays met the chalk. Thus it avoided the dampness of the valley and had supplies of spring water. Because of the extensive areas of sand overlying the clay, the lowlands of the Hampshire Basin are not as productive as those of the London Basin, though scientific treatment is resulting in greater fertility.

Towns

There is a remarkable convergence of roads at Salisbury and Winchester, the twin centres of the plain.

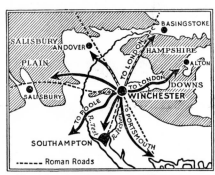

Fig. 95. THE POSITION OF WINCHESTER.

SALISBURY. This town is situated on the Avon at a point near to the convergence of five tributary streams. Thus it is a great focus of roads from, and a meeting-place for the farmers of, the clay plains and the chalk uplands. Nearby, on higher land, are the historic remains of Old Sarum, the meeting-place of the British hilltop tracks in olden times, and later the site of a strongly fortified Norman settlement.

WINCHESTER. On the Itchen is also a remarkable road centre at Winchester (Fig. 95). Once the meeting-place of Roman roads and later the capital of Wessex, it is to-day a great market centre and the gateway through which pass the main lines from Southampton to London.

There is a variety of coastal towns.

Some, to-day, are seaside resorts such as Swanage, Bournemouth, and many of the towns in the Isle of Wight, *e.g.* Ventnor. Others, such as Lymington, Christchurch, and Poole, were once busy ports, but their harbours are silted and are too small for modern ships. Weymouth is used as a ferry port from which steamers sail to the Channel Isles.

SOUTHAMPTON. On a smaller scale, Southampton stands in the same relation to the Hampshire Basin as London does to

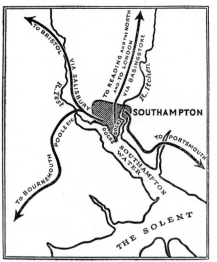

the London Basin. It is at the head of Southampton Water, a long drowned valley, at a point where the rivers Test and Itchen enter the sea (Fig. 96). As a port (see plate facing page 176) it has a number of advantages, viz:—

(*a*) Owing to its "double tides" it has the benefit of long periods of high water, during which ships can enter and leave the docks.

Fig. 96. THE POSITION OF SOUTHAMPTON.

(*b*) The triangular peninsula between the Test and Itchen provides a long waterfront for the docks.

(*c*) It is well served by railway and nearly thirty shipping lines.

(*d*) Passengers and goods landed at Southampton can reach London twelve hours earlier than by proceeding to Tilbury, so Southampton may be considered an "outport" of London.

Before the war Southampton became the premier passenger port of Britain, having displaced Liverpool. Southampton handles a tonnage of shipping greater than Liverpool does, but much of this consists of liners and the value of the merchandise handled is only one-quarter that of Liverpool. As a port for cargo it now ranks fifth. It has special facilities for the import of fresh fruit from South Africa, and for meat, flowers, vegetables, etc. Southampton imports very large quantities of crude oil for refining and also imports wool, copper, and cars. Its export trade is increasing, particularly the export of goods such as cars and textiles from the Midlands.

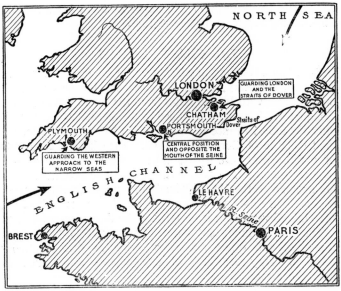

Fig. 97. THE POSITION OF THE THREE PREMIER NAVAL PORTS IN RELATION TO THE DEFENCE OF THE "NARROW SEAS".

The industries are mainly concerned with shipping and the manufacture of aircraft. The imports of crude oil have led to an oil-refining industry. The refinery at Fawley, near Southampton, is the largest in Europe with a capacity of 16 million tons a year, and a synthetic rubber plant has also been built at Fawley, which uses as raw material petroleum by-products from the refinery. The plant has a capacity of over 90,000 tons of synthetic rubber a year, the amount we at present import.

PORTSMOUTH. Situated on the north shore of Spithead, Portsmouth is the largest town of the Hampshire Basin (Fig. 97). It is a strongly fortified naval station, sheltered by the Isle of Wight, and backed by a small chalk ridge on which stand the forts protecting the harbour. Its original importance as a naval centre is due partly to its position opposite the mouth of the Seine, the natural outlet of northern France, partly to the protection afforded by the Isle of Wight, and partly to its position relative to London. It has some shipbuilding and general manufactures.

THE CHANNEL ISLES

The Channel Islands, of which the chief are Jersey, Guernsey, Alderney, and Sark, lie off the coast of Normandy. Their political link with Britain dates from the time of William the Conqueror. They were occupied by the Germans from shortly after the fall of France in the summer of 1940, until after the final collapse of Germany in 1945. They have a total area of about seventy-five square miles and a population of one hundred thousand. Like the Isle of Man, the Channel Islands are not part of the United Kingdom, but are Crown Dependencies. They have their own courts and systems of law, but the U.K. Government is responsible for their external affairs.

They are an important source of supply of early potatoes, tomatoes, and other vegetables owing to their southerly position. They are also of considerable importance as holiday centres.

CHAPTER 22

TRANSPORT

Introduction

Transport forms an important element in geographical studies. It is vital to the development of industry and commerce and to the social life of the community. Nearly 10 per cent. of the labour force in Great Britain is employed in providing transport facilities of various kinds—road, rail, waterways, pipelines, shipping, and airways. The encouragement of good communications is essential if industrial production is to increase and trade to expand.

Roads

In the Middle Ages the roads were usually maintained by the parishes who had little interest in repairing roads for through traffic. The real foundations of to-day's main road network date from 1750 when Turnpike Trusts were set up to finance road construction from tolls collected from travellers. Telford then engineered roads with easy gradients whilst Macadam introduced the cambered watertight surface of small broken stones rammed hard which was later superseded by the use of steam-rollers and "tar-macadam".

In 1888 the County Councils took over responsibility for main roads, help being provided from the Exchequer. In 1922 the roads of Great Britain were classified and numbered. The Ministry of Transport is the highway authority for all trunk roads in England and makes specific grants towards approved principal road improvements in England.

To cope with the rapid growth of traffic in the country, the Government embarked upon the construction of motorways in 1956 and hopes to have completed 700 miles of motorway in England and Wales by the early 1970s. Another important development in recent years has been the shortening of road journeys by bridging of large estuaries such as the Severn, Tay, and Forth. Also an increasing percentage of the road programme is now being devoted to urban roads where traffic congestion is acute.

Fig. 98 shows the location of the motorways and some of the important connecting roads. All motorways are denoted by the letter M (*e.g.* the London to Yorkshire motorway is M.1). Roads next in order of importance are classified as A roads, followed by B roads which are of lesser importance. Many roads are without numbers, but they are usually only of minor or local significance.

The roads of Britain are divided into zones (1-6) numbered clockwise from London, the boundaries being the trunk roads A1-A6. All roads in a particular zone are prefixed by the zone number. Thus the London-Brighton road in zone 2 is numbered A23.

Private Transport

In 1904 Great Britain had just over 8,000 cars on its roads. In 1969 the number was $11\frac{1}{4}$ million. The motor-car is the most widely used form of passenger travel and accounts for at least two-thirds of the passenger mileage covered annually in Great Britain. By 1980 it is estimated that there will be the equivalent of one car per family.

The chief advantage of the motor-car is its ability to give a door-to-door service. However, the flexibility it offers can do great damage to the quality of urban life if it is ill-used. This problem was high-lighted in the Buchanan Report of 1963 which said that we have neither the space nor the money to rebuild our cities in such a form that all journeys can be made by private car. It recognised that traffic must be eliminated from the central areas of cities to give pedestrian precincts and there should be a much greater reliance on public transport in urban areas.

Bus and Coach Travel

Since 1952 the bus and coach industry has accounted for nearly double the railway's share of total passenger mileage in Great Britain. It is best adapted to the individual require-ments of relatively light flow of passengers over relatively short

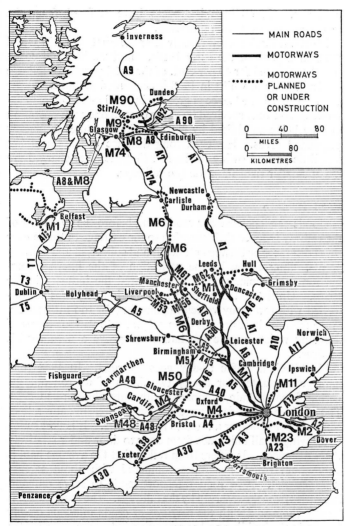

Fig. 98. MAIN ROADS. All the great centres are old towns; the new motorways pass close to, but not through, large towns.

distances. Generally, all services have suffered from the recent growth of private motoring.

Most bus services grew rapidly after the First World War and reached a peak in the early 1950s. In 1952 bus and coach travel accounted for 45 per cent. of the total passenger mileage in Great Britain, whilst in 1968 it accounted for under 20 per cent. The decline has been greatest in rural areas where many services have only survived by going over to one-man operation and by being subsidised by more profitable routes in densely populated areas. However, long distance coach travel has lost little ground owing to the fact that the fares charged are much smaller than those on the railways.

Road Haulage

Goods carriers used our roads long before the evolution of the railway reduced their function to the carriage of traffic over short distances or between railheads and collection and delivery points. Spurred on by the perfection of the internal combustion engine many newcomers entered the industry in the 1920s. Until the 1930s entry into the industry was uncontrolled with too many vehicles competing for too little traffic. Since then the industry has been subjected to various forms of licensing which require the haulier to prove a need for his services.

Most freight traffic to-day goes by road. In 1968 road haulage accounted for nearly two-thirds of all ton mileage within Great Britain, compared with only one-third in 1950. The carriage of goods by road has been increasing at a rate of some six per cent. per annum in recent years. It is best suited to carrying small unit loads from door to door under relatively short distances. It differs from rail in that the average haul is only about twenty-five miles compared with about seventy miles by rail. Also road transport tends to serve different industries from those served by the railways. The road haulier is largely concerned with the carriage of crude minerals mainly for use in the building and constructing industries and with the distribution of foodstuffs to warehouses, shops, and homes. Even so, a wide variety of goods is handled by road transport compared with other forms of transport.

Railways

The railways are distinguished by having a specialised route system for their own exclusive use. To be used economically this must be used intensively. This has meant that much reshaping has been necessary of the nineteenth century rail network that we inherited. The aim is to let the railways exploit the advantages they have over other forms of transport. To this end, the Beeching Report was published in 1963 and some of the main results of this plan are summarised below:—

(1) The closure of a high proportion of the total number of small stations and stopping passenger services.

(2) Selective improvement of inter-city passenger services and rationalisation of routes. In 1967 the main line electrification between London, the Midlands, and the North-west was completed, along with the London to Southampton and Bournemouth line.

(3) Threatened closure of many suburban lines unless proper co-ordination could be worked out with other forms of transport in the conurbations. Despite their great social benefit, especially the electrified lines in the south-eastern part of the country, many are used heavily in the peak hours only and lose a lot of money. Passenger Transport Authorities are now being established by the Government to co-ordinate transport in our conurbations.

(4) The reduction of uneconomic freight traffic passing through small stations by closing them progressively.

(5) Increase of "block" train movement which means that full train-loads of traffic favourable to rail, such as coal, iron-ore, and oil travel throughout avoiding intermediate marshalling.

(6) A network of "freightliner trains" has been built up between the main ports and industrial centres. These freightliner trains are based upon the joint use of road and rail for door-to-door transport of containerised merchandise with special purpose through-running scheduled trains providing the trunk haul between liner-train terminals.

Fig. 99 shows the main railways of Great Britain. It attempts only to show lines which carry relatively large

Fig. 99. THE MAIN RAILWAYS OF GREAT BRITAIN.

198

amounts of passengers and freight and which are likely to be selected for development in the future. Basically these lines connect the main centres of industry, population, and trade. It will be noticed that nearly all the main lines radiate from London; the only important cross-country routes are the Trans-Pennine route between Liverpool and the north-east of England via Leeds and the main line from the west of England to Yorkshire via Birmingham.

Waterways

Canals were constructed before the days of railways and properly surfaced roads in the late eighteenth century. In their heyday they carried nearly all our inland freight traffic: nowadays they handle only a fractional percentage of cargo. Canals must be absolutely level, whereas railways and especially roads can cope with gentle gradients. They entail a round-about course as well as the expensive locks or "steps" in the canal which slow down the speed of traffic.

However, relatively less power is required to move a given load over water compared with movement along roads or railways. In many instances stretches of river have been made navigable and incorporated in the canal system.

Much of the British waterways has been closed to commercial traffic though some have become sources of water supply or been developed for pleasure cruising. A small proportion of the waterways system, some 350 miles, has been retained for the conveyance of heavy and bulky goods for which there is sustained demand. Petroleum products make up 40 per cent. of all cargo on inland waterways and coal accounts for a further 30 per cent.

The main waterways used commercially to-day are the Aire and Calder Navigation, the Sheffield and South Yorkshire Navigation, the Trent Navigation, the Weaver Navigation, and the River Severn between Gloucester and Stourport. Rather different is the Gloucester to Sharpness Canal which can carry sea-going vessels of up to 750 tons capacity and the Manchester Ship Canal opened in 1894 which accommodates ocean-going vessels of up to 15,000 tons, making Manchester an important inland port.

Pipelines

Pipelines are economical when large quantities of materials are moved continuously over land. The main materials at present carried in Great Britain are crude oil, petroleum products, and natural gas. A particular advantage of pipelines is that crude oil may be unloaded from very large tankers at deep water terminals and transferred to refineries, such as Finnart to Grangemouth in Scotland, Angle Bay to Llandarcy in Wales, and Tranmere to Stanlow and Heysham in the North-west. A major scheme for a system of refined petroleum products between the Thames and the Mersey came on stream in early 1969. Since 1967 pipelines conveying natural gas have been built from North Sea gas fields to shore-reception terminals at Easington (Yorks.) and Bacton (Norfolk). From here connections are made with an existing pipeline from Canvey Island to Leeds (opened 1962 to convey imported Algerian gas) and with certain industrial centres.

Ports and Shipping

The main ports in Great Britain (calculated on the total value of exports and imports) are in order: London, Liverpool, Hull, Harwich, Southampton, Felixstowe, Manchester, Dover, Bristol, and Glasgow. Together Liverpool and London account for well over half the trade of the United Kingdom.

The most important and fastest growing import at most of our ports is petroleum which accounts for half the tonnage of imports. The main exports from this country are chemicals, iron and steel, machinery, vehicles, and cement.

The main change in the transport of goods by sea has occurred in the field of bulk cargo. Deep water berths for grain carriers are being built at the estuary of many of the established ports, such as Liverpool and Tilbury. Specialised terminals are being built for iron ore bulk carriers at Port Talbot and Uskmouth in South Wales. Immingham is to become Europe's largest shipping terminal for coal exports served by "merry-go-round" trains (which run round a circuit at the terminal and unload automatically on passing over discharge bunkers) from the East Midlands and South Yorkshire pits.

Coastal shipping is still relatively significant and accounts for 15 per cent. of freight movement in Great Britain. Coal and petroleum products make up about 90 per cent. of the cargo carried in coasting vessels. The petroleum traffic is vulnerable to pipeline competition.

Deep water berths are also being built at Tilbury, Liverpool, Southampton, and Greenock for container traffic (which at present is concentrated on a few short sea routes) to capture some of the fast developing deep-sea container traffic. A further development includes "roll-on roll-off ships". These enable fully laden lorries or cars to drive on and off ships.

The main passenger ports are Dover (which accounts for 40 per cent. of all passenger traffic in Great Britain), along with Folkestone, Harwich, and Southampton. Since 1961, more passengers have travelled abroad by air than by sea.

Airways

The total volume of traffic carried inside the United Kingdom is small compared to other forms of transport. However, airways predominate in the carriage of passengers on certain long distance trunk routes, such as between London and Scotland, Northern Ireland, and the Channel Islands. Cargo traffic by air is relatively insignificant within Britain but it accounts for over 12 per cent. of overseas trade. Passenger traffic to and from Britain by air is increasing at nearly four times the rate of sea traffic. In 1968, 16 million people arrived or left by air and 9 million by ship.

The main air ports (in terms of passengers handled) in the United Kingdom are: Heathrow, Gatwick, Manchester, Glasgow, Jersey, Belfast, Southend, Edinburgh, Birmingham, and Prestwick, given in order of importance.

Nearly two-thirds of the traffic at Gatwick and Heathrow is with the Continent, and two-thirds of the traffic at Prestwick is with North America. Apart from Manchester, the remainder are principally concerned with providing domestic flights.

CHAPTER 23

SCOTLAND

(1) THE SOUTHERN UPLANDS

Physical Divisions of Scotland

If two lines are drawn on the map of Scotland (1) from Helensburgh to Stonehaven (the Highland line), and (2) from

Fig. 100. THE DIVISIONS OF SCOTLAND.

Dunbar to Girvan, they divide the country into three well-marked physical divisions, viz. (Fig. 100):—

(1) The Southern Uplands south of the Dunbar-Girvan line.

(2) The Central Lowlands between the two lines.

(3) The Highlands north of the Helensburgh-Stonehaven line.

202

THE SOUTHERN UPLANDS

Structure and Physical Features

The Southern Uplands extend northwards from the Cheviot Hills of Northumberland, and are a dissected plateau of old rock similar to the rocks of Central Wales. The plateau is bounded on the north by the faults which run from Dunbar to Girvan, and north of which the structure is completely different. The plateau rises to well over 2,000 ft, culminating in the highlands of Merrick, Broadlaw, and Hartfell. In the south-west the Uplands are drained by the Liddel, Annan, and Nith to the Solway Firth, and in the north by the head-streams of the Clyde. The whole of the eastern half of the Uplands comprises the Tweed Basin, whose broad lower valley separates the Cheviots on the south from the Moorfoot and Lammermuir Hills on the north. The Uplands differ from the Highlands in that they are less rugged, the hills being characterised by smooth rounded outlines, the rivers are less swift, and lakes fewer in number.

Because of its altitude the region has, except in the vales, heavy rainfall (up to 60 in.) and low temperatures. The eastern lowlands of the Tweed are more sheltered, drier, and have higher summer temperatures than the west of the Uplands.

From the point of view of its agriculture the region falls naturally into three subdivisions:—

(*a*) The plains of the south and west.

(*b*) The upland zones.

(*c*) The Tweed Valley.

The Western Plains (*e.g.* Galloway)

On account of their westerly position and resultant equable temperatures and well-distributed rainfall (30-50 in.), the western plains are largely devoted to the rearing of cattle. Wheat is not extensively cultivated, arable land being used for oats, roots, and rotation grass. Because of its distance from the industrial centres, most of the milk supply is used for the making of butter and cheese, and in recent years a large number of creameries have been opened in market towns such as Stranraer and Kirkcudbright. Some milk is, however, sent by quick motor transport to Newcastle and the industrial towns of Lancashire. This is one of the most important districts in Scotland for the rearing of pigs, because they can be fed on the by-products of the creamery and cheese factory.

The slopes of the dales are used for sheep rearing, chiefly the black-faced variety, for mutton.

The market towns are not large. The population of Dumfries, the largest, is 28,000, and Stranraer comes next with about 9,000.

The Uplands

Owing to its height, low temperatures, cloudiness, thin soils, and difficult communications, the upland region is a sheep-rearing moorland, broken by valleys used for mixed agriculture. It is in many respects economically similar to Central Wales. The number of sheep per acre increases from the wetter west to the drier east, and the type of sheep reared changes also. In the west are more black-faced sheep reared for mutton, while in the east there are more white-faced Cheviot sheep, of greater importance for their wool. The upland counties of Southern Scotland, viz. Roxburgh, Selkirk, and Peebles, form part of the more important sheep-rearing region of the British Isles (see Fig. 25). The sheep farms are often as large as 5,000 acres, and consist of wide, unfenced, and uncultivated grasslands. Immediately below the open moorlands are walled fields, which were once ploughed, but which are now under permanent grass and almost as wild as the moorlands themselves. The only method of maintaining good sheep pastures on the moorland is by burning the old heather periodically to encourage the growth of young shoots, valuable for sheep grazing. At the end of the summer the sheep are rounded up, dipped, and then the surplus are sent to the sheep markets or to the lowland farms for winter feeding.

The Uplands generally are poor in minerals. Lead is mined at Leadhills in the Clyde Basin. There is a small coalfield at Sanquhar in the north-west of Dumfries which is structurally part of the Ayrshire coal basin.

The Tweed Basin

The uplands surrounding the Tweed and its tributaries are part of the great sheep-rearing area, but the lowlands of the Tweed form a distinct agricultural unit.

Drier, sheltered, and more sunny than the west, this region has a high percentage of arable land. The driest and lowest (below 250 ft) portion of the Tweed Valley is known as the Merse (Fig. 101). Throughout the district oats are the important cereal, and turnips, winter food for sheep, the

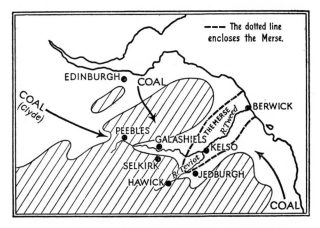

Fig. 101. THE WOOLLEN TOWNS OF THE TWEED BASIN AND THE SOURCES OF COAL SUPPLY.

important root crop. The proportion of arable land is highest in the Merse, which is very important for its barley, and which also grows considerable amounts of wheat. In these lowlands of mixed agriculture cattle are also reared, chiefly for their meat, in contrast to the dairying regions of the western plains. This distribution of dairy and beef cattle should be compared with the distribution in England, *i.e.* the gradual decrease of dairy cattle from Cheshire eastwards across the Central Plain, and the eastward increase of beef cattle.

The Tweed Woollen Industry

The middle Tweed Basin ranks next to the West Riding of Yorkshire as a woollen manufacturing region. It owes its importance to three factors:—

(1) The old-established domestic weaving industries and therefore the traditional skill in weaving.

(2) The abundant supplies of wool.

(3) The abundant supplies of soft water.

Although machinery was introduced at the time of the Industrial Revolution and operated by water power, it was not long before the district felt the great disadvantage of the distance from coal supplies. Coal is obtained to-day from three sources: (*a*) the Lanarkshire coalfield, (*b*) the Midlothian coalfields, (*c*) the Northumberland and Durham coalfield.

Because of this disadvantage the Tweed towns have had to specialise in the manufacture of goods of exceptionally high quality in order to compete with the West Riding. They manufacture tweeds, sports materials, blankets, and hosiery. High-grade goods require high-grade wools for their manufacture, and since the local wool is only suitable for coarse fabrics and carpets, much foreign wool has to be imported.

The chief towns engaged in woollen manufactures are Galashiels, Hawick, Peebles, Selkirk, and Jedburgh (Fig. 101). Hawick specialises in hosiery.

These towns are a great contrast to the industrial centres of the West Riding, for the largest, Hawick, has a population of only 16,000, while the population of Jedburgh is less than 4,000 (cf. the woollen towns of the "West of England").

Berwick, at the mouth of the Tweed, shares in the Tweed woollen industry, although its port is handicapped by the old low-arched stone bridge which crosses the river very near the sea.

The middle Tweed Valley is famous for its abbeys, whose monks did much in past ages to develop both agriculture and the weaving industry. The historical interest of these abbeys (*e.g.* Melrose) and the association of the region with Sir Walter Scott attracts a large number of tourists.

Communications

The Southern Uplands were once a barrier between the Romans and the Picts; in the Middle Ages they separated the English and Scotch; to-day they are a relatively sparsely-populated area set between the densely-populated industrial regions of Northern England and Central Scotland. The towns bordering the Uplands were formerly fortresses, guarding the natural routes; to-day the same towns are railway and road junctions controlling the same routes. Railways across the Uplands now link the important centres of England and Scotland, but even on the railways the function of the Uplands as a barrier is still evident in that extra engine-power is usually needed for the negotiation of steep gradients, as on the route from Carlisle to Carstairs (via the pass of Beattock).

The railway routes of the Uplands follow the valleys or the coastal plains (Fig. 102). They are:—

(1) The East Coast route from Newcastle through Berwick and along the east coast plain to Edinburgh. The advantages of this route are, firstly, its directness, and secondly, that there are no steep gradients.

(2) The second route ascends the Annan Valley from Carlisle, crosses the watershed to the Clyde Valley and divides at Carstairs, one branch going to Edinburgh and one to Glasgow. This is the busiest of all the Upland routes. Its obvious advantages are its directness, and the fact that it serves both the east and west of the Central Lowlands, but it has the disadvantage of steep gradients.

(3) The third route is from Carlisle along the Solway Plains to Dumfries, whence it follows the Nith Valley northwards, crosses a low watershed and reaches Glasgow via the Ayrshire lowlands. It is mainly used for traffic to the western side of the lowlands, being somewhat circuitous for through traffic to Glasgow, and serves Stranraer via Ayr.

(4) The Waverley route, now closed, went up the Liddel Valley across the watershed and down the Teviot Valley to Galashiels. Thence it proceeded up the Gala Valley, over a second watershed and down the valley of a tributary of the Esk to Edinburgh. While this route had the advantage of

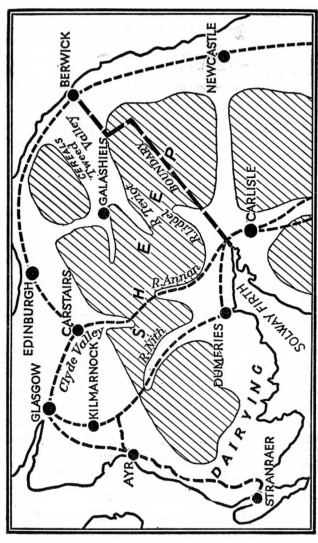

Fig. 102. The Railways of the Southern Uplands.—Shows the rail connections between Northern England and the Central Valley of Scotland. The Waverley route from Carlisle to Edinburgh via Galashiels has now been closed, as has the direct route from Dumfries to Stranraer. The London-Stranraer boat trains

bove: Stirling. Note the hills in the background, the Castle, and the River Forth.
(Valentine and Sons, Ltd.)
Below: A shipbuilding yard at Clydebank. *(John Brown and Co. Ltd.)*

Above: Loch Long, Argyleshire. (*Aerofilms Ltd.*)
Below: Looking down the pipe lines to Lochaber and the aluminium works. (*Bri(*
Aluminium Co. Ltd.)

serving the woollen towns and the "Scott" country it had two great disadvantages: (*a*) that it had two watersheds and their associated gradients to negotiate, and (*b*) that the nature of its traffic had changed. Whereas before the railway amalgamation it carried the "through" traffic to Edinburgh for the former Midland Railway from points south of Carlisle, to-day the old Midland route from Leeds to Carlisle is little used.

CHAPTER 24

SCOTLAND

(2) THE CENTRAL LOWLANDS

Relief

The Central Lowlands, or Midland Valley of Scotland, is a rift valley fifty miles wide, between two parallel sets of faults which follow the lines from Helensburgh to Stonehaven and Dunbar to Girvan.

The formation of the rift valley was accompanied by:—

(1) Submergence, which partly accounts for the long estuaries in this part of Scotland, and by (2) volcanic activity, which accounts for the presence of volcanic hills within the Lowlands (Fig. 103).

The rocks of the Lowlands are newer and often less resistant than those of the Highlands to the north, and the Uplands to the south. Hence the largest plains are to be found in this part of Scotland. Moreover, it is only in the Central Lowlands that important deposits of coal are found. Because of the rich agricultural plains and the coalfields and their attendant industries, the Central Lowlands contain 80 per cent. of the population of Scotland, although it occupies only 10 per cent. of the total area.

On the north side of the Lowlands the Highland wall rises steeply, forming a clear-cut boundary. Running parallel to the edge of the Highlands is a long line of hills composed of volcanic rock. They are broken by the transverse valleys of the Clyde, Forth, and Tay, and from south-west to north-east are known as the Renfrew Heights, Campsie Fells, Ochil Hills, and Sidlaw Hills. Between these volcanic hills and the Highlands is a broad vale composed of Old Red Sandstone, and known, east of the River Tay, as Strathmore (the Great Vale).

On the south side of the Central Lowlands the structure is not so well defined. The slope from the Southern Uplands is less abrupt than the steep Highland face. Running parallel to the edge of the Uplands is a second line of volcanic hills extending from the isolated Castle Rock in Edinburgh through

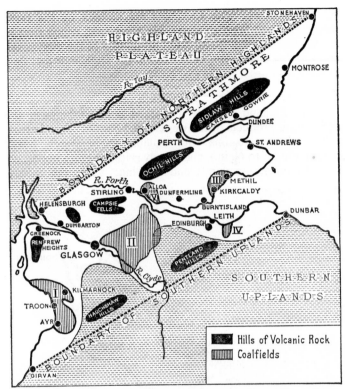

Fig. 103. Central Lowlands of Scotland, to Show Chief Hills, Rivers, Towns, and Coalfields.—I. Ayrshire Coalfield. II. Central or Lanarkshire Coalfield. III. Fife Coalfield. IV. Midlothian Coalfield. V. Clackmannan Coalfield.

the Pentland Hills and the Haughshaw Hills. Westwards of Ayrshire the island of Ailsa Craig continues this "volcanic line".

Between the volcanic hills and the Uplands, however, there is no broad vale corresponding to Strathmore. Extending northwards from the Pentland and Haughshaw Hills is a plateau region averaging 500 ft to 1,000 ft in height. This is divided into two portions by the Clyde Valley. An important feature of the relief of the Central Lowlands is the narrow "corridor" of low land which joins the Firth of Forth to the Firth of Clyde. Here is the narrowest part of Scotland, viz. thirty miles. The Lowlands are drained by the three most important Scottish rivers, viz. the Clyde, which rises in the Southern Uplands and flows north-west to the west coast, and the Tay and Forth, which rise in the Highlands and flow roughly south-east to the east coast.

Agriculture on the Central Lowlands

As in England there is a marked contrast between the agricultural products of the western and eastern coastal areas.

The western regions with equable temperatures, heavy rainfall (30 in. to 60 in.), and cloudy skies are more important for permanent grasslands and dairying; while the eastern

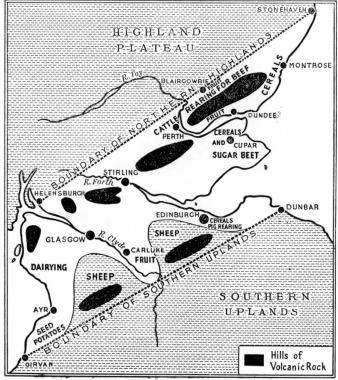

Fig. 104. CENTRAL LOWLANDS OF SCOTLAND, TO SHOW AGRICULTURAL ACTIVITIES.

regions, with rainfall below 30 in., warmer summers, and less cloud have a much greater percentage of arable land (Fig. 104).

(1) THE EASTERN MARGINS. These comprise the east coast from Stonehaven to Haddington. Agriculturally they fall into three subdivisions:—

(*a*) The Angus region, which includes the south of Kincardine and the coastal lowlands of Forfar, Perth, and Strathmore.

(*b*) The lowland fringes of Fife.

(*c*) The Lothians.

The "Angus" district. This region is noted for its cereals and fruit. This is the most northerly district of the British Isles where wheat cultivation is important. Barley is also cultivated, but the greatest acreage is devoted to oats. The rotation of crops is different from that of Eastern England. Here a six years' rotation is used, viz. oats, potatoes, wheat, turnips, barley, grass, *i.e.* cereals alternating with some non-cereal crops.

Because of the amount of sunshine, the length of the summer days, and the shelter afforded by the hills to the north, this is the most important fruit-growing region in Scotland. The greatest centre is on the sunny south-facing lands around Blairgowrie on the southern margins of the Highlands. Here raspberry-growing is pre-eminent. Another important raspberry district is the Carse o' Gowrie, the sheltered south-facing plain between the Sidlaw Hills and the Firth of Tay. Strawberries as well as raspberries are grown in the neighbourhood of Montrose. Much of this fruit is used in the jam factories of Dundee. Newtyle on the south side of Strathmore is a centre of bulb growing.

Though the demands of Dundee make dairying important in the district near that city, cattle rearing in the east is generally for beef. The rich sandstone pastures of Strathmore are famed for their herds of Aberdeen Angus and Shorthorns, and this is one of the most important cattle fattening regions in Britain.

The Fife lowlands. Here is a similar type of farming, a similar rotation of crops, and a similar importance of oats, wheat, and barley. Large-scale fruit growing is, however, absent, but sugar-beet is being increasingly cultivated.   Cupar has a sugar-beet factory.

The Lothians.   In this district, also, large crops of wheat, oats, and barley are produced.   There is here no specialisation in fruit or sugar-beet.   The presence of Edinburgh and Leith and other towns have made dairying important, and associated with the dairying industry is pig rearing.   There are more pigs per 100 acres here than in any other part of Scotland.

(2) THE WESTERN REGION.   The volcanic hills and the low plateaux to the east and west of the Clyde are all associated with sheep rearing.   The Ayrshire lowlands, particularly the northern portion of Ayrshire known as Cunningham (Fig. 106), with its equable temperatures, heavy rain, cloudy skies, and nearness to the great industrial centres of Lanarkshire, is pre-eminently a dairying region (compare Cheshire and its relation to Lancashire).   The Ayrshire breed of dairy cattle are world-famous.   It is too damp and cloudy for the cultivation of wheat or barley, so that oats is the only important cereal crop. The south of Ayrshire around Girvan, with light sandy soils, is the centre of the Scotch seed potato industry.   In the middle Clyde Valley, sheltered by the surrounding plateaux, is a region devoted to the large-scale production of tomatoes and strawberries.   The latter have given rise to an important jam-making industry at Carluke.

Industries and Towns

Over 99 per cent. of the output of coal of Scotland is mined in the Central Lowlands, this being about one-tenth of the total for Great Britain.   Whereas the coalfields of England are all associated with highland areas, the Scottish coalfields are found in the lowest basins of the Lowlands.   These coal-fields are (see Fig. 103):—

(I) The Western Basin, *i.e.* the Ayrshire coalfields.

(II) The Central Basin, *i.e.* the Lanarkshire coalfield and its eastward extension.   This coalfield is nearing exhaustion and production is falling.

(III) The Eastern Basin, *i.e.* the Fife and Midlothian coal-fields, these coal measures underlying the widest part of the Firth of Forth.

The Western Basin produces 22 per cent., the Central Basin 29 per cent., and the Eastern Basin 49 per cent. of the total Scottish production (Fig. 105). The greatest reserves of coal are in the Eastern Basin.

(I) THE AYRSHIRE COALFIELD. In this coalfield mining is scattered, and there is no great degree of industrial development. As a result there is a surplus of coal, some of which is exported through Troon, Ayr, and Ardrossan to Ireland. The chief town and industrial centre is Kilmarnock, noted for its engineering industries (Fig. 106). Ayrshire is one of the lesser woollen-manufacturing regions of Britain. The chief centres are Kilmarnock (carpets), Ayr, Dalry, and Girvan. These towns specialise in the manufacture of knitted wear, homespuns, plaids, etc. Leather industries, due to the importance of cattle rearing, are centred at Kilmarnock and Maybole. The valley of the River Irvine in Northern Ayrshire has scattered cotton-mills associated with those of the Glasgow and Paisley region. The coastal towns of Ayrshire and the islands off the coast, *e.g.* Arran, are the "play-grounds" for industrial Scotland. Prestwick has become one of the chief airports of the United Kingdom.

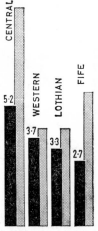

Fig. 105. COAL PRODUCTION IN MILLIONS OF TONS, 1965. See also Fig. 36.

(II) THE CENTRAL COALFIELD. This coalfield extends from the outskirts of Glasgow, south-eastwards to within about five miles of Lanark. Only a small proportion of its area lies to the west of the Clyde, but it extends east and north-east over the low plateaux and through the Clyde-Forth "corridor" to Clackmannan. It has the advantage of being served by Glasgow and the Clyde ports on the west, and by Grangemouth on the east. The Forth and Clyde canal, linking Grangemouth and Glasgow, follows the "corridor". There is a large and varied industrial development associated with this coalfield and the industrial centres fall into four groups.

(*a*) *The Clackmannan Region, North of the Forth.* This is not an important industrial area, and mining is scattered. Stirling, to the north of the coalfield, and Alloa, are centres of a small woollen industry, including the manufacture of blankets, carpets, and knitting wool.

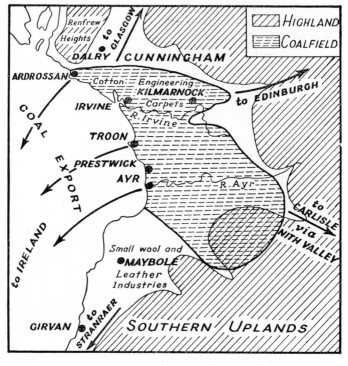

Fig. 106. THE AYRSHIRE COALFIELD.

(*b*) *The Eastern Region of the Coalfields South of the Forth.* Here, Falkirk, originally an important market town, is the centre of a district engaged in iron-working. Most of the pig-iron used is imported from the Tees district. Grangemouth, at the eastern end of the Forth and Clyde canal is an important port which not only serves the Falkirk region, but is the eastern outlet for the iron manufactures of Lanarkshire.

Oil piped from a deep water port at Finnart on Loch Long, an arm of the Clyde, is refined, and Grangemouth has the largest petroleum chemicals plant outside the U.S.A. Bo'ness, an older port, imports pit props from Scandinavia, exports coal, and has shipbuilding and aluminium smelting.

(*c*) *The Western Portion of the Coalfield in Lanarkshire.* This is one of the most important iron-working centres in Britain. Originally local supplies of black band ore were used, but, although these are not completely exhausted, the industry to-day uses cheaper imported pig-iron.

This iron industry is mainly that which is known as the "heavy" iron industry, viz. the manufacture of steel girders, bridges, the steel framework of buildings, etc. (contrast the metal industries of South Staffordshire, page 144). The best-known centres are Motherwell, Airdrie, Coatbridge, and Wishaw on the east side of the Clyde (Fig. 107). Hamilton, to the west of the river, is a coal-mining centre. South of the coalfield, near Lanark, are the series of rapids known as the Falls of Clyde. These are now used for the generation of hydro-electric power for the Clyde industries.

(*d*) *Glasgow and the Clyde Estuary.* This great industrial region is not actually on the Lanarkshire coalfield, but its industries are based on the Lanarkshire coal and the iron manufactures. From Glasgow to Greenock, a distance of twenty miles, with docks lining both banks of the Clyde, is the greatest shipbuilding district in the world, producing about one-twentieth of all the world's new ships. Some thirty shipbuilding firms have their headquarters on Clydebank, including that of John Brown and Co. Ltd, who built the *Queen Mary* and the *Queen Elizabeth* (see plate facing page 208).

Much of the success and pre-eminence of the Clydebank shipbuilding area is due to the deepening and constant dredging of the Clyde estuary, thus enabling the port of Glasgow to keep pace with the steady increase in the size of ships. The shipbuilding industry owes much to the nearby supplies of coal and iron ore, to the sheltered position of the Clyde estuary, and to the early start of the construction of steam-ships in this region, which dates from the building of the *Comet* in 1812. Some of the shipbuilding centres of the

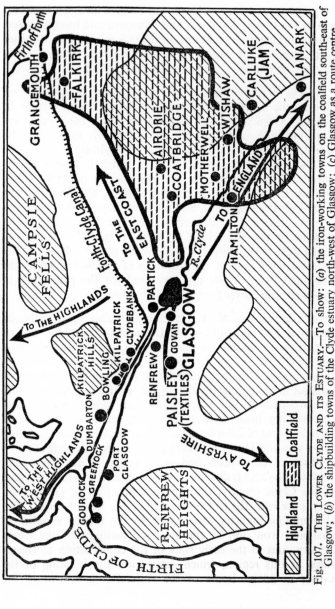

Fig. 107. The Lower Clyde and its Estuary.—To show: (a) the iron-working towns on the coalfield south-east of Glasgow; (b) the shipbuilding towns of the Clyde estuary north-west of Glasgow; (c) Glasgow as a route centre.

Clyde estuary are Partick, Clydebank, Bowling, Dumbarton, Port Glasgow, and Greenock (Fig. 107). Clydebank is also noted for the manufacture of sewing-machines. Marine engineering, *i.e.* the manufacture of boilers, marine engines, etc., ranks next in importance to shipbuilding, and is complementary to it. Glasgow is primarily an engineering centre, but it has a great variety of industries based on its imports, and on the needs of its great population. Thus there are flour mills, paper mills, soap works, oil refineries, chemical works, dye works, glass works, and a whole range of "luxury" industries, including the making of carpets, confectionery, furniture, etc. In the last twenty years the setting up of planned Industrial Estates with modern light industries has done a lot to further diversify the economic activity of the Glasgow region.

The Glasgow region is a miniature South-East Lancashire, as all branches of the cotton industry are represented, spinning, weaving, bleaching, dyeing, etc. Paisley, noted for cotton thread, is the chief centre. There are also some woollen industries in Glasgow, including the manufacture of carpets. There is a car plant at Bathgate.

Glasgow is the third city in Britain, and ranks as tenth port according to total trade (see Fig. 85). The importance of Glasgow is due to:—

(1) It was originally the market centre of the agricultural lands of the lower Clyde.

(2) At the lowest bridging point of the Clyde, it is the natural focus of land routes, (*a*) to the Highlands via Loch Lomond, (*b*) to the Forth via the Clyde-Forth corridor, (*c*) to England via the upper Clyde and Annan Valley, (*d*) to Ayrshire via the Lochwinnock Gap east of the Renfrew Heights.

(3) Situated on the west of Scotland it had the right "outlook" at the time of the rise of trade with America.

(4) It is on the only large estuary on the west coast of Scotland.

(5) It is backed by the densely-populated and highly-industrialised Central Plain.

Greenock (70,000), on the south bank of the Clyde, has sugar refineries and old trade connections with the West Indies.

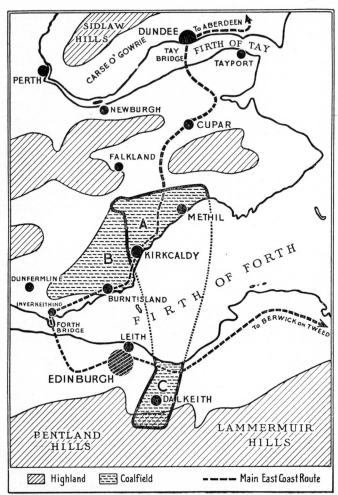

Fig. 108. THE EASTERN COALFIELDS OF SCOTLAND. A and B. Fife
coalfield (B is the concealed coalfield). C. Midlothian coalfield.

(III) THE EASTERN COALFIELDS (Fig. 108). These comprise
the Lothian coalfield on the south side of the Firth of Forth
and the Fife coalfield on the north side.

(*a*) *The Lothian Coalfield.* Situated in the counties of
Midlothian and East Lothian this field is notable for its

increased coal output in recent years. Edinburgh, the capital of Scotland, is the chief centre of this region. Many of its industries are those connected with its functions as a capital, and "luxury" industries to supply the needs of a large professional population. Thus paper-making, printing, bookbinding, brewing, and distilling, and the manufacture of biscuits and confectionery are important industries. Newer and growing industries include rubber, engineering, and electronics.

The paper industry is due to (i) the local demands for paper in connection with government departments and the university, (ii) the ease with which supplies of wood pulp can be obtained from Scandinavia and Finland, and (iii) the supplies of clean water in the Esk Valley. Brewing and distilling are connected with the local supplies of barley, though large quantities of this grain are now imported. Engineering industries are also important.

Edinburgh (Fig. 109) grew up around a volcanic hill surmounted by a castle, which guarded the east coast route between the Southern

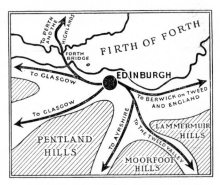

Fig. 109. THE POSITION OF EDINBURGH, to show its control of routes, and its position guarding the narrow lowland between the hills and the sea.

Uplands and the coast, the easiest entry into the Scottish Lowlands from England. As the capital of Scotland before the Union with England, it undoubtedly owed much to its strategic position. Like London, it stands on the eastern side of rich agricultural plains, and had important trade and cultural relations with Europe before the discovery of America led to a rapid growth of Glasgow, now more than twice as large as Edinburgh.

Leith is the port of Edinburgh and is the second port of Scotland, though its trade does not amount to one-third that of Glasgow. The trade of Leith is mainly connected, with the import of grain from North America, dairy produce, bacon, and wood pulp from the Baltic countries, and with the export of coal.

(*b*) *The Fife Coalfield.* The coalfield extends along the coast from Largo to Kirkcaldy, and inland its westward extension reaches beyond Dunfermline which has silk manufactures and artificial fibre textile industries. Methil is a specially-constructed coal-port, which, though small from the point of view of its population, has, owing to its coal trade, become the fourth port of Scotland.

Kirkcaldy is the centre of the linoleum industry. The jute base of the linoleum is obtained from Dundee, and the necessary cork and linseed oil are imported. Falkland, in central Fife, and Newburgh, on the northern coast of Fife, though not quite on the coalfield, are also engaged in the manufacture of linoleum. Inverkeithing, the port of the ancient city of Dunfermline, has engineering industries. At the narrowest part of the Forth estuary near Inverkeithing are the Forth road and rail bridges. Many new industries and particularly electronics are growing in central Fife and in the New Town of Glenrothes.

On the eastern shore of Fife, away from the coalfield, is St Andrews, famous for its old university and its golf links.

DUNDEE. On the north shore of the Firth of Tay, at the crossing point of the Firth of Tay by the Tay Bridge, Dundee (185,000) is not on a coalfield, but is an industrial centre, the fourth city and fifth port of Scotland. It has many important industries, the chief of which are engineering and electronics, the making of jam and marmalade, the manufacture of linen, and of hemp and jute into string, ropes, nets, sailcloth, canvas, and sacking. With the exception of local supplies of fruit, all the raw materials for these industries have to be imported, viz. pig-iron from the Tees Basin, oranges from Spain, flax and hemp from the countries of the North European Plain and Russia, and jute from India.

The origin of the linen industries of Dundee was due to local supplies of home-grown flax. Other linen-weaving centres of Eastern Scotland are Arbroath, Forfar, and Brechin.

In the course of time changes in the availability of the raw materials and in the demand for the manufactured article led textile manufacturers in Dundee to try other fibres, *e.g.* hemp for ropes, nets and sailcloth for fishing vessels, and jute and other fibres for sacking. In Dundee the manufacture of jute completely overshadows that of flax and hemp. Over 99 per cent. of the world's jute is grown in the Ganges Valley and Dundee imports its jute from East Pakistan. Dundee is now suffering from competition by increasing numbers of Indian jute mills near Calcutta, whose raw materials are close at hand.

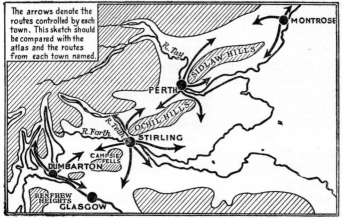

Fig. 110. THE GATEWAY TOWNS OF THE NORTHERN SIDE OF THE CENTRAL LOWLANDS.

Gateway Towns

Long before the period of industrial development the fertile plains of the Lowlands were more densely peopled than the more barren Highlands to the north and Uplands to the south. Driven outwards by the unproductiveness of their own lands, and lured by the fertility of the Central Lowlands, the hill peoples made constant raids on the rich farm lands of the plains. Added to which the Lowlands were always aware of the possibilities of attacks from England beyond the Border. In order to guard their lands they built fortresses at the important natural "gateways". Around these castles, market towns grew which centuries later became important railway centres. The strategic importance of Edinburgh guarding the main route from England has already been noted. More spectacular is the line of "castle" towns on the north side of the Lowlands (Fig. 110).

DUMBARTON. The capital of the old kingdom of Strathclyde, Dumbarton guards the route to the Western Highlands via the north bank of the Clyde estuary and Loch Lomond.

STIRLING. At the former lowest point of bridging of the Forth, with its castle perched on a plug of volcanic rock, similar to the Castle Rock of Edinburgh, Stirling controls the route between the Campsie Fells and Ochil Hills (see plate facing page 208).

PERTH. Until recently at the lowest point of bridging of the Tay, Perth guards the route between the Ochil Hills and the Sidlaw Hills which leads to the central region of the Highlands. This route follows the valley of the rivers Tay and Spey to Inverness and thence follows the east coast plains to Wick and Thurso. The recently-opened Forth road bridge near Edinburgh has greatly improved road communications between Perth and Edinburgh. Vehicles previously had either to cross the Forth by a ferry or make the considerable detour via Stirling.

MONTROSE. Situated on a "bar" and almost surrounded by water, Montrose guards the coastal route between the Sidlaw Hills and the sea.

To-day these four towns control the road and rail routes to the Highlands and later will be taken as the starting points of the railways which serve Northern Scotland.

Above: Spreading machine-cut peat in Ireland (see p. 240). (*Bord na Mona, Dublin.*)

Below: Since 1948, electricity, and the amenities electricity can provide, has been brought to nearly two-thirds of Scotland's crofters. (*North of Scotland Hydro-electric Board.*)

Above: A typical landscape in County Donegal, showing the small-holdings of the peas
farmers. (*T. H. Mason.*)

Below: Kildare. In size and general characteristics Kildare is typical of the mar
towns of Central Ireland. Notice the open market square and compare Kildare in
with an English market town, *e.g.* Shrewsbury shown on plate facing p. 113. (*Aerofilms L*

CHAPTER 25

SCOTLAND

(3) THE HIGHLANDS

The Highlands of Scotland lie north of the line from Helensburgh to Stonehaven. They can be divided into two sharply contrasting areas, viz. (*a*) the plains bordering the east coast, and (*b*) the Highlands and islands of the remainder of the region.

The Mountain Region

The true Highland zone is a plateau of ancient sedimentary, volcanic, and metamorphic rocks, which has been deeply dissected by ice and river action (see plate facing page 16). The plateau is broken into two sections by the deep rift of Glenmore, in which lie Lochs Ness, Oich, and Lochy, joined by the Caledonian Canal. To the south of Glenmore are the Grampians, higher and more deeply dissected than the North-West Highlands to the north of Glenmore. In the Grampians are Ben Nevis (4,406 ft), and Ben Macdhui (4,296 ft).

The west coast of the Highlands is of the fiord type, deeply indented with long sea lochs, the result of glaciation, faulting, and submergence (see plate facing page 209). Off this coast are hundreds of islands and islets which fall into two groups, (*a*) the Inner Hebrides, including the islands of Islay, Jura, Mull, Tiree, Coll, and Skye, (*b*) the Outer Hebrides, including Harris and Lewis, North and South Uist, and Barra. The Outer Hebrides and the Inner Hebrides are separated by a submerged rift valley known as the Minch. At the time of their formation there were extensive lava flows, the remains of which are to be seen in the basaltic heights of the Coolin Hills (Skye), Ben More (Mull), in the columnar formations of Fingal's Cave on the Isle of Staffa, and the Antrim plateau of Northern Ireland. The Outer Hebrides are, except for a portion of Harris, much lower than the Inner Hebrides.

The general slope of the Highlands is from the west to the east where the old rocks dip under the newer and less resistant rocks of the east coast plain. The western rivers are short, swift mountain torrents, while the east-flowing streams, though rapid in their upper courses, are longer.

The longest rivers are those from the Grampians, viz. the Tay flowing south-east, the Dee and Don flowing east, and the Deveron and Spey flowing north-east. The rivers of the North-West Highlands are shorter. In the courses of many of the rivers are deep long ribbon-shaped lakes, formed partly by the scooping action of ice and partly by the deposition of morainic dams across the valleys.

CLIMATE. Because of their altitude the Highlands, except on the west coast, have cold winters and cool summers and because of their exposure to westerly winds and their proximity to the main track of depressions, the rainfall is heavy (see Fig. 14). Fort William has nearly 80 in. per annum, and Ben Nevis 180 in. In addition there is a high percentage of cloudiness, and mists are common. The rainfall decreases rapidly eastwards to under 30 in. on the east coast plains.

POPULATION. Extensive areas of moorland and mountain in the Highlands are practically uninhabited. Except for a few towns on the west coast, *e.g.* railway termini, such as Mallaig, or seaside resorts, such as Oban, the population is to be found in scattered hamlets (called *townships*) on the coast and in the glens. There are few natural resources and no mineral wealth; moreover, communications are generally difficult.

AGRICULTURE. Agriculture is difficult in the Highlands. The countryside is mountainous, rainfall in the west is heavy, summer temperatures are low, and the soil is acid and peaty, requiring liming and drainage to improve it. Large sheep farms are found on the south and east margins and "crofting" on the west and north, while large areas in the higher parts are deer forests and grouse moors. Some, but not all, parts of these sporting estates could support sheep.

Each croft has a small area of arable land and a share of a large area of common hill grazing. Income is from the sale of sheep, wool, and cattle. Hay, turnips, and oats are grown as fodder crops and potatoes for the crofter's own use, or for sale. For fuel the crofter often cuts his own peats. The main problem is the small size of the croft, which leads to younger people leaving crofting, or taking an additional

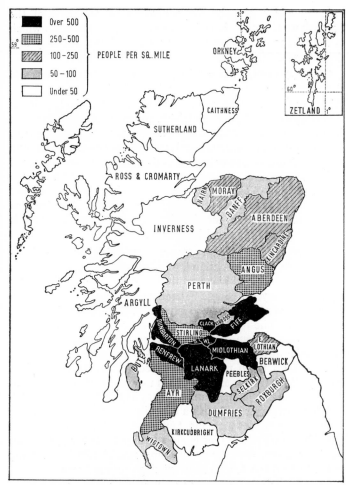

Fig. 111. POPULATION MAP OF SCOTLAND BY COUNTIES (1961).
The estimated population of Perth in 1964 gives a density of a little under 50 per square mile.

job, often to the neglect of crofting. The population is declining and is an ageing one, and this too leads to less than full use being made of the land.

In Lewis and Harris the income of the crofter is often supplemented by the making of hand-woven tweed, an industry which absorbs the equivalent of one-third of the Scottish wool crop. Knitting is important in Shetland, which is famed for the fineness of its wool and the intricacy and delicate colouring of the genuine Fair Isle patterns.

WATER-POWER. Because of the swiftness of the streams and the ample rainfall, water-power is available at many places. About one-tenth of the potential water-power of the Highlands is already used for hydro-electricity, and many other schemes are in progress. The generating stations provide employment, firstly for their construction and later for their maintenance, and the availability of power has led to the starting up of a few small industries, again providing employment. During the last ten years, supplies of electricity have been laid on to well over half the scattered farms and crofts of the Highlands. The balance (about one-quarter) of the electricity production of the Board is exported to the industrial Lowlands.

FORESTRY. The Forestry Commission holds some two thousand square miles in Scotland, of which more than one-third is already planted, and new planting is at the rate of about fifty square miles a year. Some 40 per cent. of this work is in the five Highland counties of Argyll, Inverness, Ross, Sutherland, and Caithness. The trees are mainly conifers but some oaks and beeches are grown where conditions are suitable. These National Forests are open to the public for recreational purposes and the trees when mature are felled for timber or pulping. Nearly all the timber and pit-props used in Scottish coal-mines are grown in Scotland. Fort William has an integrated wood-pulping and paper mill with a capacity of 500 tons a day.

Forestry provides permanent employment for twelve workers per 1,000 acres planted, as against two or three per 1,000 acres used for sheep, deer, or grouse, and special efforts are being made to establish forests near existing crofting areas.

WHISKY. Most of our whisky is distilled in north-east Scotland, much of it in the valley of the Spey. Exports are now worth about £175 million a year, eight times as great as those of china and pottery. The United States is our biggest customer, accounting for more than half the total.

THE TOURIST INDUSTRY. The Highlands contain the most spectacular mountain scenery in the British Isles. They provide unequalled opportunities for fishing, shooting, mountaineering, skiing, pony trekking, sailing, or simply for a quiet holiday. Consequently the tourist industry is important, bringing prosperity not only to hotel keepers, but to all sections of the community. The main difficulty is the short summer season, but the development of skiing in the Cairngorms has created a winter season in Speyside. Poor roads and lack of hotel accommodation are other difficulties this promising industry has to face. The tourist industry is found throughout the Highlands, but large resorts are found mainly on the Clyde, Rothesay and Dunoon, at Oban, and on the shores of the Moray Firth.

The Eastern Plains

The eastern coastal plains offer a great contrast to the highland areas. Here are relatively low plains partly composed of Old Red Sandstone, which yields a richer and deeper soil than the old hard rocks of the Highlands. These plains are sheltered by the mountains to the west, and the rainfall is about 30 in. per annum. Moreover, there is less cloudiness. On these plains mixed farming is practised. In the triangular plain of Caithness (where the summers are too cool for wheat or barley) oats, turnips, and potatoes are the chief crops, and cattle are extensively reared especially for meat. Further south, on the sheltered plains at the head of the Moray Firth, wheat can be grown in limited quantities, chiefly as a result of the length of the summer days and the exceptionally sheltered position. The coastlands of Nairns, Moray, and Banff, and the Buchan plain also grow oats and roots, and in particular the Buchan lowlands are famous as a cattle fattening region.

Towns of Northern Scotland. The coastal towns, Wick, Thurso, Fraserburgh, Peterhead, and Aberdeen are fishing centres. Aberdeen is second only to Grimsby in the weight of fish landed. Fraserburgh and Peterhead are centres for herring fishing. Wick and Thurso are less important. Only four towns have a population much over 10,000, viz. Aberdeen, Inverness (p. 230), Elgin, and Peterhead. Fraserburgh is just 10,000, and Wick has a population of about 7,000; Lerwick (6,000), Stornoway (5,000), and Kirkwall (4,500) are the main towns in their respective

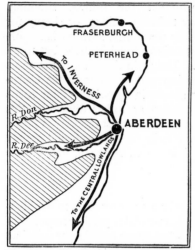

Fig. 112.   THE POSITION OF ABERDEEN.

island groups. Thurso (9,000) has more than doubled in size in ten years because of the atomic energy plant nearby at Douneray.

Aberdeen (Fig. 112), situated at the mouths of the rivers Dee and Don, is the third largest city in Scotland and has a population of over 180,000. It controls the chief route into the Highlands up the Dee Valley to Ballater, Braemar, and Balmoral. It is a university town and a fishing port, has paper and textile industries, and granite is quarried nearby.

Inverness (Fig. 113), at the north-eastern end of Glenmore, is an important route centre, and lies on the main route to Wick and Thurso. It is becoming increasingly important as a tourist centre. Shetland wool is machine-spun and returned to the Islands for knitting. A large-scale oil refinery and petro-chemical industry is to be established at Invergordon on Cromarty Firth, some sixteen miles north of Inverness.

POPULATION OF THE COASTAL PLAIN. The population of the coastal plain is over 100 per square mile, a strong contrast to the almost uninhabited moorlands. The greater

Fig. 113.   THE POSITION OF INVERNESS.

density of population of the coastal plain is the result of the drier climate, richer soils, the greater extent of agricultural land, easier communications, and the fishing industry. With the exception of Argyll, all the Highland counties have a share of the coastal plain, and the county towns are in every case on the eastern "plain" section where the bulk of the population has congregated.

Orkney and Shetland

Orkney and Shetland lie off the north coast. Unlike the Highlands they were never a Gaelic-speaking area, but had close connections with Norway. Orkney is a rich farming county, being composed of Old Red Sandstone, like the Eastern Plains, but Shetland, composed of harder rocks, similar to the Highlands, is more a crofting county, and has an important fishing industry.

The Railways of the Northern Highlands

The Highlands are served by three main railway routes from the Lowlands (Fig. 114):—

(1) From Glasgow along the northern shores of the Firth of Clyde, and along the coast of Loch Long to the northern end of Loch Lomond. Thence the railway winds northwards over the wild Rannoch Moors to Fort William, and proceeds westward to Mallaig, a ferry town for Skye.

(2) From Perth an important railway route ascends the valley of the Tay and its tributaries, the Tummel and the Garry. It passes from Glen Garry to the upper Spey by the pass of Drumochter. Kingussie, in the upper Spey Valley, is the tourist centre for the Cairngorm area. Leaving the Spey Valley the railway crosses the Monadliath Mountains to Inverness. Northwards of Inverness the railway takes a circuitous route around the head of Moray, Cromarty, and Dornoch Firths and, by following the coastal plains and the Helmsdale Valley, reaches Wick and Thurso. A branch of this railway strikes westwards from Inverness to Strome Ferry and the Kyle of Lochalsh, another centre of steamer-communication with Skye and the Western Isles.

(3) From Perth or Dundee a route follows the coastal plains through Montrose and Stonehaven to Aberdeen. It

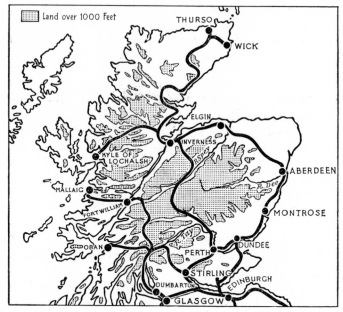

Fig. 114.   THE RAILWAYS OF NORTHERN SCOTLAND.

then turns north-westward across the Aberdeen lowland to Elgin, Nairn, and Inverness.

The west coast of Scotland north of the Central Lowlands is served by railway at only three points, viz. Oban, Mallaig, and the Kyle of Lochalsh.   Between the Kyle of Lochalsh and Thurso the coastal areas are devoid of railway communication, but the development of omnibus services has, in recent years, done much to lessen the isolation of the north-western townships and villages.

The remoteness and isolation of the Scottish islands have been greatly reduced in recent years by the growth of air transport.   Of the western islands, Islay, Tiree, Benbecula, and Stornoway, have services to Glasgow, and both Kirkwall, in the Orkneys, and Lerwick, in the Shetlands, have routes to Aberdeen and via Inverness, to Glasgow.   An Air Ambulance Service operates from Renfrew.

CHAPTER 26

IRELAND

The Ways to Ireland

Just as England is linked to the mainland of Europe by regular steamer service from ferry ports, so there are regular steamer services to Ireland. In determining routes for mail and passenger steamers, the main consideration is the saving of time, hence ferry towns are situated at points where the intervening seas are narrowest. For instance, mail and passenger boats ply between Dublin and Holyhead, a distance of sixty-one miles, but boats carrying cargo (*e.g.* live cattle), for which cheap carriage is essential, often take the longer route to Liverpool or Birkenhead, a distance of 120 miles.

The ferry services are operated by British Railways, those out of Fishguard by the Western Region, those out of Holyhead and Heysham by the London Midland Region, and those out of Stranraer by the Scottish Region. The principal routes to Ireland and the ferry ports are shown on Fig. 115. Holyhead handles more than half the passenger traffic, and Liverpool and Fishguard most of the remainder.

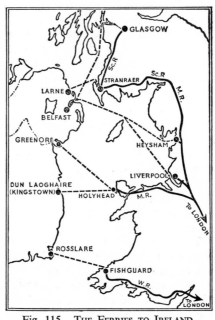

Fig. 115. THE FERRIES TO IRELAND.

Political Divisions

In Ireland there are two political units:—

(1) NORTHERN IRELAND, which sends parliamentary representatives to Westminster, and which consists of the counties Down, Antrim, Londonderry, Tyrone, Fermanagh, and Armagh, six of the nine counties of the old province of Ulster.

(2) THE IRISH REPUBLIC (EIRE), consisting of the remainder of Ireland, which is an independent Republic in an ill-defined association with the British Commonwealth, has its own parliament at Dublin.

The reasons for the separation of the Irish Republic are:—

(a) The great cultural and racial differences between the Irish and the English. Ireland was not invaded by the Romans or the Anglo-Saxons, and her peoples are descended from peoples speaking pre-Celtic and Celtic languages. In their outlook on life, language, and religion the Irish differ from their English neighbours.

(b) The grievances that Ireland has accumulated against England in past centuries, chiefly in relation to the Cromwellian invasions, the acquisition of Irish land by the English nobles, and the strong feeling that the money obtained from rentals and taxes was not used for the improvement of conditions in Ireland.

(c) The creation of self-governing Dominions within the British Empire early this century caused Ireland to demand the same privileges. It was only after a bitter struggle that self-government was granted to Eire in 1921.

The six counties of Northern Ireland differ from the Irish Republic in having fewer Roman Catholics and more people not of pure Irish lineage, largely due to the "plantation" of Scottish settlers during the reign of James I. The people of Northern Ireland have many Scottish characteristics, and are more thrifty, far-seeing, and methodical than the more carefree, happy-go-lucky, quick-tempered peoples of the south.

Relief and Structure

The study of a geological map shows striking similarities between the rocks and structure of Ireland and the west of Great Britain, and would suggest that the two islands were

Fig. 116. To Show Structural Connections between Great Britain and Ireland.

connected in early geological periods. The major points of similarity (shown on Fig. 116) are:—

(1) The old hard rocks of the Northern Highlands of Scotland are continued in the mountains of Donegal, Mayo, and Connemara.

(2) The rocks of the Southern Uplands are similar to those of the Mourne Mountains.

(3) The Welsh Mountains and the Wicklow Mountains are of similar structure.

All the foregoing mountains are characterised by the same north-east to south-west trend ("The Caledonian Trend").

(4) The rocks of South-West Ireland and of Cornwall and Devon are similar (the Armorican System).

Although the popular idea of Ireland being saucer-shaped is erroneous, nevertheless, the mountains of Ireland are arranged near the coast, but rise in detached blocks which nowhere present the length of unbroken highland found in the Welsh Mountains, the Pennines, and the Highlands of Scotland. The northern group of coastal highlands includes the mountains of Connemara and Mayo and the mountains of Donegal, the Sperrin Mountains, the Antrim Plateau, and the Mourne Mountains.

The southern group of mountains comprise Wicklow Mountains, the Knockmealdown Mountains, and the mountains of Kerry, including Macgillycuddy's Reeks with the highest mountain of Ireland, viz. Carrantuohill (3,414 ft).

Between the two groups of highlands is the Central Plain, which reaches the east coast between Dublin and Dundalk and the west coast at Galway and Limerick.

The largest river in Ireland is the Shannon (220 miles), which flows roughly north to south over the western portion of the Central Plain. In its course it passes through a number of broad shallow lakes, *e.g.* Loughs Allen, Ree, and Derg, which have been formed in some cases by the solution of limestone. After leaving Lough Derg the Shannon flows through a gap between the Slieve Bernagh and Silvermine Mountains. In this section of its course there are rapids, which have been utilised for the generation of hydro-electricity.

The River Suck and the River Brosna are the principal tributaries of the Shannon.

Other important rivers of Ireland are the Lagan, Boyne, Liffey, and Slaney, draining to the east coast; the Barrow, Nore, Suir, Blackwater, Lee, and Bandon, draining to the south coast (note the parallelism of the courses of the four last-named); and the Foyle and Bann draining to the north coast. Except for the Shannon, the rivers flowing to the west coast are short and unimportant.

Climate

The outstanding features of the climate of Ireland are its humidity and its equability. Winter temperatures never fall below 5° C. (*41° F.*), and the average July temperatures are always below 15° C. (*59° F.*) (see Figs 11 and 12), except in the south. Thus everywhere the mean annual range of temperature is less than 10 C.° (*18 F.°*) [compare London with a range of over 13 C.° (*24 F.°*)].

As Ireland is further west than Britain it receives the full force of the rain-bearing westerlies and cyclonic storms. The rainfall of Ireland is therefore heavy, but, because of the breaks in the mountains of the west, the winds carry the rain inland, and the strong contrasts in rainfall distribution found in Britain are absent in Ireland   The rainfall is neither so heavy near the west coast, nor so light near the east coast as in England, and it is more evenly distributed over the whole country (see Fig. 14). Two small mountainous areas on the west have over 80 in. of rainfall, viz. the mountains of Kerry and Connemara. Only a small area around Dublin has less than 30 in., and the remainder of the Central Plain has between 30 and 40 in. (contrast the English plain with an average rainfall of less than 30 in.).

Agriculture

The climate of Ireland strongly influences agricultural activities. Over most of Ireland the summer temperatures are generally too low for the ripening of wheat and barley, so that oats is the most widely distributed cereal crop (see Figs. 18, 19, and 20). Production of oats is about 300,000 tons a year, with wheat over 400,000 and barley over 800,000 tons.

The district with the highest summer temperatures, viz. the south-east in the valleys of the Suir, Nore, Barrow, and Slaney, has the greatest acreage devoted to cereals. The warm winters (particularly in the south-west) allow the growth of grass almost throughout the year, so that there is a high percentage of permanent pasture devoted to cattle rearing. The humidity of the atmosphere, the absence of any well-defined dry season, and the prevalence of cloud, have resulted in that greenness of the Irish pastures which have earned for Ireland the name "Emerald Isle". The climatic conditions are ideal for the production of grass and for dairying, and it is largely on the methodical organisation of the dairying industry that the future prosperity of Ireland depends. That Ireland has not yet developed her agricultural industries to the full is shown by the following figures for 1968-9:—

	SIZE IN SQ. ML.	VALUE OF ARABLE PRODUCE IN £ MILLION	VALUE OF DAIRY PRODUCE AND MEAT IN £ MILLION
England and Wales	65,700	339	1,280
Ireland	31,800	65	340
Scotland	30,400	64	171

The first column shows that Ireland and Scotland are approximately the same size, and each is about half the area of England and Wales. Bearing this fact in mind, the second column shows the relative unimportance of the Irish arable cultivation. Relatively (*i.e.* per square mile) the arable production of England and Wales is nearly three times that of Ireland. Nevertheless, in recent years there has been a considerable increase in Eire in the amount of barley and wheat grown, largely as a result of Government subsidies.

The third column indicates that, although the value of animal products in Ireland is twice as great as that of Scotland, dairy produce and meat in England, in relation to size, is nearly twice as valuable as in Ireland. With the increase in cereal production noted above, there has been a decrease in the production of wool, pigs, and eggs.

Industry

The predominance of agriculture in Ireland is partly due to climatic conditions, partly to the national characteristics, but chiefly to lack of economically workable mineral wealth, particularly of coal and iron.

Coal is worked only in three places, viz.:—

(1) At Dungannon in County Tyrone.

(2) In the south of County Monaghan.

(3) In Kilkenny.

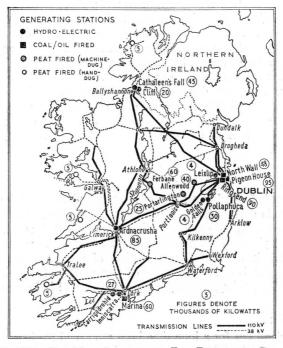

Fig. 117. THE MAIN LINES OF THE EIRE ELECTRICITY GRID.

The large areas of coal measures which are shown on a geological map, in Limerick and Clare, do not contain seams of coal thick enough to be worked. Peat, from the peat bogs, is the usual domestic fuel in the rural areas, and coal and oil have to be imported. For this reason, the Industrial Revolution which took place in Britain in the nineteenth century, did not occur in Ireland. This meant that the chief manufacturing towns of Ireland were the ports where coal could be imported. Now, the development of the electricity grid and the availability of a surplus of labour (Ireland is the only Western European country that has one) is leading to some development of light industry elsewhere, mainly connected with agriculture. During the last twenty-five years, industrial production as a whole in the Irish Republic has doubled and the manufacture of clothing, boots and shoes, hosiery, vehicles, and light engineering products has increased fourfold. Industry in Northern Ireland is discussed on pp. 245-7.

In the last few years, improvement in techniques, and the rising value of metals, have made it worth while to work some previously uneconomic deposits of zinc, lead, copper, and silver, and new discoveries are still being made, *e.g.* in Tipperary and Galway. Most of the ore mined is exported to Europe through small west-coast ports. In 1969 ore containing 6,000 tons of copper and 65,000 tons of lead were exported.

Peat

Peat is formed as a result of the accumulation and decay of plants in shallow lakes and swamps. It has been used as fuel for centuries, but digging has been mechanised since 1924 and to-day yields over 4 million tons per annum. Three-quarters of this is used in the generation of electricity while the remainder is put to a variety of uses such as for fuel, deep litter for poultry, packing early potatoes, and in horticulture.

Tourism

Ireland has for a long time been renowned for its excellent river and lake fishing. However, the unspoilt natural scenery is probably Ireland's greatest asset and within recent years, the tourist industry has developed to a very large extent. It is an activity in which the Irish, with their flair for meeting people, excel. The development of tourism in the Irish Republic is conducted by the government-sponsored Irish Tourist

Board. The areas being developed by them as tourist centres are to be found in the mountain periphery of Ireland, the sole exception being the Shannon Waterway. To-day earnings from tourism rank as the biggest invisible export and Ireland derives a higher proportion of its external revenue from tourism, about one-eighth, than any European country except Spain and Austria.

Distribution of Population

The absence of highly-developed industrial areas reflects on the size of the towns and cities of Ireland.

(1) There are only three large cities: Dublin, Belfast, and Cork. The fourth town is Limerick (58,000) and the fifth Londonderry, with a population of about 55,000.

(2) All the towns with a population of over 10,000 are either (*a*) on the coast where market towns have the additional function of a port, or (*b*) are included in the linen towns of the Lagan Valley. Among these towns are (i) Limerick (58,000), Waterford (30,000), Wexford (13,000), Tralee (12,000), Galway (26,000), Sligo (13,000), Dundalk (22,000), Drogheda on the coast; (ii) Lisburn (22,000), Lurgan (21,000), Portadown (21,000), Newry (12,000), Newtownards (13,000), and Ballymena (16,000) in the linen district of Northern Ireland.

(3) With the exception of the linen towns, all the inland towns of Ireland have populations of less than 10,000, and often less than 5,000. Thus in type they are similar to very small English market towns.

The population is much more evenly distributed than it is in Great Britain. Except for the mountainous western areas there are few regions of scanty population, but on the other hand, there are no very densely populated areas comparable to the English coalfields and the Metropolitan area.

The Trade of Ireland

Both Northern Ireland and Eire send the bulk of their exports to Great Britain, from which they derive most of their imports. Thus the importance of Great Britain as a market for Irish goods, and of Ireland as a market for the manufactures of Britain, should not be minimised. The exports of Northern Ireland differ from those of Eire. Less than half the exports of Northern Ireland are of agricultural origin (*e.g.* dairy produce, eggs, fat cattle and sheep, potatoes, etc.), and the rest of the exports are manufactured goods, *e.g.* linen and ships. In contrast, two-thirds of the exports of Eire are of agricultural origin, and counting industrial exports derived mainly from agriculture this rises to over three-quarters, a higher proportion than for any other temperate country except New Zealand. Live animals constitute over one-third of the exports of Eire. With increasing home consumption, Eire's exportable surplus of agricultural products is now decreasing compared to twenty years ago.

Manufactured goods normally make up about 50 per cent. of the imports of both the political divisions of Ireland, and both countries import petroleum, coal, grain, maize, and fertilisers, and tea, sugar, and other products of tropical origin.

Railways of Ireland

Public transport, road and rail, has been nationalised in both Northern Ireland and the Irish Republic. Dublin is the great route centre of the railways of the Irish Republic and Belfast the centre of those of Northern Ireland.

Throughout Ireland, as in Britain, uneconomic rail routes are being closed, and road transport links substituted. Only about one-fifth of the total freight traffic is now carried by the railways, and in Ulster the only freight services are the express routes from Belfast to Londonderry and from Belfast to Dublin.

In the Republic railways radiate from Dublin like the ribs of a fan, southwards to Wexford, south-westwards to Cork and Limerick, westwards to Galway, Westport, and Sligo, and northwards to Belfast. In Northern Ireland a line runs to Belfast, and thence north of Lough Neagh and via the lower Bann valley and the north coast plain to Londonderry.

In addition to the routes given above there is an outer semi-circular route running from Sligo through Athenry, Limerick, and Tipperary to Waterford and Wexford.

The Five Divisions of Ireland

Ireland may be divided into a number of well-defined natural regions (Fig. 1), viz:—

(1) Northern Ireland (as limited by the political boundary).

(2) The mountains of the north and west including the mountains of Donegal, Connemara, and Mayo.

(3) The mountains and vales of the south-west.

(4) The mountains and vales of the south-east.

(5) The Central Plain.

NORTHERN IRELAND

Relief and Occupations

RELIEF. The simplest idea of the relief of Northern Ireland is to regard the lowlands as a cross, with Lough Neagh at the intersection of the two arms. The four lowland arms of the cross are the valleys of the Bann and Blackwater draining into Lough Neagh; of the Bann flowing out on the north; and the valley of the Lagan flowing eastwards from the Mourne Mountains to Belfast Lough (Fig. 118). In the four quadrants are the highland areas, viz:—

(*a*) Between the lower Bann and the Lagan Valley is the Antrim plateau, which is mainly composed of basalt, a black volcanic rock which sometimes splits so as to form hexagonal columns. This is well seen at the Giant's Causeway. Some of the cliff scenery is spectacular, belts of black columnar basalt alternating with layers of white chalk. In some parts of the plateau the chalk is exposed at the surface, and gives rise to typical chalk country, treeless downs, white roads, and sheep rearing. Lough Neagh was formed by the subsidence of a portion of basalt plateau.

(*b*) Between the Lagan and the upper Bann are the Mourne Mountains, composed of rocks similar to those of the Southern Uplands of Scotland. The north-western edge of the Mourne Mountains is a fault line continuous with that of the Dunbar-Girvan fault in Scotland.

(*c*) Between the upper Bann and the Blackwater the hills (Armagh Heights) are lower than, but similar in structure to, the Mourne Mountains.

(*d*) Between the Blackwater and the lower Bann are two distinct areas. The first, immediately north of the Blackwater, is a region of rolling country and low heights mainly composed of limestone and Old Red Sandstone. This region is structurally a continuation of the Scottish rift valley, and there is a small area of exposed coal measures just to the west of the Lough Neagh at Dungannon. Further north are the

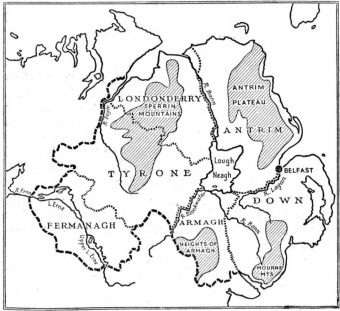

Fig. 118. Northern Ireland, to show the Chief Relief Features and the Six Counties.

Sperrin Mountains, composed of ancient rocks similar to those of the Scottish Highlands.

The western boundary of Northern Ireland is the River Foyle, whose broad vale lies between the Sperrin Mountains and the mountains of Donegal.

Agriculture. The agricultural activities of Northern Ireland may be generalised as sheep rearing on the uplands, and other forms of farming in the river lowlands. Sheep rearing is most important on the uplands of County Down (cf. The Southern Uplands), and on the north of the Antrim plateau, especially where there is chalk downland. Of the cereals, oats are cultivated throughout the lowlands, but the acreage devoted to barley and wheat is almost negligible, and is mainly in the sheltered south-east of County Down (see Figs. 18, 19, and 20). Cattle rearing is important everywhere below 600 ft, but there are a few areas of major importance, viz. the damp lowlands of Fermanagh, the lowlands surrounding Lough Neagh, and in the neighbourhood of Belfast (Island Magee). Cattle rearing for beef is especially important in the sandstone regions of the Lagan Valley (compare the sandstone plains of Eastern Scotland).

Potatoes, and especially seed potatoes, are grown for export. The rearing of poultry and the production of eggs for export is of great importance, especially around Ballynahinch, a town about fifteen miles south of Belfast. On account of the cool summers, fruit growing is relatively unimportant, the largest output being from Armagh. Around Comber, near Belfast, there is some market gardening.

INDUSTRIES. In spite of the absence of adequate supplies of coal and iron, Northern Ireland has two important manufacturing industries, viz. shipbuilding and linen. A more recent industry is aircraft building.

The shipbuilding industry, which specialises in liners and motor ships, is centred at Belfast, supplies of coal and iron ore being obtained from Ayrshire and Lanarkshire.

Northern Ireland is the most important linen-manufacturing district in the British Isles, and its development was due to the local supplies of flax and the fact that the river water is free from lime, a fact important for "retting", *i.e.* the separation of the fibres from the stem by soaking. The industry now relies entirely on imported flax.

The chief centre of the linen industry is Belfast (380,000). It is also to be found in every town and village of Northern Ireland, but notably in the lowlands west of Belfast, at such towns as Lisburn, Lurgan, Newtownards, Portadown, Banbridge, Ballymena, and Larne. In the Foyle Valley,

Londonderry, Lifford, and Strabane are noted for the manufacture of linen garments, *e.g.* shirts.

With the exception of Belfast and Londonderry, the towns engaged in linen manufacturing are all small (comparable in size with small English market towns). None of them has a population greater than about 20,000, so that in this, the greatest manufacturing region of all Ireland, there is a complete absence of the densely-crowded industrial towns such as are associated with the Lancashire cotton industry.

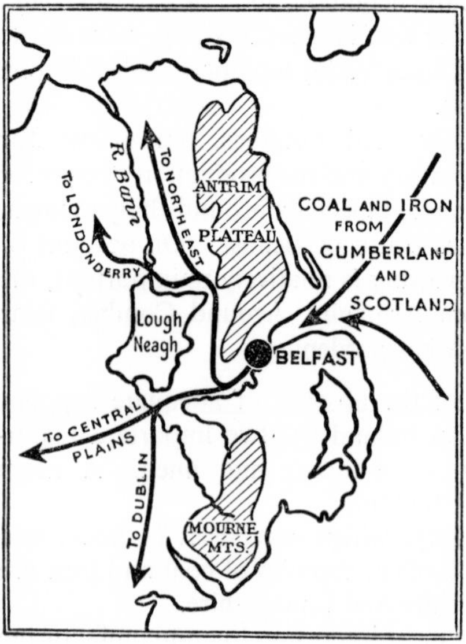

Fig. 119. THE POSITION OF BELFAST.

The linen industry is declining, mainly owing to failing markets because of foreign tariffs and competition from synthetic textiles. Nevertheless, Ulster still exports some £16 million of fine quality linen, largely to the United States. Belfast also manufactures jute and hemp, and distils whiskey. Recent new industries include aircraft and guided missiles, electronic computers, and petroleum refining.

Londonderry, at the lowest bridging point of the River Foyle, is the outlet for dairy produce and linen goods from the Foyle lowlands. It has ship-repairing yards, and manufactures synthetic rubber.

Unemployment has been a problem in Ulster for many years and this has not been helped by the decline in the linen industry. Every effort is therefore being made to encourage new industries. Some of the linen towns are turning also to other textiles, *e.g.* Carrickfergus (rayon), Coleraine (acrilan),

Newtownards (nylon hosiery), Donaghadee (carpets). Northern Ireland now produces one-fifth of the United Kingdom's man-made fibres. Larne has started making turbines and Lurgan (22,000) optical lenses, and food-processing industries such as meat canning are increasing.

Fig. 120.   THE LINEN TOWNS OF NORTHERN IRELAND.

THE IRISH REPUBLIC

The Mountains of the West and North-West

RELIEF AND CLIMATE.   This district includes the mountains of Connemara, Mayo, and Donegal, regions of boggy uplands, and rugged peaks, such as the Twelve Pins of Connemara and Mount Errigal in Donegal.   These mountains are composed of ancient rocks, and are similar in type to the Highlands of Scotland.   They are the regions most remote from contact with modern development (with them in this respect should be included also the western peninsulas of Kerry), and in them the Irish language and Irish customs have survived more strongly than elsewhere. It is here that the descendants of the earliest inhabitants of Britain are to be found.

The exposure to Atlantic winds, hard rocks, thin soils, damp atmosphere, and the remoteness and inaccessibility of these regions have all contributed to their backwardness.

AGRICULTURE AND POPULATION. As in the Scottish Highlands, the population is extremely scanty, much of the highland being uninhabited. Hamlets and small villages are clustered around the coast and in the more fertile valleys (see place facing p. 225). Although the density of population is so low, these districts are often referred to as the "Congested Areas" of Ireland, because the small proportion of cultivable land is insufficient to support the population. The farmer's income is mainly from the sale of calves to the larger farms in the east, for fattening. Pigs and poultry are also kept. The chief crops grown are oats and potatoes. Sheep are reared on the hill slopes and from their wool Irish homespuns and Donegal tweeds are made as cottage industries. Knitting and hand embroidery are carried out largely on a factory basis to-day, in various centres throughout Donegal, while hand-knotted carpets are made at Killybegs. Though much has been done to improve the standard of living, it still remains low, and there is a high percentage of emigration from this region to the industrial areas of Britain and to America. There are no large towns, the chief being Sligo (13,000) and Westport (3,000), where the railways reach the coast, and Donegal (2,000), Letterkenny and Ballina, all of which are market centres.

The Mountains and Vales of South-West Ireland

STRUCTURE AND RELIEF. Structurally, this region is part of the old Armorican system of highlands which is continued in Cornwall and Brittany. The most striking feature of the relief is the series of east to west mountain ranges composed of Old Red Sandstone. The intervening vales are composed of Carboniferous Limestone. Originally, parallel consequent streams* flowed southwards, and lateral east-west tributaries

* See *Foundations of Geography*, Preece and Wood, p. 24.

developed along the limestone vales. As the result of river-capture the present river system has evolved. The rivers Bandon, Lee, Blackwater (and the Suir of the south-eastern region) all flow eastwards in broad longitudinal valleys, but before reaching the sea turn sharply southwards (compare the Wealden rivers, page 179). Wind gaps (the valleys of the original south-flowing stream) notch the sandstone ridges and make communication from Cork northwards, and from valley to valley, relatively easy. Consequently the railway from Cork to Limerick makes use of some of them (*e.g.* the gap at Mallow).

In the west of the region is the high sandstone mass of Macgillycuddy's Reeks, which is a barrier to communication between the coastlands of Kerry and the rest of Ireland. The coastline is of the "ria" type, *i.e.* long drowned valleys separated by hilly peninsulas. This district, like Connemara, Mayo, and Donegal, was until recently very isolated. Much of the highland is inhospitable, boggy, and unproductive, and the population correspondingly scanty. The beauty of the mountain, lake, and coastal scenery, and the mildness of the winters, are making this an increasingly popular tourist region. As in Cornwall, plants characteristic of the Mediterranean grow in the open, because of the absence of frost.

DAIRYING AND AGRICULTURE. The heavy rainfall, warm winters, cool summers, and fertile soil all combine to produce pasture land unsurpassed by that of any other section of the British Isles. For this reason, this area, especially the Golden Vale (see Fig. 121) is the greatest dairy farming region in Ireland. Most of the milk is dealt with by co-operative creameries, cf. Denmark. Since Ireland has not a large population, there is a large surplus of milk which is made into butter and cheese, mainly for export to Britain. The skimmed milk is used for feeding pigs and there are bacon factories at Limerick, Tralee, and Cork. To the north of Cork, most of the cattle are reared for beef while in the uplands, especially in Kerry, sheep are reared. An increasing number of poultry is kept.

County Cork is one of the chief grain producing areas in the Irish Republic. Oats are the chief cereal crop and barley, potatoes, and turnips are grown. Market gardening is increasing in importance in Kerry and West Cork on account of the mild winters which allow the production of early vegetables, cf. Cornwall. Cork (125,000), the second port of the Irish Republic, is a large city situated at the lowest bridging point and head of navigation of the River Lee (see Fig. 121). The lower harbour of Cork, at Cobh (Queenstown) on Great Island, is a calling port for transatlantic liners. Cork exports live cattle, dairy produce, and bacon, and imports large quantities of coal and maize, the latter for the feeding of cattle.

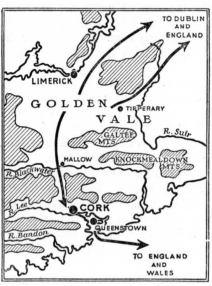

Fig. 121. To show: (*a*) The parallel arrangement of hills and valleys in the hinterland of Cork. (*b*) The gaps in these hills which facilitate communication inland. (*c*) The position of Cork as an export centre for dairy produce from the Golden Vale. (*d*) The relative unimportance of Limerick as a port for the Golden Vale.

It is a cathedral and university town, and is becoming an important industrial centre with steel works, motor car and rubber manufactures, knitwear and ready-made clothing factories and a petroleum refinery, which supplies most of the Republic's needs, in addition to industries associated with agriculture such as milling, milk processing, brewing, and distilling. Killarney (7,000) is an important tourist resort. It also manufactures cranes. Whiddy Island in Bantry Bay is being developed as a one-million-ton storage depot for oil, to be brought in by 300,000-ton tankers.

The other towns of the region such as Tipperary (5,000), Mallow, Mitchelstown, and Tralee (11,000) are mainly market and service centres concerned with food processing.

The Mountains and Vales of the South-East

The south-east of Ireland consists of two regions: (*a*) the Wicklow Mountains, and (*b*) the land drained by the rivers Suir, Nore, Barrow, and Slaney.

(*a*) The Wicklow Mountains, extending from Dublin south-eastwards, are high mountains similar in structure to the Welsh Mountains. They rise to over 3,000 ft (Lugnaquilla 3,039 ft), and are dissected by U-shaped valleys, often containing ribbon lakes such as those at Glendalough. These uplands are one of the most important sheep rearing areas in Ireland (see Fig. 25), the sheep being brought down to the lowlands in winter. In the sheltered valleys mixed agriculture is practised. The largest town of this area is Bray (13,000), an important tourist resort.

(*b*) The remainder of the south-east is a rich agricultural region. As in the rest of Ireland, cattle rearing, both for meat and milk, is the main type of farming. Much of the meat is exported through Dublin and Waterford, while the milk is sent to co-operative creameries, or in the north to supply the Dublin market. Pigs and poultry are also reared. Because of the higher summer temperatures and the low rainfall, this region is the most important in Ireland for the cultivation of cereals especially wheat, oats, and barley. Root crops are also important, being used mainly as foodstuffs, and some sugar-beet is grown. An increasing amount of small fruits and vegetables are being produced.

The most extensive coal deposits in Ireland occur between the Nore and Barrow valleys but the output is small and there is no important industrial development. Most of the towns, such as Kilkenny (11,000), Carlow, Enniscorthy, New Ross, and Clonmel (10,000), are market centres whose industries are largely associated with agriculture, *e.g.* flour milling, meat canning, tanning, brewing, woollen manufacture. Wexford (13,000), on the Slaney, is a small port and manufactures a variety of iron goods including agricultural machinery.

Waterford (30,000) on the Suir, is also a port handling mainly agricultural products. In addition to agricultural manufactures, there is a glassworks which specialises in high quality cut glass production.

The Central Plain

STRUCTURE AND RELIEF. The Central Plain is a low plain, rarely rising to 300 ft, covering the whole of Central Ireland and extending to the east coast between the Wicklow Mountains and the Mourne Mountains, and to the west coast at several points where there are breaks in the coastal mountains, at Limerick, Galway, and Sligo. A geological map shows that this plain is almost entirely composed of Carboniferous Limestone. This is misleading, for, except to the west of the River Shannon, the limestone rarely appears at the surface, but is covered by a thick mantle of glacial clays (cf. the pasture lands of Cheshire) and of peat.

A large portion of the plain is drained by the River Shannon, but much of the eastern half of the plain is badly drained. Around the headwaters of the Brosna and the Boyne in the counties of West Meath and Offaly are extensive bog lands. The greatest difficulty of the bog lands is communication and many of the original roads keep to the crests of low, elongated glacial ridges (called eskers) which rise above the level of the bogs. An almost unbroken line of eskers extends westwards from Dublin across the plain, giving that city a natural line of communication with its hinterland.

AGRICULTURE. The damp lowlands of the Central Plain give rise to excellent cattle pasture. In this region the emphasis is on beef cattle. The farms to the west of the Shannon are small, generally less than twenty acres, and these breed calves which are sold at the many cattle fairs throughout the country. These calves are brought to the eastern part of the Central Plain for fattening prior to export. The farms here are relatively large and therefore more suitable for this purpose than those in the west. Half a million live cattle are exported annually through Dublin and other east coast ports to England.

Dairying and market gardening are important in the immediate hinterland of Dublin, cf. other large cities in the British Isles. Sheep are reared for mutton in the drier areas to the north of this region and in the east of County Galway where the limestone is drift-free. Poultry farming is also important. In County Kildare, especially near the Curragh race course, horses are bred.

Throughout the plain, potatoes are an important crop due to the clayey soils but particularly in the west where it is too wet for cereals. Oats and root crops are grown in the east around Dublin and in County Meath.

Fig. 122. The Position of Dublin.

The towns here are mainly market centres concerned with the processing of agricultural produce, *e.g.* Athlone (11,000), Longford, Mullingar, Ballinasloe, Tullamore, etc., though some have manufacturing industries as well, such as carpets and furniture at Navan and cutlery and rope at Newbridge.

Dublin (570,000). At the lowest bridging point of the Liffey and one of the few ports of the east coast, Dublin is the natural outlet of the Central Plain. Its position is convenient to trade with Britain through Liverpool (see Fig. 122), while it is the focus of routes from all parts of Ireland. It was originally a Norse settlement built on two low hills which afforded dry ground. To-day, Dublin is the seat of government and administrative centre and is an important ecclesiastical centre. It is also a great cultural centre with two universities. Like most capital cities, other than those, such as Washington and Canberra, specially laid out as government centres, it has numerous and varied industries including the manufacture of beer, whiskey, biscuits, clothing, and tobacco as well as motor car assembly and light engineering works, and a range of other light industries. Dublin airport, like those at Belfast and Cork, is mainly concerned with services to Britain and the Continent.

LIMERICK (51,000) is situated at the lowest bridging point of the Shannon but, as a port, it is overshadowed by Dublin and Cork because of their proximity to Britain. However, several routes converge here and Limerick's main function is as a market centre. Its industries are largely based on agriculture, *e.g.* flour milling, bacon curing, fertiliser manufacture, milk processing, and tanning, but it also manufactures clothing and cement while its hand-made lace is world-famous. Fifteen miles west of Limerick lies Shannon Airport. As well as the airport handling several transatlantic flights daily, an industrial estate has been established, producing lightweight, high value goods for export by air. Being within the customs free zone, this estate functions in the same way as a free seaport, and is in fact the first industrial estate of its kind in the world. Shannon handles about five per cent. of all the Republic's exports.

GALWAY (26,000) used to function as a port trading with Spain and North America but this has declined owing to the unsuitable harbour and to-day the port is used only by a few fishing boats and the steamer which plies between Galway and the Aran Isles, thirty miles west. To-day, Galway acts as a market centre, supplying goods to rural areas rather than processing products. It is a university city but its greatest importance, together with its twin settlement of Salthill, is as a tourist centre.

DUNDALK (22,000) and Drogheda (18,000) are also ports on the east coast, importing coal and manufactured goods from England, and are small industrial towns manufacturing such things as beer, tobacco, footwear, etc. Cement manufacture is important in Drogheda.

CHAPTER 27

FOREIGN TRADE, POWER, POPULATION

Foreign Trade

The United Kingdom is, after Holland, the most densely-populated country in the world, and only about half of the food we require can be produced at home. We are able to buy the other food we need because we are a nation of manufacturers and sell large quantities of manufactured goods to other countries. Not only do we have to import food but also much of the raw materials required for our manufactures, *e.g.* wool, cotton, rubber, iron ore, and many other things. Consider the summary table of imports and exports below.

SUMMARY OF TRADE 1970

	Imports (£M)	Exports (£M)
Food and Drink, Tobacco	2,052	515
Raw Materials and Fuel	2,310	480
Manufactures	4,580	6,808
Miscellaneous	110	261
Total	9,052	8,063

It will be noted that food and drink, and raw materials and fuel, each make up about one-quarter of the total imports. The manufactured goods that make up the remainder of our imports cover a very wide range of articles and no one class of article greatly predominates.

Our exports, on the other hand, consist almost entirely of manufactured articles (about 85 per cent.). Raw materials exported are about 6 per cent. Food and drink exported includes such items as cocoa and chocolates, biscuits, and especially whisky (£211 million), the last named being our principal export to the United States (£104 million). A more detailed table showing our chief imports and exports is given on page 256.

Our best customers in 1970 were the United States (12 per cent. of our total exports), Western Germany (6 per cent.), the Netherlands, the Irish Republic, Sweden, and Australia (4½ per cent. each), France and South Africa (4 per cent. each). The chief sources of our imports were the United States (13 per cent.), Canada (7½ per cent.), Western Germany (6 per cent.), the Netherlands (5 per cent.), Sweden, France, and the Irish Republic (4 per cent. each), and Denmark, Australia, and South Africa (3 per cent. each).

Not so very many years ago the other members of the Commonwealth provided half our imports and took half our exports. This proportion has been falling steadily in recent

TRADE OF THE UNITED KINGDOM 1970

Principal Imports (in £ millions)		**Principal Exports** (in £ millions)	
Petroleum	925	Machinery	1,642
Non-ferrous metals ..	609	Vehicles, ships, and aircraft	1,080
Meat	438	Chemicals	786
Fruit and vegetables ..	380	Electrical goods	579
Cereals and feeding stuffs..	371	Iron and steel	348
Beverages and cocoa ..	289	Beverages	245
Timber	239	Petroleum products ..	176
Wood pulp and paper ..	198	Clothing, footwear	159
Dairy produce	186	Woollen goods	115
Iron ore and scrap iron ..	113	Paper..	89
Tobacco	110	Rayon goods	85
Wool	96	Cotton goods	45
Cotton	50	Coal	29
Rubber	58	Miscellaneous manufactures	572
Total Imports	**9,052**	**Total Exports**	**8,063**

years and is now down to little more than one-fifth. On the other hand, our trade with the countries of Western Europe, and especially with the countries of the Common Market (France, Western Germany, Italy, Belgium, the Netherlands, and Luxemburg) has increased markedly. In 1970, the countries of the Common Market took 20 per cent. of our exports and provided about 21 per cent. of our imports. The countries of E.F.T.A., the European Free Trading Association (Norway, Sweden, Denmark, Finland, Austria, and Switzerland) took nearly 16 per cent. of our exports and provided nearly 15 per cent. of our imports.

Britain was the first country in the world to develop large-scale industries, and hence to be able to export large amounts of manufactured goods which other countries were unable to make for themselves. For many years before the war, however, British exports had been decreasing. Although Britain

SOURCES OF OUR CHIEF IMPORTS

Wheat: Canada (55%).
Australia.
U.S.A.

Sugar: Mauritius (25%).
Australia.
Jamaica.
Fiji.

Tea: India (35%).
Ceylon (30%).
Kenya.

Coffee: Uganda (30%).
Brazil (25%).
Kenya.

Cocoa: Ghana (60%).
Nigeria (30%).

Beef: Argentine (55%).
Uruguay.
Australia.
Eire (live cattle).

Bacon: Denmark (75%).
Poland.
Eire.

Mutton: New Zealand (90%).
Australia.

Petroleum: Libya (20%).
Kuwait (20%).
Saudi Arabia.
Iran.

Butter: New Zealand (30%).
Denmark (25%).
Australia (15%).

Cheese: New Zealand (35%).
Irish Republic (15%).
Australia.
Denmark.

Wool: Australia (40%).
New Zealand (20%).

Cotton: U.S.A. (20%).
Sudan (12%).
Turkey (12%).

Flax: Belgium.

Rubber: Malaya (50%).
Canada (8%).
U.S.A. (8%).

Timber: U.S.S.R. (20%).
Sweden (20%).
Finland.
Canada (20%).

Iron Ore: Canada (25%).
Norway.
Liberia.

Tin: Bolivia (80%).

Tobacco: U.S.A. (50%).
Canada.
India.

had a big start as an industrial nation, other nations had begun to develop their own industries and thus to supply themselves with the kind of goods which hitherto they had bought from us, and even to out-sell us in other markets as well. Every country tries to develop its own industries because they provide additional employment and the value of the output per worker from industry is usually much greater than that from agriculture or even mining. The greater the value of the goods produced by a country, the more money its citizens can earn, and hence the higher their standard of living.

The United States, France, Germany, and Belgium, were among the first to become industrialised. More recently the same thing has been happening in Asian countries such as Japan, India, and China, and in the Commonwealth, especially Canada, and elsewhere. In many cases factories were equipped with machinery bought from Britain. The low standard of living in some countries, especially in Asia and hence the cheapness of the labour, has enabled these countries in some cases to sell textiles and other manufactures at a lower price than we can do ourselves, although this tends to be true only for cheaper qualities (see page 122).

Half a century ago when our manufactures had to withstand but little competition from other countries, cotton and woollen textiles,

Fig. 123.   THE COAL-EXPORTING AREAS.

machinery, ships, and coal, accounted for a very large proportion of our total exports. While these are still important items in our list of exports (page 256), with the exception of machinery they no longer occupy the commanding position they once did. A number of new industries have developed based on modern scientific discovery and invention: the manufacture of cars, trucks, aircraft, of artificial or synthetic fibres, such as rayon and nylon, the electrical industry, including telegraphy, wireless, television, and radar, and the chemical industry, including fine chemicals, dyes, plastics, drugs, synthetic fertilisers, pesticides, etc. In these and many similar fields British scientific skill has led to the development of new industries providing employment for our people and producing goods which overseas countries are willing to buy. The economic importance to our country of such discoveries and inventions as nuclear power, radar, penicillin, and jet-aircraft engines, will be clear. The future of our export trade seems to lie increasingly with such new industries and with the success of our scientists in keeping in the van of progress, which involves the spending of very large sums of money on research and on the development of new ideas.

As an example of a new large-scale industry in this country we may take petroleum refining. Refined petroleum costs much more than crude oil. Until recently nearly all the oil we used was refined where it was produced. We have now built in the United Kingdom a number of large refineries, *e.g.* the plant at Fawley near Southampton, the largest in Europe, which in all are capable of refining over one hundred million tons of oil, much more than our total consumption in 1950. There are now large refineries at Shellhaven and Coryton in Essex, on the Isle of Grain, at Llandarcy and Milford Haven in South Wales, at Stanlow on Merseyside, at Heysham, at Grangemouth, and at Belfast. During the refining of petroleum a variety of valuable by-products can be obtained for use in our chemical industries, and in 1970 we exported nearly £175 million worth of refined petroleum products, besides obtaining large quantities of raw materials for the manufacture of synthetic detergents, certain plastics, synthetic fibres such as "terylene", synthetic rubber, and so on.

In the case of older industries, such as textiles, there is an increasing tendency to specialise for export in high quality goods, in the manufacture of which our technical skill and long experience are valuable assets.

Sixty years ago the U.K. exported over ninety million tons of coal a year (see pages 77-8), worth about £600 million at present prices. But between the wars the trade declined, partly owing to the increased use of oil in ships and factories, partly owing to the development of hydro-electric power, *e.g.* in Sweden and Italy, and partly to the development of new mines in countries, *e.g.* Australia and South Africa, which had previously imported from us.   Overseas markets once lost are not easily regained and more recently demand has itself fallen, both at home and abroad, mainly owing to the increased use of fuel oil for heat and power.   Our present export is only about 3 million tons a year.   It seems, at any rate for the present, as if we are now over-producing coal.

Invisible Exports

It will be seen from the table on page 255 that we had in 1970 an adverse balance of trade of £989 million, *i.e.* we imported goods worth £989 million more than we exported. At first sight, therefore, it would appear that we had been living greatly above our means and were not paying our way. But certain other factors have to be taken into account, factors often referred to as *invisible exports.*

Our imports are valued at the British port of entry.   A part of this value represents the cost of shipping the goods to us, and has to be paid not to the country from which the goods came but to the country whose ships carried them.   The United Kingdom has the largest merchant fleet in the world, nearly one-fifth of the total world shipping, and carries about half our imports.

Our exports are likewise valued at the British port of exit. Our overseas customers have to pay the cost of shipping, again about half to British companies.   And our ships also carry much foreign merchandise from one foreign port to another.   The earnings of our shipping vary somewhat from year to year, but in 1968 were over £900 million and represent an invisible export.

In the days when we were a great manufacturing country with few competitors, we acquired great wealth, some of which we used to make investments in foreign countries.   During the War of 1939-45 we had to sell these foreign investments worth about £4,000 million and use the money so obtained to buy food and munitions.   During the last twenty years, however, we have invested some £3,000 million abroad and the income from this represents an invisible export of about £1,100 million considerably offset, however, by the interest we have to pay foreign countries for the money they invest in the U.K.

There are other invisible exports such as the payment for various business services we undertake for foreign countries particularly insurance (mainly fire and marine insurance), the financing of international trade, and the overseas earnings of British oil companies and air lines.

Money spent in this country by foreign tourists (nearly £300 million) is another invisible export, slightly more than that spent abroad by our own tourists.

Only when all these invisible exports and various other adjustments, such as government expenditure abroad, are taken into account can we find whether the total amount due to us from foreign countries in a given year exceeded that which we owed to them, *i.e.* whether we had a favourable *Balance of Payments*.

During the War of 1939-45 we had a very large adverse balance of payments and it was not until 1950 that, by increasing our exports and restricting our imports of consumable goods we were able to show a favourable balance of payments. Although we have had unfavourable balances in 1964, 1965, 1967, and 1968, over the seventeen years 1954-70, we have had favourable balances ten times and unfavourable balances seven times.

Power in Britain

For a century and a half, England's success as an industrial nation has largely been based on her good supplies of coal, which have been used to produce steam power. Other conditions, are, of course, essential for the success of any industry such as the supply of raw materials, good communications, good markets, and good labour supply. To-day, through the great development of world-wide communications, raw materials are almost equally available to every nation, and it seems that, in the near future, the most successful manufacturing countries will be those that have the cheapest and most efficient power supplies.

The present age is seeing a great development of electricity, and, if economically produced, this is a very cheap form of power. It is, moreover, very convenient in use, and it can be transmitted considerable distances, so that a large area can be supplied by a suitable network of cables (a "grid"). Electricity, however, has to be generated from other sources of power—coal, petroleum, natural gas, nuclear energy, or falling water. Falling water can be used to drive dynamos and electricity produced in this way is referred to as hydro-electricity. Coal, petroleum, and natural gas can be burned to produce steam, which can also drive dynamos. Electricity produced from dynamos driven in this way is called thermal electricity. Nuclear energy is also converted into electricity by way of steam power so this electricity is thermal electricity but it is usual to refer to it separately as nuclear power.

Very wet and mountainous countries, such as Norway, Sweden, and Switzerland, have the best natural advantages for the development of hydro-electric power. In Great Britain there are few large waterfalls, and, although the mountainous areas have a heavy rainfall, they are not very high, so that, as far as hydro-electric power is concerned, we cannot hope to compete with countries such as Switzerland. In Britain about 85 per cent. of our electricity is thermal, generated by using about 50 million tons of home-produced coal and 10 million tons of imported oil. Our thirteen nuclear power stations between them account for nearly one-eighth of our electricity, while the hydro-electric station in the north of Scotland, together with a few in South-West Scotland and North Wales, altogether supply only one-fiftieth, so that about two-thirds of our electricity is generated from coal.

Britain was the first country to plan the large-scale industrial generation of electricity from nuclear energy and up to the present we have produced as much electricity this way as all the rest of the world put together. Our rate of production is still increasing but it now seems likely that the originally planned rate of increase may be slowed down because of the discovery within the last four or five years of large amounts of natural gas in the North Sea off the coasts of Yorkshire and East Anglia.

This gas is being piped ashore and fed into a "grid" of underground pipes and will in due course be available in almost all parts. It is expected that in the early 1970's this natural gas will supply 10 per cent. of our total energy requirements. This natural gas is by far the cheapest form of energy available although for the present the Government, as part of its overall fuel policy, is selling it to the consumer at getting on for ten times its raw cost.

So far as we in Britain are concerned, in the changing pattern of fuel use this century, the sole loser has been coal. The change over of ocean-going vessels to oil burning has almost wiped out our ships' bunker trade. Our export trade is negligible because our former customers have either (as in Australia) developed their own source of fuel or (as in Western Europe) increasingly use other forms of energy. Our railways no longer use solid fuels and oil has also made inroads on domestic heating.

In 1913 our coal production was 287 million tons, in 1956, 214 million tons, in 1968, 164 million tons, and it is expected to be about 156 million tons in 1970. In many of our old pits the most easily won coal has already been mined and what is left is much more expensive to produce. The National Coal Board is proposing to close about one-third of all our present pits and concentrate production on the newer, larger, and more mechanised pits where the coal can be mined much more cheaply. This considerable shrinkage of one of our large industries presents a major social, as well as economic, problem and one that affects more than the coal-mining industry itself.

The replacement of coal by electricity in large industrial areas will mean that the air will be purer and more free from the smoke which at present pollutes it. The cleaner and clearer atmosphere must inevitably have a beneficial effect on the health, efficiency, and contentment of workers in large urban areas. The availability of supplies of electricity is leading to the greater development of manufacturing industries, and particularly light industries, in districts not on the coalfields. This is especially noticeable in South-East England and the Midlands.

In 1970, our fuel requirements were supplied as follows (values in equivalent amounts of coal in millions of tons):

coal 156, oil (almost all of it imported) 145, hydro-electricity 2·2, nuclear energy 11, natural gas 16.

Distribution of Population

In 1801 the population of England and Wales was 8,892,536. One hundred and sixty years later, at the Census of 1961, it was 46,071,604, and increasing at the rate of about 230,000 a year.   The average population is 790 to the square mile, which is the highest population density for any country in the world with the exception of the Netherlands and Mauritius.   The population of Scotland has increased from 1,608,420 in 1801 to 5,178,490 in 1961 with a density of 174 to the square mile. During the last twenty-five years the population of the United Kingdom has increased by six million or by about 1 in 8.

Not only has the population of Great Britain increased rapidly, but great changes have taken place in the distribution of the people.

Before the Industrial Revolution, when England was mainly an agricultural country, the majority of the inhabitants lived in the fertile lowlands which lie south of the Pennines and east of Wales, and the greatest centres of population were around London and Bristol.

The Industrial Revolution caused a great movement of people from country districts to towns, and, in particular, to the great new towns of the coalfields.   This meant that the centres of densest population moved from South-Eastern England to Northern England and South Wales.   Although the south-eastern plains are more densely populated now than they were in 1801, they now contain a smaller proportion of the total population than they did in 1801.

The last thirty years or so has seen a new trend.   The great trade depression of the early 1930's hit the industrial areas of Wales and the North of England very hard, and between 1931 and 1951 the population of South Wales, South-East Lancashire, and Durham actually decreased despite the fact that England and Wales, as a whole, increased by about 4 million.   The greatest increases in population were seen in the South-East, whose newer industries were better able to withstand the depression.   Dagenham in Essex, a new town engaged in motor car manufacture, increased from 9,000 in 1921 to 89,000 in 1931 and 114,000 in 1951. On the other hand, the population of the administrative County of London has fallen by nearly one-third since 1931 and is still falling. However, this is not because of any fall in industrial activity but because improvements in public transport and the increased use of cars has enabled many people to live further from their work. The decrease in population shown in the 1961 Census for other big cities such as Birmingham, Glasgow, Liverpool, and Manchester is probably due to the same cause.

The population of England and Wales increased by two million, or 5 per cent., between 1951 and 1961, including a net immigration of 352,000, largely West Indians. But all the great conurbations show increases less than the national average (although in the case of the West Midlands only slightly so), as do the London region and all other regions except the Midlands, East, South-East, South, and South-West, which have increases greater than the national average. Thus, on balance the migration of people from the older industrial areas of the north to the newer industries further south is still continuing.

Only three English counties actually decreased in population between 1951 and 1961—the counties of London, Middlesex, and Cornwall. The population of the administrative County of London decreased by well over one million over the last thirty years. In Wales, Pembrokeshire, Glamorgan, and Monmouth, in the south, together with Cardigan, Anglesey, and Flint, all show increases, while all the hill counties show decreases. Even for the former group, however, the increases are less than the excess of births over deaths, showing that on balance people are moving away.

Industrial counties, such as Lancashire, Glamorgan, Warwickshire, Durham, and Staffordshire have more than 1,000 persons per square mile, as have the counties of Essex, Kent, Surrey, Hertfordshire, and Middlesex, which are adjacent to the London area. Cheshire, too, with its many industries, its agriculture, and residential areas for Lancashire, comes within this group, as does Nottinghamshire.

Counties that have much agricultural land, but which have some industrial areas or are near large population centres, have a density varying from 500 to 1,000 people per square mile. Included in this group are such counties as Sussex, Monmouth, Worcestershire, Hampshire, Leicestershire, Berkshire, Gloucestershire, Derbyshire, and Bedfordshire.

The counties mainly dependent on agriculture only have under 500 per square mile (average 300-350). Examples are Dorsetshire, Cambridgeshire, Somerset, Devonshire.

Finally, the very mountainous counties have less than 100 people per square mile. The only English county with such a low average is Westmorland, but it is true of many of the Welsh counties, and of the mountainous counties of Scotland. In these areas the land is too unproductive to support a flourishing agricultural population. Radnorshire has an average less than forty persons per square mile, and the population of the whole county is about the same as that of an English market town. Anglesey has 52,000 inhabitants, and an average density of 187 per square mile. It is, for Wales, a well-populated county, yet there are in England and Wales 184 towns which contain more than 50,000 people including the "New Towns" of Basildon, Crawley, Harlow, and Hemel Hempstead, and nearly seventy of these contain more than 100,000 people (see page 268).

Large industrial areas usually spread over parts of more than one county and we shall therefore be able to appreciate better the relative importance of the main areas, or *conurbations* as they are sometimes called, from the table on page 268.

It will be noted that London has a population as large as all the industrial areas of the North and Midlands combined, and that, with the exception of the West Midlands, all these areas have increased in population at a rate less than the average for the whole country (5·2 per cent.).

The table on page 269 shows the chief occupations of our population. Notice the large proportion (over 45 per cent.) of essential but non-productive occupations—professional and financial services, distributive trades, transport and communications, and public administration. There are nearly a quarter of a million teachers, for example, and half a million engaged in road transport.

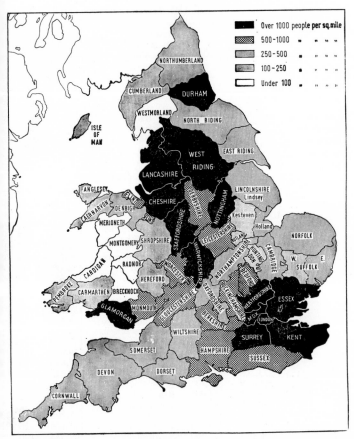

Fig. 124. ENGLAND AND WALES—DENSITY OF POPULATION BY COUNTIES (1961).

The numbers engaged in cotton, woollen, and rayon manufactures are approximately as 3 : 2 : 1. In the engineering group we have 300,000 engaged in making cars and cycles, 150,000 on aircraft, and 200,000 on ships.

AREA AND POPULATION OF THE MAIN CONURBATIONS, 1961

	POPULATION	INCREASE OR DECREASE SINCE 1951 (per cent.)	AREA (square miles)	DENSITY (per square mile)
Greater London	8,172,000	− 2·1	670	12,200
S.E. Lancashire	2,427,000	+ 0·2	380	6,400
W. Midlands ..	2,344,000	+ 4·6	269	8,700
W. Yorkshire ..	1,703,000	+ 0·6	481	3,500
Merseyside ..	1,386,000	0·0	147	9,400
Clydeside ..	1,081,850	+ 2·4	324	3,300
Tyneside ..	852,000	+ 2·0	90	9,500

POPULATION OF CHIEF TOWNS

	1961	1951		1961	1951
London	3,195,114	3,348,336	West Ham ..	157,186	170,98
Birmingham ..	1,105,651	1,112,340	Salford	154,963	178,03
Glasgow	1,054,913	1,089,555	Bournemouth ..	153,965	144,72
Liverpool.. ..	747,490	789,532	Blackpool ..	152,133	147,13
Manchester ..	661,041	703,175	Hendon	151.500	155,83
Dublin	550,000*	537,600	Wolverhampton	150,385	162,66
Leeds	510,597	504,954	Stockport ..	142,469	141,66
Sheffield	493,954	512,834	Birkenhead ..	141,683	142,39.
Edinburgh ..	468,378	466,770	Derby	132,325	141,26
Bristol	436,440	442,281	Luton	131.505	110,37
Belfast	435,000*	444,000	Huddersfield ..	130,302	129,02
Teesside	392,000*		Hornchurch ..	128,127	104,09.
Nottingham ..	311,645	306,008	Wembley	124,843	131,36
Coventry	305,060	258,211	Norwich	119,904	121,22
Hull	303,268	299,068	Reading	119,870	114,17
Bradford	295,768	292,394	Walsall	117,836	114,57
Leicester	273,298	285,061	Ipswich	117,325	104,78
Newcastle ..	269,389	291,723	Oldham	115,426	121,21
Stoke-on-Trent	265,506	275,095	Romford	114,579	88,00.
Cardiff	256,270	243,627	Thurrock.. ..	114,302	82,10.
Croydon	252,387	249,592	Preston	113,208	119,24
Portsmouth ..	215,198	233,464	Tottenham ..	113,126	126,92
Harrow	208,963	219,463	South Shields ..	109,533	106,598
Southampton ..	204,707	178,326	Walthamstow ..	108,788	121,069
Plymouth.. ..	204,279	208,985	Dagenham ..	108,363	114,55
Sunderland ..	189,629	181,575	St Helens.. ..	108,348	110,27
Aberdeen.. ..	185,379	163,252	Newport	108,107	106,42
Ealing	183,151	187,306	Oxford	106,124	98,747
Dundee	182,959	177,333	Blackburn ..	106,114	111,217
Ilford	178,210	184,707	Northampton ..	105,361	104,429
Willesden.. ..	170,835	179,647	East Ham ..	105,359	120,873
Swansea	166,740	160,832	York..	104,468	105,419
Southend.. ..	164,976	151,830	Gateshead ..	103,232	115,017
Brighton	162,757	156,440	Wallasey	103,213	101,369
Bolton	160,887	167,162			

* estimated

CHIEF OCCUPATIONS, 1970

	Millions	% of total
Total Working Population	25·2	100·0
Professional and Financial Services	3·7	14·5
Engineering, Shipbuilding, and Vehicles	3·4	12·4
Distributive	2·7	10·7
Other Services	1·9	7·4
Miscellaneous Manufactures	1·6	6·4
Transport and Communication	1·6	6·1
Public Administration	1·4	5·5
Building and Construction	1·3	5·2
Food, Drink, and Tobacco	0·8	3·4
Textiles	0·7	2·6
Paper, Printing, and Publishing	0·6	2·6
Chemicals	0·5	1·9
Clothing and Shoes	0·5	1·9
Mining and Quarrying	0·4	1·7
Agriculture and Fisheries	0·4	1·6
Gas, Water, and Electricity	0·4	1·6
Armed Forces	0·4	1·5

QUESTIONS

1. Enumerate the geographical factors which may have contributed to the advance of the British Isles.

2. Make a sketch-map of the chalk and limestone belts of South-East England. Name the chief hill systems, mark the scarp slopes, and insert the names of the chief mining and quarrying districts.

3. Suggest reasons for the development of industries in the south of England during recent years.

4. Compare climatic conditions in (a) Cornwall and Lincoln, (b) Cumberland and Kent.

5. Explain the meaning of the following terms: secondary depressions, rain-shadow, anticyclones, insular climate.

6. Draw temperature and rainfall graphs to represent conditions in the four climatic quadrants of the British Isles:—

		J.	F.	M.	A.	M.	J.
Temp. °C.	A. Cambridge	3·1	3·9	5·5	8·3	11·2	14·9
	B. Valentia	7·0	6·5	7·4	9·2	11·2	13·8
	C. Nairn	3·0	3·2	4·3	6·7	9·4	12·6
	D. Fort William	3·7	3·8	4·7	7·3	9·8	13·0

		J.	A.	S.	O.	N.	D.
Temp. °C.	A. Cambridge	16·8	16·4	13·9	9·4	5·9	3·3
	B. Valentia	15·0	15·2	11·6	10·7	8·7	7·4
	C. Nairn	14·1	13·7	11·6	7·7	5·0	3·1
	D. Fort William	13·9	13·6	11·8	8·1	7·8	4·5

		J.	F.	M.	A.	M.	J.
Temp. °F.	A. Cambridge	37·5	39·0	41·9	47·0	52·2	58·8
	B. Valentia	44·6	43·8	45·4	48·5	52·2	56·9
	C. Nairn	37·4	37·7	39·8	44·1	49·0	54·7
	D. Fort William	38·7	38·8	40·4	45·1	49·7	55·4

		J.	A.	S.	O.	N.	D.
Temp. °F.	A. Cambridge	62·4	61·5	57·1	48·9	42·6	38·0
	B. Valentia	59·0	59·3	56·6	51·3	47·6	45·4
	C. Nairn	57·4	56·7	52·9	46·0	41·0	37·5
	D. Fort William	57·1	56·5	53·2	46·6	44·0	40·1

		J.	F.	M.	A.	M.	J.
Rainfall in Inches	A. Cambridge	1·5	1·4	1·3	1·5	1·9	2·2
	B. Valentia	5·6	4·9	4·1	3·9	3·1	3·5
	C. Nairn	2·0	1·8	1·9	1·5	1·8	1·8
	D. Fort William	8·7	6·9	7·0	4·0	3·5	3·5

		J.	A.	S.	O.	N.	D.
Rainfall in Inches	A. Cambridge	2·5	2·4	2·0	2·4	2·0	1·6
	B. Valentia	3·7	5·1	4·6	5·5	5·5	6·5
	C. Nairn	2·7	2·4	2·2	2·3	2·4	2·2
	D. Fort William	4·6	6·9	8·2	7·9	7·5	11·3

7. Account for the summer maximum of rainfall in South-East England.

8. How may the work of local government benefit from the possession of accurate and detailed rainfall statistics of an area?

9. What do you understand by the terms:—mixed farming, permanent grassland, crop-rotation, and intensive farming?

10. Compare and contrast the farming activities in—

(*a*) Cheshire and Cambridge;

(*b*) Somerset and Kent.

11. What are the chief developments in recent years in the farming activities of England? Give examples.

12. Trace outline maps of Cornwall and Devon and indicate—

(*a*) the physical features;

(*b*) summer and winter isotherms and annual rainfall;

(*c*) products;

(*d*) towns and rail communications.

13. Draw a sketch-map of Somerset, and on it summarise the chief facts given in the text.

14. Describe the position of Bristol, account for its growth and importance in comparison with Liverpool.

15. On a map of Wales insert the chief rivers and show how the main railways make use of these valleys and the coastal plains.

16. Account for the decline in coal exports from the British Isles.

17. Give in tabular form the main sources of supply of the metals used in the smelting industries of South Wales. Name the ports of export.

18. Illustrate by a sketch-map the statement that "The Cumbrian Mountains form a dome-shaped area from which the rivers drain radially". Name the rivers, the chief lakes, and routes.

19. It has been suggested that a direct motor road across Morecambe Bay should be made to connect the Cumberland coalfield with North Lancashire. What advantages would accrue from such an undertaking?

20. Compare and contrast the industrial activities of Cumberland and Northumberland.

21. Explain why the city of Durham has not developed along the same lines as Newcastle.

22. Draw a sketch-map of Northumberland and Durham, marking the 1,000-ft contour, the chief rivers, extent of coalfield, chief coal ports, and industrial centres.

23. Explain why the York, Derby, and Nottingham coalfield has the greatest output of any British coalfield.

24. Account for the development of the Yorkshire woollen industry.

25. Trace the development of the metallurgical industries of the Sheffield area.

26. Draw sketch-maps to illustrate the position of Derby, Nottingham, and Leicester.

27. Give an account of the farming activities of Yorkshire.

28. Indicate on a sketch-map the five regions of Lincolnshire. Mark the positions of the chief industrial centres.

29. Describe the east coast of England between the Tees and the Wash, accounting for variations.

30. Account for the development of any three industries connected with the Lancashire coalfield.

31. Draw a sketch-map of the Manchester Ship Canal indicating the industrial towns it serves.

32. In which parts of the British Isles are salt deposits worked? Give a list of the various industries dependent upon the salt industry.

33. Compare the positions and trade of Liverpool and Hull. Give sketch-maps.

34. Draw a sketch-map of the physical features of the Central Plain of England.

35. Describe the position of Birmingham and account for the varied nature of the city's industries.

36. On a large map of Central England mark the extent of the Midland coalfields, naming the chief towns and the industries connected with each.

37. Define the extent of the Fenlands and account for their formation.

38. "Luton is typical of many towns in Southern England which have attracted new industries." Find six other towns which could be included in such a list and state the industries which have been developed.

39. Compare the Fenlands and the Plain of Somerset as regards physical features, climate, occupations, and sites of settlements.

40. "The manufactures of East Anglia are based upon the farming activities of the region." To what extent is this true?

41. On a map of East Anglia mark distinctively—

> (*a*) the chief fishing ports;
> (*b*) the chief ferry ports;
> (*c*) the county towns;
> (*d*) the manufacturing centres.

42. Explain why the towns and ports of East Anglia are not to-day as important as they were in the Middle Ages.

43. Draw a map of the Thames Basin and divide it into five main regions. Give a brief description of any two of the regions.

44. Show how farming activities vary within the Thames Basin with soil conditions.

45. Compare the sites of Swindon and Crewe as centres for the railway systems they serve.

46. Name the countries of origin and the ports of export of the commodities named on page 174.

47. What are the advantages and disadvantages of the concentration of population and industries around London?

48. What is meant by entrepôt trade? Give three examples of ports in other continents which depend on this type of trade for much of their commerce.

49. Trace the changes which have occurred in the location of the English iron industries from the days of the Wealden industry.

50. Draw a sketch-map to illustrate the position of Canterbury.

51. Mark on a map of the English coast, between the Humber and the Solent, the chief routes linking Great Britain and the Continent.

52. Show on a sketch-map the convergence of roads upon Salisbury and Winchester.

53. Compare the farming activities carried on in the Hampshire and London Basins.

54. Compare the advantages of Southampton and Liverpool—
        (*a*) as passenger ports;
        (*b*) as cargo ports.

55. Compare the plains of Galloway and the Tweed Valley.

56. Show on a sketch-map the close connection between relief and railway routes across the Southern Uplands.

57. Why was the east coast route to Scotland more important than the west until the nineteenth century?

58. Account for the woollen industry of the Tweed Valley. How does it differ from West Yorkshire industry?

59. Give an account of the farming activities of the Central Lowlands of Scotland.

60. Draw a detailed map of the industrial regions of the Central Lowlands.

61. Compare and contrast the development of the Lanarkshire and Lancashire coalfields.

62. Describe the various textile industries carried on in the Central Lowlands.

63. Under the headings (*a*) Physical Features, (*b*) Climate, (*c*) Economic Resources, compare the Highlands of Scotland and the mountains of Wales.

64. Describe and account for the distribution of population in Scotland.

65. Compare the distribution of population in Scotland and Eire.

66. Describe a railway journey from Perth to Inverness.

67. Write a description of the life of the "Crofters".

68. Account for the division of Ireland into two political divisions.

69. Explain clearly why pastural occupations are more important than cereal cultivation in Ireland.

70. Draw a map showing the chief steamship routes between the United Kingdom and Ireland. Give distances.

71. Give a geographical account of Northern Ireland under the headings (*a*) Position and Relief, (*b*) Climate, and (*c*) Occupations.

72. Compare Dublin and Limerick as outlets for the produce of Central Ireland.

73. What steps are being taken to improve farming and industrial conditions in Eire?

74. Give the position of the following and account for the importance of each: Valentia, Cobh, Greenore, Galway, and Waterford.

75. Construct a railway map of Ireland, using the information given on page 242.

76. The value of the annual imports into the United Kingdom is always in excess of the exports. How can this fact be explained?

77. Give in tabular form two countries and the probable exporting ports from which the imports given on page 256 will come.

78. Why has the export of coal been of great value to the development of industry in Great Britain?

79. Why is it that countries such as Switzerland make greater use of water power for the generation of electricity than England does?

80. Give as many examples as you can of industries which depend for some processes upon the salt industry. State the areas in the British Isles producing salt.

81. Name four important shipbuilding regions in Great Britain and account for their importance.

82. State where each of the following is made or produced in Great Britain: kaolin, soap, linoleum, rayon, beet-sugar, paper.

83. Find examples, other than those mentioned in the text, of towns in Great Britain at (*a*) a gap; (*b*) a bridging point; (*c*) a river confluence; (*d*) a river bend; (*e*) head of an estuary. Give a sketch-map to illustrate each answer.

84. Plan a seven-day tour on the Scottish railways, stating the places at which you would stop and the things you would like to see. Calculate the mileage covered.

85. Draw a large sketch-map of *one* important industrial area of England, and summarise on it—

    (*a*) sources of raw materials and chief foodstuffs;

    (*b*) holiday resorts within fifty miles radius of the chief town;

    (*c*) means of transport;

    (*d*) ports serving the area.

86. Describe and account for the distribution of population in (*a*) Aberdeenshire, (*b*) Warwickshire, (*c*) Westmorland, (*d*) Norfolk, (*e*) Buckinghamshire, (*f*) Somerset, (*g*) Shropshire, (*h*) Northumberland.

87. Describe the characteristics of the coast of West Scotland and contrast them with those of South-West Ireland.

88. Account for the importance of Glasgow as a port. Why are there no other first class ports on the west coast of Scotland?

89. Give in tabular form the chief imports into Scotland, naming their probable destinations and uses; the chief coal exporting ports; the chief packet stations.

90. What is meant by: fen, dissected plateau, scarpland, rift valley, boulder clay? Give examples of each within the British Isles.

91. Draw a map of the Trent Basin indicating the industrial areas within the basin. Describe and account for the agricultural activities of the basin.

92. Describe, with reference to definite examples, the scenery of (a) a clay plain; (b) a granite upland; (c) a limestone plateau; (d) a chalk plateau.

93. What are the chief characteristics of the trade of each of the following: Harwich, Hull, Southampton, Cardiff, Liverpool, London?

94. Account for the importance of (a) Torquay as a holiday resort; (b) Carlisle as a railway centre; (c) Manchester as a port; (d) Holyhead as a packet station.

95. Describe the scenery and economic importance of the Pennines. Show on a sketch-map how communications are affected by these highlands.

96. Describe and compare the past and the present distribution of important wool industries in Great Britain.

97. Compare the climatic conditions on the two sides of the Irish Sea and explain differences.

98. What factors determine the temperature of a region? Illustrate your answer by reference to temperature conditions in the British Isles.

99. Describe and, as far as you can, account for the position of the chief lakes of Ireland, mentioning the rivers with which each is connected.

100. Give an account of the distribution of the iron and steel industry of the United Kingdom, pointing out changes which have occurred in the relative importance of different regions during the last century.

101. Locate the chief industrial areas of Scotland and Ireland; contrast their natural resources and show how far these explain their respective manufactures.

102. Give an account of the trade relationship between (a) England and South Africa; (b) England and the United States; (c) England and Australia.

103. What is the Continental Shelf? In what ways has it affected the economic development of the British Isles?

104. Where are the principal leather-manufacturing centres of Great Britain? As far as you can, explain the reasons for the growth of the industry.

105. Name the principal industries which are located around the lower Mersey and the Mersey estuary. Explain why these industries have developed there.

106. South Wales imports quantities of foodstuffs, timber, and metal ores. Explain why these are imported and whence they are obtained.

107. What are the conditions necessary for the growth of an important fishing port? Name the chief fishing ports of Britain and show how they satisfy the conditions you have outlined.

108. What do you understand by textiles? Where are the principal textile manufacturing centres of the British Isles?

EXAMINATION QUESTIONS

The following questions have been reproduced by permission of the various Examining Bodies concerned from examination papers at the Ordinary Level of the General Certificate of Education.

(*C.*) Cambridge, (*L.*) London, (*N.*) Northern Universities, (*O.*) Oxford, (*O. & C.*) Oxford and Cambridge Joint Board.

1. Life is far easier and more pleasant in England south of the Thames estuary than in Scotland north of Glenmore. Show to what extent *geographical* conditions are responsible for this contrast. (*O. & C.*)

2. With the aid of sketch-maps or diagrams, describe, in order, the scenery of the areas that would be crossed in travelling along a direct line drawn (*a*) from London to Brighton, and (*b*) from the north coast to the south coast of Devon. (*O. & C.*)

3. Describe and suggest reasons for the more important types of farming found in each of *two* of the following areas:—

    (*a*) South-Eastern England (Kent and Sussex).

    (*b*) The Lowlands of Scotland.

    (*c*) The Midland Plain of England. (*C.*)

4. Discuss the physical and economic conditions which help to explain the importance of *three* of the following occupations in the areas indicated: dairy-farming in Cheshire, fruit growing in Kent, potato cultivation in Central Ireland, sheep rearing in Central Wales. (*O. & C.*)

5. Using as illustrations *either* Wales, north of the Brecon Beacons, *or* Cornwall and Devonshire, show how the relief and climate of a region in which people live influences their life and their work. (*C.*)

6. Where and under what conditions in the British Isles is wheat cultivated on a large scale? (*L.*)

7. Describe the geographical factors which have contributed to the growth of Britain's fishing industry. Mention the main fishing grounds frequented by British vessels and state the chief ports to which the catch is brought. (*L.*)

8. Choose *three* fishing ports in Great Britain, one on the east coast, one on the south coast, and one on the west coast, and explain the reasons for the situation and importance of each. (*O.*)

9. The Central Plain of Ireland, East Anglia, and Kent are all farming areas. For each area, name the *two* most important farm products, and explain carefully the particular advantages of the area for the production of the goods named. (*O.*)

10. Coal production is one of the most important foundations of British industry.

(*a*) For each of the following state the location of a British coalfield which illustrates the feature named:—

(i) a concealed coalfield;

(ii) submarine mining;

(iii) the mining of more than one type of coal.

(*b*) Show what is meant by the following terms, using diagrams where suitable:—

(i) a concealed coalfield;

(ii) opencast working;

(iii) anthracite.

(*c*) Choose *either* the South Wales coalfield *or* that of Northumberland and Durham. Draw a sketch-map of the area to show the extent of the coalfield and mark and name *two* important towns and *two* rivers. Name *two* manufacturing areas which have developed on or near the coalfield, and suggest reasons for the growth of each. (*N.*)

11. Describe with the aid of a sketch-map how routes are related to relief in *one* of the following areas: (*a*) the Southern Uplands of Scotland; (*b*) Wales; (*c*) South-East England. (*L.*)

12. Give *two* reasons why *each* of the following is important:—

(*a*) The British Isles are situated on a broad part of the continental shelf of Europe.

(*b*) No part of Great Britain is far from the sea.

(*c*) The position of Great Britain's chief lowlands is in the south-east of the island. (*C.*)

13. Describe, by reference to the ports of Great Britain, some of the geographical conditions which favour the development of a great seaport. (*O. & C.*)

14. Select *four* minerals, other than coal and iron, found in the British Isles. Locate areas in which each mineral is mined or quarried, and describe some of its uses. (*O. & C.*)

15. Among British coalfields some are important as exporters, some as areas for the manufacture of iron and steel and their products, and some for industries other than those concerned with metals. Give *one* example of a coalfield from each of these groups. Explain how local conditions have helped to bring about the utilisation of the coal in the way mentioned.

Illustrate each example by means of a map. (*N.*)

16. Iron and steel and heavy engineering industries are well developed in both the Glasgow and the Sheffield areas.

Suggest reasons for the presence of iron and steel production in each area and give an account of the main products of their engineering industries.

Illustrate your answers by drawing a sketch-map of each area. (*N.*)

17. Choose *two* of the following: dairy produce; woollens; early vegetables. For *each* of the *two* (*a*) name the chief areas of production in the British Isles; (*b*) state the chief reasons for large-scale production in these areas; (*c*) name *two* areas from which the product is imported to supplement or compete with the British product. (*O.*)

18. Textile materials are made at Belfast, Selkirk, Pontypool, Macclesfield, Coventry, Leicester, Dundee. Select *three* of these towns and for each of the chosen *three* give an account of the textile industry located there, the sources of the raw materials used, and the nature of the goods produced. (*O.*)

19. Describe and explain the characteristic features of the relief and drainage of *three* of the following: Antrim plateau, Dartmoor, Fens, Mendips, Salisbury Plain. (*O. & C.*)

20. Illustrating your answer with a sketch-map, discuss the geographical factors concerned in the industrial development of the English Midlands, noting the distribution of the chief industries. (*O. & C.*)

21. The coastal towns named in each of the groups (*a*), (*b*), (*c*), are situated in the same county, but owe most of their importance to very different geographical factors:—

(*a*) Barrow-in-Furness, Blackpool, Liverpool.

(*b*) Hull, Middlesbrough, Scarborough.

(*c*) Bournemouth, Portsmouth, Southampton.

Selecting *one* of the groups, mark the towns named on *one* sketch-map, and describe the conditions which have favoured their development.

(*O. & C.*)

22. Draw a large sketch-map of North-Eastern England to show the position and extent of the Northumberland and Durham coalfield. Mark and name *three* rivers and *four* important towns. Name *three* manufacturing industries which have developed on or near the coalfield and give reasons for the growth of each. (*C.*)

23. With the aid of sketch-maps, describe the geographical factors which have contributed to the importance of:

(*a*) Liverpool *or* Southampton as a port.

(*b*) Leeds *or* Swansea as a manufacturing town.

(*c*) Crewe *or* Reading as a railway route centre. (*C.*)

24. Draw a sketch-map of North-East England, north of the Tees. Mark and name *two* rivers, the area of high ground, *one* important seaport, *one* important inland city, *one* important railway centre. Shade the coalfield. State briefly details of the occupations of the inhabitants of the three towns named. (*O.*)

25. Write an orderly geographical account of *one* of the following: the Hampshire Basin, East Anglia, the Weald. (*L.*)

26. Name *one* important manufacturing industry which is carried on in each of *three* of the following coalfields and show, in each case, how geographical factors have promoted the growth of the industry named: (*a*) Northumberland and Durham, (*b*) North Staffordshire, (*c*) Lanarkshire, (*d*) South Wales. (*O. & C.*)

27. Describe the influence of position, physical features, and natural resources upon the occupations of the people in *either* (*a*) Yorkshire, east of the Vale of York; *or* (*b*) Northern England, west of the Eden Valley (*i.e.* the Cumbrian Peninsula). (*O. & C.*)

28.   From the six towns, Aberdeen, Blyth, Bradford, Goole, Grimsby, and Swansea, select *three* so as to include *one* manufacturing town, *one* coal-exporting port, and *one* fishing port.   Show for each town chosen how geographical factors have favoured the development of its principal occupation; illustrate your answers with sketch-maps.   (*N*.)

29.   Draw a sketch-map of the Midlands of England (Midland Triangle) showing and naming the chief highlands and rivers.   On the map show, by shading, the position of *three* important coalfields.   Mark or name an important town on, or near, each coalfield.   Write a *brief* account of the *agricultural* activities of the Midlands.   (*O*.)

30.   Explain the importance for farming of *three* of the following: the Golden Vale; the Carse o' Gowrie; the Scilly Islands; the Cheshire Plain.   (*O*.)

31.   Illustrating your answer by sketch-maps, describe the geographical factors which have contributed to the importance of (*a*) *either* Liverpool *or* Hull as a seaport, (*b*) *either* Birmingham *or* Leeds as a manufacturing town.   (*L*.)

32.   Write a geographical account of *either* (*a*) the London Basin, *or* (*b*) the Hampshire Basin and the Isle of Wight.   (*O. & C*.)

33.   Compare the life and activities, from season to season throughout the year, of a shepherd of the Welsh or Scottish highlands with those of a farmer mainly concerned with dairy farming *or* fruit growing *or* market gardening.   (*O. & C*.)

34.   Analyse carefully the factors which led to the establishment of the shipbuilding industry on (*a*) Clydeside, (*b*) Tyneside, and give an account of the subsequent growth and importance of this industry in each of these two areas.   (*O. & C*.)

35.   Scotland, north of the Central Lowlands, has few inhabitants. (*a*) State *three* factors which have caused this low density.   (*b*) Explain how each factor has operated.   (*c*) Locate *one* area of North Scotland which has more than the average population density and give reasons to account for this higher density.   (*O*.)

36.   The following statements indicate differences in the density of population in parts of Scotland:—

Lower Clyde Valley: Densely populated.

North-east coastal plain: Moderately populated.

The Highlands: Sparsely populated.

Explain *two* reasons for the stated density in *each* area.   (*O*.)

37.   Select *two* of the following: Manchester; Leeds; Dundee; Belfast; Cardiff; Reading.   For *each* selected place and its immediately surrounding area, state *three* predominant reasons for the concentration of population there nowadays.   Add a sketch-map for each to illustrate the written answer.   (*O*.)

38. Discuss the relief features of that part of the mainland of Scotland which lies north of the Central Lowlands, and (*b*) discuss their influence on the distribution and activities of the inhabitants. (*O. & C.*)

39. Choose *three* of the following towns and show how the importance of each has been influenced by its position: Aberdeen, Carlisle, Edinburgh, Inverness, Perth, Stirling. (*L.*)

40. (*a*) On a large sketch-map of South Wales:—

(i) Shade the high ground, naming the most prominent part.

(ii) Mark and name *two* rivers.

(iii) Mark by a dot and name *three* towns on the coast and one inland.

(iv) Shade the coalfield.

(*b*) Give details of the occupations of the inhabitants of *three* of the towns marked on the map. (*C.*)

41. Account for the fact that more people live in Glamorganshire than in any other Welsh county. (*L.*)

42. Describe the positions of *three* of the following Irish towns and discuss the geographical factors which have helped or hindered the growth and development of each of the towns selected: Belfast, Cork, Dublin, Galway, Limerick, Londonderry. (*O. & C.*)

43. Explain why in Eire:

(*a*) The annual range of temperature is small in the south-west of the country.

(*b*) Manufacturing industries are less important than farming.

(*c*) There are no very large seaports on the west coast. (*O. & C.*)

INDEX

Doncaster, 99, 105
Donegal, 248
— Mts, 43, 236, 242, 244, 247
Dorchester, 186
Dorking, 182
Dorset, 57, 185, 265
Douglas, 88
Douneray, 230
Dover, 9, 177, 183, 184
Dovey, R., 69
Dowlais, 78
Down, 234, 244
Drogheda, 241, 253-4
Droitwich, 7, 147
Dublin, 20, 40, 201, 232, 241, 242, 250, 252, 267
Dudley, 143, 145
Dumbarton, 219, 226
Dumfries, 37, 204, 205
Dunbar, 202, 203, 210
Dundalk, 241, 253
Dundee, 33, 213, 222-3, 267
Dunfermline, 222
Dungannon, 6, 239, 244
Dungeness, 177
Dunoon, 229
Durham, 10, 94, 98, 264

EAST Anglian Heights, 8, 156, 165
Ebbw, R., 70, 76
— Vale, 78, 79
Eden, R., 85, 86, 87
Edge Hill, 8
Edinburgh, 210, 214, 221, 267
Egremont, 87
Elan, R., 80
Electricity, 10, 88, 228, 236, 261-3
Elgin, 229, 232
Ely, 31, 153, 154
Engineering, 52-4, 74, 86, 96, 97, 103, 107, 123, 133, 137, 153, 155, 160, 165, 175, 182, 219, 222, 253, 268
Epping, 168
Epsom, 168
Erith, 168

Ermine Street, 117, 199
Errigal Mts, 247
Esk, R., 207, 221
Eskdale, 111, 112
Eskers, 251
Esparto, 124
Essex, 27, 31, 43, 156, 157, 264
Eston Moor, 96
Evesham, Vale of, 33, 35
Exe, R., 60, 61, 63
Exeter, 60, 63, 102
Exmoor, 60, 65
Exports, 255-61
— Invisible, 240, 260-1

FAL, R., 60
Falkirk, 216
Falkland, 222
Falmouth, 61
Fawley, 68, 191, 259
Fens, the, 65, 152-5
Fenton, 126, 127
Fermanagh, 234, 244
Ferryhill Gap, 98
Ferry Ports, 183-4, 233
Fertilisers, 97, 160, 253, 259
Festiniog, 7, 73
Fife, 27, 31, 213-4
— Coalfield, 222
Filey, 112
Fishguard, 71, 233
Fishing, 2, 3, 44, 62, 79, 88, 115, 118, 229, 231
Flamborough Head, 8, 113
Flax, 223, 245, 257
Fleetwood, 44
Flint, 73, 74, 264
Flowers, 34
Fogs, 15
Folkestone, 182, 184
Forestry, 45, 228
Forfar, 213, 222
Forth, R., 210, 212, 222, 224
Fort William, 226
Fosse Way, 63, 118
Fowey, 63, 127
— R., 61
Foyle, R., 237, 244, 246
Fraserburgh, 44, 229

Frodingham, 9
Frome, 66
— R., 186
Fruit, 31-3, 62, 81, 142, 153, 179, 213, 256
Furness, 6, 83, 88
Fylde, 129

GAINSBOROUGH, 118
Galashiels, 206
Galloway, 203
Galway, 43, 241, 242, 251, 252, 253
Gannister, 104
Gateshead, 98, 267
Gatwick, 173, 201
Giant's Causeway, 243
Gillingham, 181
Girvan, 203, 210, 214, 215
Glamorgan, 75, 264
Glasgow, 201, 217, 219, 264, 267
Glass, 98, 103, 130, 147, 175, 219, 251
Glastonbury, 66
Glenmore, 225, 230
Glenrothes, 222
Glossop, 120
Gloucester, 148, 198
Gloves, 40, 111, 146
Golden Vale, 249
Goole, 115
Goring 161, 165
Grampians, the, 225, 226
Grangemouth, 215, 216, 217, 259
Granite, 7, 62, 73, 85, 148, 230
Grantham, 100, 118
Graphite, 85
Great Ouse, R., 150, 154
Greenock, 217, 219
Grimsby, 44, 100, 118
Guildford, 182
Gwent, plain of, 36, 70, 72, 73
Gypsum, 147

HALIFAX, 103
Hambledon Hills, 111
Hamilton, 217

PRINTED IN GREAT BRITAIN BY UNIVERSITY TUTORIAL PRESS LTD

FOXTON, NEAR CAMBRIDGE